Financial Wellness

A Proven Process to Change Your Behavior and Start Winning with Money

TARAS COLLUM, SR.

© 2015 Taras Collum, Sr.
All Rights Reserved.

No part of this publication may be reproduced, stored in a retrieval system, or transmitted in any form or by any means, electronic, mechanical, photocopying, recording, or otherwise, without the prior written permission of the publisher. Permission requests should be sent to Taras Collum, Sr.: taras@tarasTheBull.com.

ISBN 10: 0692356452
ISBN 13: 978-0692356456 (Financial Wellness)

Discounts are available through Taras the Bull™ LLC for books ordered in bulk. Special consideration is given to financial coaching seminars including adult and continuing education and online mediums, post-secondary business classrooms, and seminar-style instructional outlets. Inquire via email to Taras Collum, Sr.: taras@tarasTheBull.com. Taras Collum, Sr. is a financial wellness educator, speaker, and coach.

Taras the Bull™ is a registered trademark product. For more information about Taras the Bull products and services, visit tarasTheBull.com

Contents

Introduction	1
Chapter 1: Financial Wellness	3
Chapter 2: Financial Wellness in the Workplace	5
Chapter 3: Financial Coaching and Financial Planning	9
Chapter 4: Career Questionnaires	31
Chapter 5: Banking Basics	55
Chapter 6: College Planning Tips	97
Chapter 7: Insurance	135
Chapter 8: Mortgage Mechanics	167
Chapter 9: Home Buyer Basics	187
Chapter 10: Credit and the Pitfalls of Borrowing Money	213
Chapter 11: Understanding Bankruptcy	233
Chapter 12: Credit Repair Tips	249
Chapter 13: Cash Flow Planning	267
Chapter 14: Investing	293
Chapter 15: Retirement Options	315
Chapter 16: Estate Planning	345
Chapter 17: Business Coaching	373
Conclusion	377
Testimonies	379
About the Author	391
Glossary	393
Appendix: Forms	417

Introduction

Financial wellness is a process that begins first with dealing with any financial emergency, then developing financial goals and achieving them over a period of time. How you want to or plan to spend your money requires that you first establish a budget, or cash management plan. Without a written budget to guide your finances, you will undoubtedly develop a spending pattern that is not conducive for personal financial success.

Today, spending patterns reveal much about the character of the person. If you are someone who spends more money than the total amount of money coming in, then you will always live in deficit, never fully able to move beyond common financial obstacles. Obstacles to financial success are not just driven by the idea that you are not earning enough money to live; but obstacles to financial success are primarily driven by the idea that you are not managing what you earn.

> **A budget/spending plan is a road map for your money.**

In addition, if you continue to charge a credit card to the maximum and pay only the minimum due or fail to pay it at all, then you are developing the habit of paying only what's required and/or running away from the problem. Essentially, you can be accused of just doing the bare minimum to survive. You don't have a goal to get out of and stay out of debt.

Therefore, developing a written budget for where you want to direct your money is all-important within the context of achieving personal financial success. In addition, developing financial goals will help you aim above your present economic condition. If you are constantly living paycheck to paycheck, but you don't establish a goal that will usher you out of this type of system of thinking, then this will be your reality for now and for future years to come. When considering the budgeting process, ask yourself these preliminary questions:

- What is my goal for managing expenses?
- What are my current expenses?
- Of all my expenses, which ones can I do without?
- Am I including retirement planning, life insurance, health insurance and giving as necessary expenses?
- Does food expense exceed any other type of necessary expense?
- Where do I see myself in the next 5 years? The next 10 years?

> **All good financial plans should include saving and giving.**

These are questions that you need to ask yourself in order to create financial goals. With this in mind, this book is a guide to the financial wellness industry as well as a workbook to help you develop, sustain, and monitor financial goals as you endure this journey towards financial freedom. Please read the book. You will gain insight into the industry as well as learn how to implement a financial wellness program in the workplace, save for an emergency, management money, tips to help you repair your credit, overcome bankruptcy, prepare for retirement and how to leave a lasting legacy.

Thank you for reading *Financial Wellness*.
God bless you.

Taras Collum, Sr.

CHAPTER 1

Financial Wellness

WHAT IS FINANCIAL WELLNESS?

Financial Wellness means having healthy habits about how we use money, including spending, saving, giving, investing and growing, and creating security and safety. Financial Wellness considers the big financial picture. Then, it helps the individual or an organization create a unique, working plan to achieve their financial goals. According to Dave Ramsey's *Financial Peace University*, most people experience a major life-changing event once every ten years. Financial Wellness includes creating a plan that will protect against the financial catastrophes that befall many people as a result of these cyclical, life-changing events. A Financial Wellness Plan also includes finding the right life insurance plan to provide an income for dependents and family members when a wage earner passes away unexpectedly.

Financial Wellness emphasizes unbiased financial education about healthy financial habits in spending, saving, investing, and giving. When people and companies learn healthy money habits, they can change their behaviors with money. Think about it: We all know we need to save for a rainy day and for retirement, but how many of us actually do? Financial Wellness teaches people and companies how to create a complete financial plan for spending, saving, giving, budgeting, debt reduction, risk management, retirement planning, and cash flow management. Financial Wellness education helps people and companies make informed financial decisions using sound judgment, common sense, skill, and discipline.

Financial Wellness education does not focus on selling insurance and investment products. Buying insurance and investment products from financial representatives who may be biased is not a Financial Wellness Program. Instead, Financial Wellness focuses on education, structure, and changing behaviors involving money.

CHAPTER 2

Financial Wellness in the Workplace

WHAT IS A FINANCIAL WELLNESS PROGRAM?

A **Financial Wellness Program** is an educational experience designed, taught, and delivered to employees by an independent financial education company. It teaches employees how to save money, manage income, reduce stress, reduce and eliminate debt, and prepare for retirement. Employees will benefit from an unbiased financial education company that has no ulterior motive to sell investment or insurance products. Employees <u>without</u> financial education suffer the stress of merely hearing many investment options from financial salespeople. In this situation, employees feel ill-equipped to pick an investment plan without knowing anything about the plans other than they have one. But, employees <u>with</u> financial education will be empowered, and they will learn how to choose wisely and make sound decisions that are in their best interests. Employers also benefit from using an independent financial educator. Employers do not want to be held liable for giving financial planning advice, but they realize their employees need guidance nevertheless. **Implementing a Financial Wellness Program in the workplace boosts company morale, reduces absenteeism, increases employee retention, increases workforce stability, and increases productivity – all while increasing the employer's bottom line.**

Personalized Financial Wellness Programs will meet the needs of the individual by answering questions and not just defining financial terminology. We all know we need to save money, but <u>how</u> can we do it consistently and systematically? How do we create a functioning budget that really, truly works? How do we get our spouse on the same page about money so we can work together instead of against each other? Think about it: If one spouse is trying to save while the other is spending, what type of plan is that? It is a plan for destruction, discord, and frustration that leads to a strained, unsatisfying relationship. In addition, a good Financial Wellness Program will educate participants so they can in turn teach their children how to manage money. This will change one's family tree and change the culture of a company. So, how do we teach our children to manage money effectively? These are questions a good

Financial Wellness Program answers. A holistic, unbiased Financial Wellness Program encompasses all aspects of the personal finance world:

- budgeting and planning for emergencies
- dealing with debt collectors and creditors
- saving for an emergency fund
- communicating about money with one's spouse or partner
- teaching children about money
- planning for retirement
- paying for college
- managing one's credit score
- strategizing to pay off debt quickly
- buying a home or other real estate and real property
- choosing the right mortgage loan
- understanding the importance of insurance
- investing for retirement
- estate planning

A good Financial Wellness Program complements an employer's current retirement and benefits plan. When employees develop consistent, healthy spending and saving plans, they can truly maximize the benefits their employer offers. Employees can save more for retirement instead of borrowing against or depleting their retirement funds for emergencies.

A Financial Wellness Program should be tailored to the needs of both the employer and the employees. The best results come from Financial Wellness Programs designed to fit the unique structure of a specific business, not from a one-size-fits-all approach. Because each organization is different, a successful Financial Wellness Program accommodates the existing workplace culture. For example, if an organization has a lunch hour, it can use that hour as a lunch-and-learn session. Each shift can have its own lunch-and-learn session. Or, entry-level workers can have an independent session, mid-level employees can have their own sessions, and executive employees can have their own. Or, everyone can be together in one room as an organization.

When an organization brings on a new employee, the orientation process should include an introduction to the Financial Wellness Program. Employers are often frustrated that their employees do not take full advantage of the benefits offered to them. This may be due to a lack of a clear plan or just a lack of knowledge. With a Financial Wellness Program in place, employees can truly understand the benefits their employers offer, and how to use them most effectively for their unique situation.

> **Financial Wellness is a process, not a one-day event.**

Sometimes, employers ask investment advisors to come in and offer products to the employees. A Financial Wellness Program, however, helps the employees understand what is in those products, what they mean, and how to pick the ones that are best for them. The independent financial education company does not earn a sales commission on the products or services that the employees choose in their benefits package. They simply want to <u>educate</u> people on what is right for them.

To serve the best interests of employers and employees, an independent, unbiased financial coach should teach the Financial Wellness Program. The Financial Wellness Program should provide options for different learning styles. The options should include: (1) Online education that empowers employees to learn at their own pace and share the experience with their family, (2) live, engaging, interactive, fun workshops, and (3) one-on-one financial counseling from an unbiased financial coach with a passion for teaching, not selling. A good Financial Wellness Program will also provide continued support for further insight, accountability, and monitoring to sustain positive results. Remember: Financial wellness is a process, not an event.

No one is immune from financial stress. Most Americans live paycheck-to-paycheck. A June, 2013 survey by Bankrate.com found 27 percent of respondents had zero emergency savings. Another 23 percent had some savings, but not enough to cover three months living expenses. That means more than half of Americans lack the savings to deal with emergencies or a sudden loss of income. Therefore, the entire organization should have access to the Financial Wellness Program – everyone from the entry-level employees to the most influential executives. A Financial Wellness Program will increase employee retention and satisfaction, something that benefits both employers and employees alike, and directly contributes to a company's bottom line.

CHAPTER 3

Financial Coaching and Financial Planning

Learning Objectives

- Define Financial Coaching.
- Define Financial Planning.
- List the types of financial plans.
- Complete a sample Financial Coaching Worksheet.
- Complete a sample Financial Planning Worksheet.

WHAT IS FINANCIAL COACHING?

Financial Coaching is defined as a process that guides the creation of a financial plan and the development of a detailed strategy. A **financial coach** is a professional who prepares financial plans that cover multiple aspects of the personal finance environment. The financial coach carries out additional functions. Their responsibilities include providing guidance regarding cash flow management, education planning, retirement planning, risk management, investment planning, tax planning, estate planning, insurance planning, and business succession planning. A good financial coach does not sell investments or insurance and are not sponsored by a large corporation. Therefore, a financial coach is unbiased and their primary responsibility is to teach personal finances.

It is not always an easy task to reconcile the complex world of personal finance. Clients seeking the services of a financial coach often need help with creating personal finance goals and ensuring that they are sustained, navigating through the sea of investment and estate planning options, understanding how financial decisions affect all areas of personal finance, and developing personal financial transition goals for the next chapters of their lives.

A financial coach will help clients create goals and reach targets, develop and update realistic plans, and make sound decisions where personal finances are concerned. When deciding to work with a financial coach, consider the character of the individual. A financial coach who is primarily interested in selling you products, but not interested in helping you to determine how best to meet your needs on a quality basis, will more than likely prevent you from reaching your goals, provided your goal is not to buy more products.

Therefore, it is important to develop a plan that is realistic and executable. The plan the financial coach creates with you must be clear and sound enough to implement. It is important to have a checklist for the purposes of measuring progress.

Small business owners must consider the risks associated with their legal structure. Owners of sole proprietorships assume the largest risk. In legal terms, a sole proprietorship is not a separate entity from its owner. Liabilities that the business owner encounters will be the sole responsibility of the owner. This means that the assets of a business owner operating as a sole proprietorship may be subject to loss or judgment. By purchasing basic business and liability insurance, the business owner can ensure that his or her assets are protected from judgment.

Concept Checker	*What is financial coaching?*

Case Study:
Tim and Angela Talk to a Financial Coach

Tim and Angela Taylor were up to their eyeballs in debt. They had been married for nine years. They had three children and were sick and tired of living paycheck to paycheck. Together, their monthly take-home household income is $6800 per month. They feel they make good money but can't seem to save any.

The financial coach built rapport with Tim and Angela. The financial coach asked the couple a series of questions to assess their financial standings. For the first time in nine years, the couple was able to discuss the money stress without arguing and blaming one another.

When Tim and Angela left the consultation, they had hope that one day they would have an emergency fund just in case the car started making noise, or if there was an unplanned expense. They motivated to pay off their debt, including their student loan debt, credit card debt, family debt and automobile debt.

With the financial coach, Tim and Angela learned that their debt was stifling their ability to save for retirement, preventing them from buying a home, and preventing them to contribute towards college for their three kids. Tim and Angela hoped that by they could begin investing and building wealth within 18 months with the guidance, accountability, and expertise of their financial coach.

By following their financial coach's recommendations, Tim and Angela were able to pay off $56,000 in debt in 12 months, on a combined salary of $115,000 per year. They are now realizing the dream of home ownership, paying for their kids' college, building wealth, and giving as they always desired.

> By following the plan that the financial coach created with them, Tim and Angela felt as if they had received a pay raise. They seemed to have more money and were able to pay off more debt than they had originally imagined. They also became more aware of where their money was going and began behaving better with their finances.

WHAT IS FINANCIAL PLANNING?

Financial Planning is the process of buying and selling investments such as mutual funds, stocks, bonds, and insurances such as life insurance and annuities. A **financial planner** is a licensed professional who advises clients on which investments and insurances are best for them according to their risk tolerance. Typically, there is not a lot of hand holding and accountability for the one purchasing the investments and insurances. Although a financial planner is equipped to help individuals with budgeting and prioritizing expenditures, their primary function is advising people on buying and selling insurance products and investment products for wealth creation and wealth building.

TYPES OF FINANCIAL PLANNING

There are different types of financial planning practices. For example, retirement planning is a process by which individuals determine how to prepare for the next transition in their lives, which may begin at age 59½. Retiring individuals are urged to save at least 10–15% of their annual income, create an emergency fund, and pay down debt.

On the other hand, estate planning is a process of arranging for the disposal of an estate. The process is used by individual and legal professionals to eliminate uncertainty over the administration of an estate through probate and maximize the value of an estate through the reduction of tax liabilities. Estate planning involves the creation of wills, trusts, beneficiary designations, powers of appointment, and property ownership rights.

These are just examples of the different types of financial planning solutions provided by certified and licensed professionals in the field of financial advisory services.

Concept Checker	*What is financial planning?*

Certified Financial Planner

A **Certified Financial Planner** (CFP) is a professional certification mark conferred to financial planners by the Certified Financial Planner Board of

Standards, Financial Planning Standards Council in Canada, and affiliated organizations in coordination with the Financial Planning Standards Board (FPSB), the organization that owns the CFP mark outside of the United States.

Prospective financial planners must meet education, examination, experience, and ethic requirements before receiving the designation.

Education

Prospective financial planners must complete a bachelor's degree from an accredited college or university. In addition, students must demonstrate mastery of a minimum of 100 topics on integrated financial planning. The following topics cover traditional planning areas:

- General Principles of Finance and Financial Planning
- Insurance Planning
- Employee Benefits Planning
- Investment and Securities Planning
- State and Federal Income Tax Planning
- Estate Tax, Gift Tax, and Transfer Tax Planning
- Asset Protection Planning
- Retirement Planning
- Estate Planning
- Financial planning and consulting

Students must complete the course training in the aforementioned topic areas before they can sit for the CFP Board Certification Examination, which lasts for ten hours. The bachelor's degree in any discipline is required for certification. However, it is not a requirement to take the examination.

There are exceptions. Individuals who already hold a professional designation that has been pre-approved by the CFP Board are not required to register for or take the exam. Individuals under this category include the following:

- PhDs in business, economics
- Attorneys
- Certified Public Accountants (CPA)
- Chartered Certified Accountants (ACCA)
- Chartered Accountants (CA)
- Chartered Wealth Managers (AAFM)
- Chartered Life Underwriters (CLU)
- Chartered Financial Consultants (ChFC)
- Chartered Financial Analysts

Prospective financial planners (students) and individuals who have received these designations are still responsible for adherence to ethics and continuing education requirements and must abide by the policies expressed in the CFP Board Code of Ethics and Professional Responsibility. To maintain certification, a license holder is required to complete at least thirty hours of continuing education and pay a licensing fee every two years.

Work Experience

After a candidate passes the examination, he or she must provide proof of extensive work experience in the field. The CFP Board defines work experience to mean the delivery of all or part of the personal financial planning process to a client. This definition references the act of supervising, directing support, and teaching. The delivery of personal financial solutions must fall under one or more of the following primary elements of financial planning:

- **Relationship:** Candidates demonstrate experience in establishing and defining the client relationship.
- **Data:** Candidates gather client data and personal goals.
- **Evaluation:** Candidates analyze and evaluate the client's financial status.
- **Recommendations:** Candidates develop and present financial planning recommendations and suggest alternatives where and when appropriate.
- **Implementation:** Candidates implement financial planning recommendations.
- **Monitoring:** Candidates monitor financial planning recommendations.

> **Both financial coaches and financial planners follow this process.**

After the candidate passes the exam and meets the work experience requirement, he or she must complete three years of full-time or part-time experience in the field and two years of full-time experience as an apprentice; and pass an extensive background check.

Related Designations

The financial planning field includes related designations where individuals serve in multiple industries such as investment management, financial analysis, risk management, and financial reporting. The following related designations are options for seasoned professional financial planners who desire to provide solutions through multiple outlets:

- Chartered Financial Consultant
- Chartered Financial Analyst
- Chartered Alternative Investment Analyst
- Financial Risk Manager
- Certified Public Accountant
- Registered Investment Advisor

These industry designations all have basic entry requirements that require the completion of a four-year degree.

Chartered Financial Consultant

The **Chartered Financial Consultant** (ChFC) is conferred by The American College and it is an "Advanced Financial Planning" designation. The ChFC professional assists individuals, small business owners, and professionals with information about financial planning. Topics include income taxation, retirement planning, estate planning, investments, and insurance. To earn the designation, candidates must complete nine courses and an exam. Six of the nine courses are required to complete the Certified Financial Planner program. Candidates must complete the program at an accredited institution or through an accredited program.

Concept Checker	What are the types of financial planning?

Chartered Financial Analyst

The **Chartered Financial Analyst** (CFA) is a professional credential offered by the CFA Institute. Candidates who complete the program and related requirements will be awarded the CFA charter and will become officially a CFA charter holder. The CFA designation is typically awarded to investment professionals in the fields of investment management and financial analysis (of bonds, stocks, and derivative assets).

To become a charter holder, candidates must demonstrate evidence of completion of four years of work experience. Prospective charter holders must successfully complete the CFA Program, become a member of the CFA Institute and submit application for membership with a local CFA member society, and ethically abide by the *CFA Institute Code of Ethics and Standards of Professional Conduct*. To be sure, the CFA Program takes approximately four years to complete.

Chartered Alternative Investment Analyst

The **Chartered Alternative Investment Analyst** (CAIA) is a professional designation awarded through the CAIA Association. It is typically available for investment professionals who complete a course of study and two examinations. The alternative investments industry deals primarily with investment professionals who are familiar with asset classes such as hedge funds, private equities, real assets, commodities, and structured products. The program provides finance professionals with a broad knowledge of alternative investments. The CAIA program is divided into two levels: Level I curriculum and Level II curriculum.

The Level I curriculum centers on the fundamentals of the alternative investment markets. On the other hand, Level II centers on advanced topics. The Level I exam comprises 200 multiple-choice questions; it covers some of the following topics:

- Professional Standards and Ethics
- Introduction to Alternative Investments
- Hedge Funds
- Real Assets
- Risk Management and Portfolio Management

The association recommends that candidates study for the exam at least 200 hours. The Level II exam covers such topics as Hedge Funds and Managed Futures, Asset Allocation and Portfolio Management, Manager Selection, Due Diligence, and Regulation.

Financial Risk Manager

The **Financial Risk Manager** (FRM) is an international professional certification offered through the Global Association of Risk Professionals. Candidates for the designation must complete a rigorous program that is two-part and practiced-oriented. The exam covers the topic of financial risk management. Candidates must demonstrate two years of work experience in financial risk management.

Risk management professionals analyze, control, and assess potential credit risk, market risk, and liquidity risk and typically work in investment banks and asset management firms. Top employers of FRM holders are Deutsche Bank, HSBC, and UBS, three of the major global financial services firms.

Certified Public Accountant

The **Certified Public Accountant** (CPA) is a type of qualified accountant in the United States. Candidates for the CPA designation must pass the Uniform Certified Public Accountant Examination and meet state-based education and experience requirements. Most U.S. states require CPAs to be licensed in order to attest to the validity of a company's financial statement. When employed by a corporation or an association, a CPA operates in multiple areas of finance. These areas include the following:

- Assurance and Attestation Services
- Corporate Governance
- Corporate Finance
- Financial Accounting
- Financial Planning
- Venture Capital
- Income Tax
- Management Consulting

These are some of the major areas CPAs are licensed to work in and must demonstrate proof of certification.

Registered Investment Advisor

The **Registered Investment Advisor** (RIA) is a registered professional with the Securities and Exchange Commission or a state securities agency. The RIA is classified as an Investment Adviser (IA) and the designation is often referenced in the Investment Advisers Act of 1940.

An Investment Adviser is defined as an individual or a firm in the business of providing advice about securities and receiving compensation for the advice on investing in stocks, bonds, mutual funds, and/or exchange traded funds. An RIA is generally paid a percentage of the value of the assets, an hourly fee, a fixed, or a commission on the securities sold.

Concept Checker	*Describe work experience requirements for a CFP.*

An IA has a fiduciary duty to provide a standard of care that falls under the guidelines of the statute. The investment adviser is also required to register with a state securities agency if managing assets totaling less than $100 million. However, if an investment adviser manages assets in excess of $100 million, then the adviser must register with the U.S. Securities and Exchange Commission (SEC).

An agent of the RIA (or IA) who provides investment advice is called an Investment Adviser Representative (IAR). An IAR must complete the FINRA Series 66 and the Series 7 (or Series 6) exams. An IAR may petition to waive the exam requirement if he or she possesses a pre-qualifying designation such as Certified Financial Planner (CFP), Chartered Financial Consultant (ChFC), Personal Financial Specialist (PFS), Chartered Financial Analyst (CFA), or Chartered Investment Counselor (CIC).

Financial Planning Disclosures

The CFP Board requires a Financial Planner to satisfy requirements of Rules 1.2, 1.3, and 2.2 of the Rules of Conduct, which outline specific information with regard to disclosures to prospective clients before and after the prospect of entering into an agreement. The agreement must stipulate that the licensed provider is entering into an agreement to provide financial planning services.

For this reason, a standard Financial Planning Disclosure and Agreement is composed of multiple parts and outlines the duties of the financial planner.

Part One

Part One of a financial planning disclosure agreement outlines the contact information of each party entering into the agreement.

Part Two

Part Two of a sample agreement defines the "Services to be Provided" with the client. In this part of the agreement, the obligations of the client and the financial planner are structured in detail. Examples of obligations and responsibilities are defined as follows:

- The defining of financial planning goals, needs, and objectives
- The gathering of data
- The determining of results made to the client's current course of action
- The determining of recommendations to the client's current course of action
- The determining of implementation priorities
- The determining of monitoring responsibilities

This section of a sample agreement further describes the firm the certified professional (i.e., certificant) works with to provide financial advisory services.

Part Three

The third part of a sample agreement outlines the material information relevant to the relationship between the client and certified professional. This section provides a description of how the certificant will be compensated for services provided; a description of costs incurred charged separately to the client; a description of additional sources of compensation, direct or indirect; and a description of compensation paid to an affiliate or affiliated entity of the certificant or certificant's employer.

This section also provides an outline of conflicts of interest the certified professional may have; and the limitations placed on products, services, and/or solutions.

Part Four

The last section of a sample agreement represents additional information regarding termination responsibilities and adherence to standards of professional conduct that govern the field.

Elements of the Financial Coaching and Financial Planning Process

Relationship

The certified professional establishes a relationship with the client by explaining issues and concepts related to the financial coaching and financial planning process. The certified professional explains specific information concerning the services he or she provides and clarifies the responsibilities between both parties.

Client Data

The financial coach or financial planner gathers client data which includes goals. The professional interviews the client about his or her financial resources, expectations, and current obligations. During the interviewing process, the financial coach or financial planner also determines the client's current needs and priorities, assesses the client's value and belief system, and determines the client's aptitude for risk tolerance.

Evaluation

The financial coach or financial planner analyzes the client's financial status by evaluating current cash flow needs, risk management, investments, employee benefits, taxes, estate planning objectives, and related needs.

Recommendations

The financial coach or financial planner develops and presents to the client recommendations necessary for meeting financial coaching and planning goals and objectives. The client receives the recommendations and the financial coach or financial planner works with the former to ensure goals are met and are revised when appropriate.

Implementation

The financial coach or financial planner helps the client put the plan into action. Implementation includes coordinating with professionals such as accountants, attorneys, real estate agents, stockbrokers, investment advisers, and insurance agents.

Monitoring

The financial coach or financial planner monitors and reviews the soundness of the recommendations periodically, making necessary changes in consultation with the client. This process involves evaluating changes with tax laws and making appropriate recommendations to meet financial coaching and planning objectives.

Case Study:
Scott Talks with a Financial Planner

Understanding the process of implementation is important to clients who are unfamiliar with the process of financial coaching and planning. Scott Sims found it to be vital to his progress.

Scott Sims was a novice investor. To begin his journey towards sound financial health which includes choosing fixed income investments, Scott sought the services of a financial planner to get started. Part of his goals was also to create a will and an estate plan. The certified financial planner Scott chose possessed multiple designations, which gave him the confidence needed to trust the planner. Scott spoke with Tim Nassau about the evaluation process as well as the implementation process.

Tim evaluated Scott's current financial status. Scott had massive debt obligations, but a sound credit score. Tim advised Scott to choose fixed income products that would preserve his capital and increase rate of growth periodically. In other words, Scott did not want to take on too much risk at the beginning.

Tim evaluated the data, created sound goals in coordination with Scott, and made recommendations that were suitable for Tim at his current financial state. One of the recommendations Tim made to Scott was to begin paying down the debt and establishing a high-interest yield savings account for the remaining debt.

This would make it easier to pay the debt and earn interest at the same time. The major goal that Scott preferred was the one where he could preserve his principal.

By following Tim's goal pattern, Scott was able to pay two major debt obligations and begin the process of choosing small investments. In about six months, Scott plans to develop additional sets of objectives that will include some risk to his principal. With Tim as a financial planner, Scott feels confident that he will meet his goals.

This beginner's story to sound financial health is important to every individual who wants to begin entering the investments market but who also has current debt obligations that are hindering this type of goal. Scott and Tim developed a goal where the former could still pay his debt and set up a brokerage account for investment trading.

BUSINESS PLANNER

Businesses entering the financial planning services industry or any industry for that matter must consider the importance of obtaining business insurance. Any sound financial plan will reference this issue. The purpose of insurance coverage for small businesses is to transfer risk that you can afford in the form of a premium in order to cover a risk that you cannot afford. Insurance is important to your business relationships and can be beneficial to cover a broad range of losses. There are different types of business insurance available.

Business Property Insurance

Property insurance covers buildings. Coverage is typically required if you own the building your business occupies. However, in cases where you lease premises, the landlord may provide the coverage. Business personal property includes tables, desks, chairs, and equipment. Tenant's improvements are also included. Business property insurance covers loss of income and loss caused by an earthquake.

Liability Insurance

A standard Comprehensive General Liability policy covers third parties in the event of personal and advertising injury; fire legal liability; products; medical expense and payments; general liability; and damage control.

Worker's Compensation Insurance

If your business has employees, by law you are required to have a worker's compensation policy. A startup organization may be eligible for their state's compensation fund. Worker's compensation insurers provide risk management and loss of control services.

Employment Practices Liability Coverage

Employment Practices Liability Coverage is typically appropriate for coverage against losses associated with wrongful termination and sexual harassment lawsuits.

When considering a business insurance policy, shop around for the best rates for premiums that won't break your budget.

Chapter Key Points

Financial Coaching is defined as a process that guides the creation of a financial plan and the development of a detailed strategy. A **financial coach** is a professional who prepares financial plans that cover multiple aspects of the personal finance environment. The plan created by the financial coach and the client will consist of an emergency fund of three to six months of household living expenses and paying off debt.

Financial Planning is defined as the process of buying and selling investments such as mutual funds, stocks, bonds and insurances such as life insurance and annuities. A **financial planner** is a licensed professional who advises clients on which investments and insurances are best for them according to the client's risk tolerance.

There are different types of financial planning. For example, retirement planning is a process by which individuals determine how to prepare for the next transition in their lives, which may begin at 59½. Retiring individuals are urged to save at least 10–15% of their annual income, create an emergency fund, and pay down debt.

A **Certified Financial Planner** (CFP) is a professional certification mark conferred to financial planners by the Certified Financial Planner Board of Standards, Financial Planning Standards Council in Canada, and affiliated organizations in coordination with the Financial Planning Standards Board (FPSB), the organization that owns the CFP mark outside of the United States.

The **Chartered Financial Consultant** (ChFC) is conferred by The American College and it is an "Advanced Financial Planning" designation. The ChFC professional assists individuals, small business owners, and professionals with information about financial planning.

The **Chartered Financial Analyst** (CFA) is a professional credential offered by the CFA Institute. Candidates who complete the program and related requirements will be awarded the CFA charter and will become officially a CFA charter holder.

The **Chartered Alternative Investment Analyst** (CAIA) is a professional designation awarded through the CAIA Association. It is typically available for investment professionals who complete a course of study and two examinations.

The CFP Board requires a Financial Planner to satisfy requirements of Rules 1.2, 1.3, and 2.2 of the Rules of Conduct, which outline specific information with regard to disclosures to prospective clients before and after the prospect of entering into an agreement.

CHAPTER KEY TERMS

Certified financial planner: term refers to a professional certification mark conferred to financial planners by the Certified Financial Planner Board of Standards, Financial Planning Standards Council in Canada, and affiliated organizations in coordination with the Financial Planning Standards Board (FPSB).

CFP: acronym stands for Certified Financial Planner.

Chartered Alternative Investment Analyst: term refers to a professional designation awarded through the CAIA Association.

Chartered Financial Analyst: term refers to a professional credential offered by the CFA Institute. Candidates who complete the program and related requirements will be awarded the CFA charter and will become officially a CFA charter holder.

Chartered Financial Consultant: term refers to a professional who assists individuals, small business owners, and professionals with information about financial planning.

Financial coach: term refers to a professional who prepares financial plans that cover multiple aspects of the personal finance environment.

Financial coaching: term refers to a process that guides the creation of a financial plan and the development of a detailed strategy.

Financial planner is a licensed professional who advises clients on which investments and insurances are best for them according to the client's risk tolerance.

Financial planning - is defined as the process of buying and selling investments such as mutual funds, stocks, bonds and insurances such as life insurance and annuities.

Financial Risk Manager: term refers to an international professional certification offered through the Global Association of Risk Professionals.

IA: acronym stands for Investment Adviser.

IAR: acronym stands for Investment Adviser Representative

Registered Investment Adviser (RAI): term refers to a registered professional with the Securities and Exchange Commission or a state securities agency.

GROUP WORK PROMPT

Visit the CFP Board website. Review the sample exam questions. As a group, answer the questions. Begin the process in class and complete the exam as a group out-of-class. Answer as many questions as you can. Be prepared to discuss your answers.

HOMEWORK EXERCISE

For homework, visit the Scottrade website. Review the company's Investment Advisor Services Agreement. You can access the PDF here.

http://www.scottrade.com/documents/alt/AdvisorServicesAgreement.pdf

Review the document, noting information specific to you as the client. Write a comparison paper analyzing the company's current product offerings as they are specific to your financial planning goals. The paper should be no more than six total pages, excluding the bibliography.

HELPFUL WEBSITES

eHow.com: Risks in Starting a Sole Proprietorship
http://www.ehow.com/list_6813867_risks-starting-sole-proprietorship.html

AARP: 10 Steps to Take So You Can Retire
http://www.aarp.org/work/retirement-planning/info-10-2012/10-steps-to-plan-for-retirement.html

Certified Financial Planner Board of Standards
https://www.cfp.net/become/examinee_agreement.asp

CHAPTER FORMS

On the next pages are all of the forms discussed within this chapter. You may photocopy, scan, and print them out. Some forms you will need to complete the group work and the homework.

Assessment

1. What is financial coaching?
_____
_____
_____

2. What primary role does a financial coach play within the context of advisory services?
_____
_____
_____

3. What is a financial planner?
_____
_____
_____

4. What primary role does a financial planner play within the context of advisory services?
_____
_____
_____

5. **True or False.** A Certified Financial Planner is a type of professional certification mark conferred upon investment professionals.

6. **True or False.** A Certified Public Accountant must pass the Uniform Certified Public Accountant Examination.

7. **Match the Acronym.**
   - A. CFP   Chartered Financial Analyst _____
   - B. ChFC   Certified Public Accountant _____
   - C. CA   Certified Financial Planner _____
   - D. FPSB   Chartered Life Underwriters _____
   - E. ACCA   Chartered Financial Consultant _____
   - F. CAIA   Financial Risk Manager _____
   - G. FRM   Chartered Analyst _____
   - H. CPA   Financial Planning Standards Board _____
   - H. RIA   Chartered Alternative Investment Analyst _____
   - I. IA   Chartered Certified Accountants _____

FINANCIAL COACHING INTERVIEW QUESTIONNAIRE & WORKSHEET

When seeking the advisory services of a financial coach, use the following document to prepare your answers for the meeting.

1. What prompted you to seek out a financial coach?

_____
_____
_____

2. What is going well with your finances?

_____
_____
_____

3. What is *not* going well with your finances?

_____
_____
_____

4. What are your goals for your time with your coach?

_____
_____
_____

5. At the end of your coaching package, what do you hope to have accomplished?

_____
_____
_____

6. Where do you see yourself in the next year? 5 years? 10 years?

_____
_____
_____

7. Do you currently use a working/functioning budget?

   Yes or No

8. What are you willing to sacrifice to see the results you want?

_____
_____
_____

9. Are you committed to not borrowing? Is your spouse committed to not borrowing?

   Yes or No

FINANCIAL WELLNESS | 29

FINANCIAL PLANNING INTERVIEW
QUESTIONNAIRE & WORKSHEET

When seeking the advisory services of a financial planner, use the following document to prepare your answers for the meeting.

Current Status

Age: _____
Net Monthly Salary _____
Monthly Expenses _____
Disposable Income _____

Current Investments and Insurance

Investment Type #1 _____ Maturity _____
Investment Type #2 _____ Maturity _____
Insurance Type #1 _____ Premium _____
Insurance Type #2 _____ Premium _____
Related Investments _____ Maturity _____

Current Financial Goals

Goal #1: _____

Goal #2: _____

Goal #3: _____

Goal #4: _____

Goal #5: _____

Current Emergency Fund

Fund Type #1: _____

Fund Type #2: _____

Fund Type #3: _____

Research & Cost Considerations

Term Insurance
_____
_____
_____

Health Insurance
_____
_____
_____

Child Education Funding
_____
_____
_____

Goal Planning

Annual Vacation Fund
_____
_____

Retirement Fund
_____
_____

Home Loan Fund
_____
_____

Annual Child School Expenses Fund
_____
_____

Estate Planning Fund
_____
_____

Notes
_____
_____
_____
_____

CHAPTER 4

Career Questionnaires

Learning Objectives

- Define career questionnaire.
- List the types of career questionnaires.
- Complete a sample career questionnaire.

WHAT IS CAREER QUESTIONNAIRE?

A **career questionnaire** is defined as a list of probing questions about an individual's skills, preferences, interests, and plans. The purpose of a career questionnaire is to help guide and direct an individual towards a career. A career questionnaire is equally important for an individual who wants to change careers. The most important thing to remember is that a career questionnaire is a tool by which to measure your strengths, weaknesses, and determination of life goals.

Career questionnaires often ask personal questions particularly about your personality. For example, a career questionnaire might ask a question to determine if you are an introvert or an extrovert. A career questionnaire might ask if you have completed education beyond the secondary level. Further, a career questionnaire might ask if you like working alone or in groups.

It is important to answer the questions on a career questionnaire truthfully to determine what type of career might be suited for your capability, personality, and attitude. If you love working with people, then you can expect this to be a question on a career questionnaire. If you love performing or conducting research, then a career questionnaire might benefit you in directing your energies to the most likely environment.

Always remember that a career questionnaire is just one of many options to use when determining which career to choose. It is important to always do your research. Take your own personal assessment of your likes and dislikes. This will help to guide you on the road towards success.

Small business entrepreneurs who are faced to wind up their businesses and go back to work will find a career questionnaire to be of great benefit. Changing careers is not easy and it requires patience on your part and due diligence. In addition, adding career counseling as a business solution will allow you the opportunity to add more skills to your skillset as well as add a revenue-generating segment to your business solutions. Consider both options as a possibility when determining the best solution to a current business problem.

TYPES OF CAREER QUESTIONNAIRES

A **career questionnaire** is defined as a self-assessment tool used by career counselors and organizations to measure a respondent's primary and secondary interests, career choice, and aptitude for job placement. Career questionnaires must be designed scientifically. They typically provide insight into the respondent's psychology, personality, temperament, aptitude, and attitude.

There are different types of career questionnaires that help respondents assess their current interests, transforming hobbies into prospective careers. For example, the Kids' Career Questionnaire is a type of personalized test for kids that fall under the age group of eight to thirteen. The questionnaire helps kids develop and analyze their life goals. On the other hand, a general Job Questionnaire is designed to help respondents assess and evaluate their current workplace skills. Employees respond to questions concerning current computer-based and organizational skills.

| Concept Checker | *What is a career questionnaire?* |

Different types of career questionnaires are formatted according to a prescribed purpose and are targeted to a specific age group. Age groups range from secondary and undergraduate students to prospective university graduates and applicants. Career counselors at all levels help respondents assess their core interest areas and develop them into a pursuit towards a career and/or life-long dream.

The Career Counselor

The **career counselor** is a type of individual who specializes in career coaching. Career counselors have similar aims as marriage and psychological counselors. Their purpose is to provide support to clients who are in the process of making complex decisions regarding career selection, career change, and career transition.

Career counselors often use techniques to focus the client on a particular type of aim that might include joining professional organizations specific to their field and enrolling in professional development coursework to improve prospects for work.

Career counselors work with many types of people, from adolescents contemplating career options and experienced professionals seeking a career change to parents who want to return to work after raising a child and related people seeking employment.

Career counselors are subject to the guidelines of one or more certifying bodies and are expected to behave professionally according to ethical standards.

Review the guidelines stipulated by the National Board for Certified Counselors and Affiliates, Inc. for more information about certification and credentialing.

| Concept Checker | *What is a career counselor?* |

Career Questionnaire Format

A **career questionnaire format** is a structured document that serves as the basis for different types of questionnaires targeted to multiple student and non-student groups. The format provides sections for the following:

- Name
- Address
- Gender
- Age
- Class/Grade
- School/College
- Email

The rest of the document provides sections for four major types of questions. The structure of each question is developed differently based upon the type of career questionnaire. No one career questionnaire is like its counterpart. There is a possibility that one career questionnaire will not have the same questions as another.

However, keep in mind that most career questionnaires are structured using one or more of the same first four questions. These questions are structured differently for each targeted group.

The sections that follow only represent samples of how the first four questions are structured for the high school age group.

First Question

The first sentence contains questions related to current student involvement in social groups, hobbies, and interests. In addition, questions are framed to provide multiple choice options so that a student/non-student can mark the item that is of most interest to him or her.

Second Question

The second sentence provides a more focused question. It asks the respondent about his or her participation in various projects. This type of question is geared towards the high school student who is required to complete a school science project or who registers for a campus-based competitive event. The respondent answers questions about the type of projects he or she has completed over a particular period (i.e., summer).

Third Question

The purpose of the third sentence is to target the respondent's comfort zone. For example, the questions of a standard questionnaire designed for high school students will ask if the student is comfortable with computers, adventure, sports, or television. These questions tend to help the career counselor delve deeply into the psyche of the respondent.

Fourth Question

The fourth category sentence targets the inherent nature of the respondent. The purpose of this type of question is to help the respondent think about their psychological attributes. For example, questions are structured to determine if the respondent is an extrovert or an introvert, creative or intellectual, and smart or good looking. The possible answer to the question is part of a multiple-choice set of predetermined responses.

The standard questions that form a career questionnaire are important because they measure the respondent's ability to think about how he or she has made decisions leading up to the moment of completing the questionnaire.

Sample Career Questionnaire Example

A **sample career questionnaire example** is a type of document that provides insight into the types of questions generated to measure a respondent's interests. The following three questions are examples of the types of questions asked on a sample questionnaire.

Question #1: Which of the following activities do you participate in?

This type of question prompts the respondent to think both about past and current events. Some questionnaires allow for the selection of one or more responses. On the other hand, some questionnaires allow the respondent to choose the response that best reflects his or her interests. Typical responses might include the following:

- Environmental campaigns
- Organizing an event
- Working with computers
- Outdoor-related activities

The responses are general. Respondents are not typically allowed to write in an answer. Instead, they must choose from among the responses provided. This practice calls into question the true validity of the career questionnaire. To measure the respondent's attitude within the context of the questionnaire, he or she should be able to write in an answer, which allows the career counselor to obtain specific data.

Question #2: Which of the following qualities represents a description of you?

This is another type of question where the respondent must identify an adjective that best describes his or her current and/or present interests or responsibilities. In essence, the respondent should know the right adjective within which he or she fits. For example, typical multiple choice options would be one or more of the following:

- Planner
- Computer geek
- Independent
- Social networker

These responses allow the respondent to self-identify with a group and/or category. These responses also help the respondent to focus his or her energies on a single aspect of his or her character, one that particularly serves as a description for others.

Lastly, all career questionnaires ask the same standard questions regarding aptitude.

Question #3: Which of the following subjects do you like the most?

This type of question provides multiple choice answers, but is structured in a way that ensures the data collector receives a specific response. The following responses are specific to this type of question:

- Mathematics
- English
- Science
- History

Some questions provide more specific responses such as the following:

- Chemistry
- Physics
- Life Science
- Earth Science
- Geography

Other career questionnaires do not provide enough details and leave the last category "Others" to chance. It is important to note that "Technology" is not a common response category. Instead, past career questionnaires only use "Computer Geek" to refer to technology-based fields. However, "Computer Geek" is an example of a description and not a subject.

This is exactly the problem that Jennifer Scott had with her school's questionnaire. There were many options on the questionnaire that didn't fit with Jennifer's aptitude.

> **Case Study:**
> **Jennifer's Problem with Career Questionnaires**
>
> Jennifer Scott is a high school student who is about to graduate in May. She wants to attend a local junior college because her grades are not as high as her counterparts. She is also considering a job to gain experience.
>
> She completes a job questionnaire offered by the career counselor. Some of the questions on the questionnaire were great. She answered them without any problems. However, there were some questions that did not offer the appropriate response. Jennifer loves computers, but she loves software writing. She writes code when she has some spare time.
>
> In a time where social media is becoming the norm, the questionnaire doesn't have a question about the Internet, let alone about Facebook, Twitter, and Google. These are all of Jennifer's likes. She thrives in this environment.
>
> Choosing "Computer Geek" to reflect one of many qualities is just not a good fit for Jennifer. Even though Jennifer knows what she likes, she completes the career questionnaire not truly feeling guided towards any direction.
>
> Jennifer's issue with the career questionnaire is common. Most questions on a sample questionnaire are outdated and don't fit within a twenty-first century environment. It is important that career counselors and certifying bodies develop questions that are also specific to an industry. When considering career questionnaires, keep in mind that each type of questionnaire may not always provide the guidance you need. It is important to research the field you may be interested in to gain more insight.

The career questionnaires at the end of this chapter are in standard formats. They offer more responses specific to a twenty-first century, technology-laden environment.

BUSINESS PLANNER

It is important that business owners provide sound solutions within an ever-changing environment. As the Internet and technology in general continue to grow exponentially, to stay competitive, business owners will need to diversify their products. This includes adding social media expertise and Internet marketing to a current product line.

In addition, it is important that business owners also tap into non-traditional, industry-specific resources. Adding paralegal and publishing solutions to a graphics design business will provide the necessary solutions for a diverse clientele.

Because clients may struggle with personal financial management, adding financial and investment advisory services may be the key to increasing your bottom line. Tax preparation services are another option.

These are all suggestions that should be considered when developing strategic objectives for one or more business segments. The goal is to provide both unique and comprehensive solutions that will ensure continued business with a client.

When considering career counseling as a business segment, or purposes related to a career change, it is important to note that there are specific licensure requirements. A career counselor must be licensed to provide counseling services in a public and/or private capacity. The National Board for Certified Counselors (NBCC) provides guidelines for certification. The NBCC is just one of many certifying bodies that require career counselors to be licensed and offers the standard certification designation called National Certified Counselor (NCC).

Prospective career counselors must complete a master's degree or higher in counseling and 48 hours of graduate-level, credit coursework. A survey of coursework titles includes the following:

- Human Growth and Development Theories in Counseling
- Group Counseling Theories and Processes
- Professional Orientation to Counseling
- Counseling Field Experience

Graduate students must also pass the National Counselor Exam (NCE) and provide documentation of a minimum number of hours in counseling supervision over a certain period of time after completing the master's degree. The NBCC offers three types of specializations for mental health, school counseling, and addictions counseling.

These are the general guidelines for the counseling certification. Visit the organization's website for more information about how to apply for certification.

Chapter Key Points

A **career questionnaire** is defined as a list of probing questions about an individual's skills, preferences, interests, and plans. The purpose of a career questionnaire is to help guide and direct an individual towards a career.

It is important to answer the questions on a career questionnaire truthfully to determine what type of career might be suited for your capability, personality, and attitude.

A **career questionnaire** is defined as a self-assessment tool used by career counselors and organizations to measure a respondent's primary and secondary interests, career choice, and aptitude for job placement.

The **career counselor** is a type of individual who specializes in career coaching.

A **career questionnaire format** is a structured document that serves as the basis for different types of questionnaires targeted to multiple student and non-student groups.

A **sample career questionnaire example** is a type of document that provides insight into the types of questions generated to measure a respondent's interests.

When considering career counseling as a business segment, or purposes related to a career change, it is important to note that there are specific licensure requirements. A career counselor must be licensed to provide counseling services in a public and/or private capacity.

CHAPTER KEY TERMS

Career counselor: term refers to a type of individual who specializes in career coaching.

Career questionnaire: term refers to a self-assessment tool used by career counselors and organizations to measure a respondent's primary and secondary interests, career choice, and aptitude for job placement.

Career questionnaire format: term refers to a structured document that serves as the basis for different types of questionnaires targeted to multiple student and non-student groups.

NBCC: acronym stands for National Board for Certified Counselors.

NCC: acronym stands for National Certified Counselor.

NCE: acronym stands for National Counselor Exam.

Sample career questionnaire example: A type of document that provides insight into the types of questions generated to measure a respondent's interests.

Group Work Prompt

As a group, review the guidelines required to become a career counselor by visiting multiple websites. Outline the guidelines on multiple sheets of paper. Turn a typed version in for credit. Work on the project in-class; finish it up as a group at home.

Homework Exercise

As a business owner it is important to offer a diversified portfolio of products to ensure you are able to meet the demands of multiple clients. Because this is important to consider, you must also be aware of the dangers of overextending the company into many areas.

For homework, consider the idea of diversifying your company product line. Outline and describe your current company's product offerings. Debate whether adding "career counseling" as an advisory solution would be a sound decision. Develop an analysis evaluating such a potential decision.

Helpful Websites

National Board for Certified Counselors
http://www.nbcc.org/

National Career Development Association
http://www.ncda.org/

Assessment

1. What is a career counselor?
   _____
   _____

2. What are some types of questions a career questionnaire may ask? Include two.
   _____
   _____

3. Write responses to the following example question: Which of the following subjects do you like the most?

   a. _____
   b. _____
   c.
   _____
   d. _____

4. As a business owner, how important is it to your business to create and offer a diversified portfolio of product offerings?
   _____
   _____

5. What are some of the certification requirements for becoming a licensed career counselor?
   _____
   _____

Chapter Forms

On the next pages are all of the forms discussed within this chapter. You may photocopy, scan, and print them out. Some forms you will need to complete the group work and the homework.

FINANCIAL WELLNESS | 43

BASIC CAREER QUESTIONNAIRE (HIGH SCHOOL)

Name: _____

Current Course: _____

Graduating Year: _____

Address: _____

City, State, Zip: _____

Email Address: _____

1. When participating on a team, how do you identify yourself in relationship to your teammates?

    a. Competitor
    b. Fellow student
    c. Team partner

2. Of the following responses, which of the two represents your preferences?

    a. Team-structured events
    b. Indoor events
    c. Outdoor events
    d. Individual events

3. Rank the following subjects under each column according to preference.

General	*Science*	*Social Science/Business*
a. English_____	Life Science_____	Accounting_____
b. Science_____	Earth Science_____	Psychology_____
c. History_____	Chemistry_____	Economics_____
d. Math _____	Physics_____	Law_____

4. Which of the following represents a primary interest? Rank according to preference.

Sports _____ Photography _____ Boating ___ Computers ____ Technology ___

5. Which of the following appeals to you most? Rank according to preference.

Nike __ Apple ___ Sony __ Wall Street __ Facebook __ Twitter __ UNICEF ___

6. What word best describes you and how you think? _____

CAREER QUESTIONNAIRE (SUBJECT-BASED)

Name: _____

Current Course: _____

Graduating Year: _____

Address: _____

City, State, Zip: _____

Email Address: _____

Please answer the following questions.

1. What is your favorite subject interest?
   _____
   _____

2. What is your preferred method for learning? Reading? Video instruction? Lecture? Explain.
   _____
   _____

3. Do you plan to choose this subject as a major in college?
   _____
   _____

4. What are some requirements for the major?
   _____
   _____

5. What do you hope to do with a degree in the major?
   _____
   _____

6. How long do you want to study for this degree?
   _____
   _____

7. What have you done to prepare for the major?
   _____
   _____

8. Do you plan to enroll in advanced coursework to gain more insight about the major?
_____
_____

9. How would you rate your overall efforts to prepare for the major on a scale of 1 to 10? Provide a reason.
_____
_____

10. Have you established transitional goals?
_____
_____

KIDS' CAREER QUESTIONNAIRE

Name: _____

Age: _____

Current Course: _____

Graduating Year: _____

Address: _____

City, State, Zip: _____

Email Address: _____

Please answer the following questions.

1. What do you want to become when you grow up?
    a. Doctor
    b. Lawyer
    c. Scientist
    d. Mathematician
    e. Own your own business
    f. Other: _____

2. How much money you want to make?
    a. $5,000 dollars
    b. $10,000 dollars
    c. $1,000,0000 dollars
    d. $50,000 dollars

3. Which of the following would you choose as a career? Rank 1 to 4.

Police _____ Doctor _____ Lawyer _____ Judge _____

4. Which is your favorite subject?

History _____ English _____ Math _____ Science _____ Writing _____

5. If you became a teacher, what subject would you like to teach?

_____

JOB QUESTIONNAIRE (WORKPLACE SKILLS)

Candidate's Name: _____

Address: _____

City, State, Zip: _____

Email Address: _____

Department and Designation (if employed): _____

Please answer the following questions.

1. Are you currently working?
_____

2. How long have you worked for the organization?
_____

3. Which of the following do you possess?

a. High School Diploma/GED
b. Associate's degree
c. Bachelor's degree
d. Master's degree
e. Doctorate degree
f. Vocational training certificate

4. What is your computer literacy?

a. Expert
b. Use some computer programs/software
c. Knowledge of computer hardware
d. Create computer software

5. What are your organizational skills?

a. Sales and marketing
b. Public Relations
c. Human Resource Management
d. Leadership Management

JOB APPLICATION QUESTIONNAIRE

Job Title: _____

Job Code: _____

Name: _____

Address: _____

City, State, Zip: _____

Email Address: _____

Please answer the following questions.

1. How did you come to learn about this position?

Newspaper _____ Television ad _____ Friends/Family _____
Company website _____

2. What other positions have you applied for with the company?

Job Title: _____ Job Code: _____

3. Application Type

Online _____
Telephone _____
In person _____
Mail _____
Email _____

4. Have you read the company profile? Yes _____ No _____

5. What is your preferred start date? _____

Job Search Questionnaire

Job Title: _____

Job Code: _____

Name: _____

Address: _____

City, State, Zip: _____

Email Address: _____

Home Phone: _____ Cell Phone _____

Alternate Phone: _____

Please answer the following questions.

1. Job Experience: Years _____ Months _____

2. Which company did you work for prior to coming here?
_____

3. Description of the company.
_____
_____

4. What was the title of your position?
_____

5. What were your responsibilities?
_____
_____

6. What was your ending salary/wages?
_____

7. How did you find out about this employment opening?
_____

8. Do you have an updated resume?
_____

9. What is your preferred pay rate/salary?
_____

10. Do you have any computer skills?
_____

11. Describe how your skills closely match the requirements of the job.
_____
_____
_____
_____
_____

CHAPTER 5

Banking Basics

Learning Objectives

- Define bank and banking.
- List categories of banking.
- List the two standard types of banking accounts.
- Create banking management goals.
- Complete a sample check form.
- Create payment management objectives.

WHAT IS BANKING?

Banking is defined as a process of depositing and withdrawing money from a bank. A **bank** is a type of financial institution and a financial intermediary that provides for the acceptance of customer deposits of which it channels through lending activities. A bank typically uses customer deposits within multiple capital markets.

Banks tend to be highly regulated in many countries and they operate under the fractional reserve banking system, which is a type of practice where the bank holds customer reserves of deposited funds to meet minimum capital requirements and to satisfy demands for payment. The reserves are typically small and banks lend out the rest to generate profit.

Because banks use depositor funds to establish and sustain profit objectives, it is important for a customer to choose the best institution not just for location purposes, but also for long-term objectives that might include one day applying for a home mortgage loan or a car loan or even a business loan.

When considering a bank, research the institution's general practices. How does the bank put customer deposits to work? What is the bank's lending practices? What is the bank's policy on college and retirement planning? What products does the bank offer that are necessary for my life planning objectives? In order to answer these questions, you will need to know what your life planning objectives are within the contexts of establishing both short-term and long-term objectives. Be wise in determining if the bank you choose offers safety, depositor insurance, and convenience. It is not enough to have an account at a bank that is a block away from your apartment. It is important to know if that bank provides additional opportunities to help you meet your long-term objectives.

For this reason, small business entrepreneurs interested in locating a bank that will meet their lending needs must review business banking opportunities. Not every bank provides loans to small businesses where revenues are below $25,000 per year. Some banks only work with small businesses where net revenues begin at and exceed $250,000 per year. Before establishing a business banking relationship with an institution, visit multiple locations and gather as much information necessary to help you determine the best banking option for your business.

TYPES OF BANKING

There are different types of banks. Banking activities are usually divided into multiple categories. For example, retail banking is typically for individuals and small businesses. **Retail banking** is defined as the process by which banks conduct business and execute transactions with consumers instead of corporations. See the list below for a description of the different types of retail banks.

Business banking, on the other hand, is defined as the process by which institutions provide services to mid-market businesses. Business banking institutions are considered to be commercial banks that accept deposits, give business loans, and offer basic investment products. **Corporate banking** is typically directed at larger business entities.

Concept Checker	*What is banking?*

Private banking is typically tailored directly to high net worth individuals and families where private banks provide wealth management services. The term "private" does not refer to an unincorporated business; instead, it refers to the type of personal customer service that is contrary to the practices of mass market retain banking.

Investment banking is defined as the process by which financial and banking institutions enter the financial markets. An **investment bank** is a type of financial institution that provides assistance to individuals, corporations, and governments by helping each raise capital through underwriting or by acting on the client's behalf as an agent in issuing securities.

Underwriting is a process that large financial services providers use to determine the eligibility of customers that want to receive the institution's products. A **financial services provider** is typically a bank, an insurer, and/or an investment house. Products provided by the financial services provider include equity capital, insurance, mortgage, and/or credit. Investment banks also assist companies with other activities that include mergers and acquisitions; provide services that include market making and derivatives trading; and offer fixed income instruments, equity securities, and foreign exchange commodities.

As noted above, there are different types of retail banks that provide a multitude of services. Below is a list of the most common, but it is not comprehensive.

- **Commercial bank:** This is a general term used for normal banking. It is different from an investment bank. Commercial banks normally deal with deposits and loans from large businesses and corporations.
- **Community bank:** A community bank is a locally-operated financial institution that provides community empowerment. This type of bank essentially serves the community through partnership and customer decision-making.
- **Community development bank:** A community development bank is a regulated institution that provides financial services and typically credit to underserved markets and populations.
- **Credit union:** A credit union is a not-for-profit cooperative that is owned by the depositors. Membership in a credit union is typically restrictive to employees of a specific company, residents of a certain neighborhood, members of a labor union, and immediate families. A **cooperative** is an association of one or more persons that cooperate for a mutual, social, economic, and cultural benefit.
- **Postal savings bank:** A postal savings bank is associated with a national postal system.
- **Private bank:** A private bank manages the assets of high net worth individuals. Private banks typically require a one million dollar opening deposit, but many banks have lowered the entry requirement.
- **Offshore bank:** An offshore bank is located in non-U.S. jurisdictions. Offshore banks offer low taxation and minimum regulation. In some cases, offshore banks are considered private banks.
- **Savings bank:** A savings bank primarily accepts savings deposits, but may also offer some retail banking products.
- **Direct or Internet-Only bank:** A direct or Internet-only bank is a type of institution without any physical bank branches. It wholly operates on a network of computers.

These are the types of banking institutions. To determine the institution that will be best for your banking objectives, research each type before depositing any money.

There are some general things you need to know about banking, beginning with understanding standard banking policies concerning typical products.

The Checking Account

The **checking account** is a standard product offered to each depositor. A checking account is protected by FDIC insurance, which is a type of insurance that guarantees the safety of deposits in banks that are members of the **Federal Deposit Insurance Corporation**. The FDIC is a United States government corporation that operates as an independent agency. The FDIC was created by the Glass-Steagall Act of 1933, which assures depositors that their money is insured up to $250,000; this means that deposits are insured for each depositor and for each bank.

To be sure, the FDIC does not provide depositor insurance for credit union members. Insurance is provided by the **National Credit Union Administration** (NCUA), which is an independent federal agency that was created by the U.S. Congress for the purposes of regulating, chartering, and supervising federal credit unions.

Concept Checker	*What are the types of banking?*

The standard checking account allows depositors to pay bills by writing a check on the account; access account information 24 hours a day online; and withdraw funds via an ATM and/or debit card. In essence, the checking (and savings) account is one of many money management tools that help depositors establish a budget, keep track of money and activities, and build a financial relationship with a banking (or credit union) institution. Before continuing, complete the following exercises.

Activity #1: Creating a Checking Account Management Objective

1. Why do you want a checking account?

_____
_____

2. For what purpose will you use a checking account?

_____
_____

3. Create a money management objective for a checking account.

_____
_____

After you have answered the questions and created the objective, review multiple types of checking accounts offered by one or more institutions to determine if your objective(s) align with one or more of the banking products.

Shopping

When considering opening a checking account, shop around for multiple options. Keep an organized list of what each institution offers in terms of the minimum opening deposit required, the monthly fee charged, the minimum daily balance requirement, and fees for nonsufficient funds transactions. Below is a definition of each of these terms as well as others that are specific to the industry.

Minimum Opening Deposit

Financial institutions typically require a minimum deposit to open a checking account. Each institution is different, but the standard rate is set between $25 and $400 depending on the type of checking account.

Monthly Fee

The **monthly fee** for a checking account is defined as your payment for using the account to the institution for managing it. Some checking accounts don't assess a monthly fee; this policy is typically based upon the minimum daily balance requirement. Some institutions waive the fee if you have money deposited into the account automatically. Automatic deposits typically include direct deposit through an employer. When choosing a bank, ask about the requirements for the minimum balance; ask if it has any correlation to the closing of an account.

Minimum Daily Balance Requirement

The **minimum daily balance requirement** is defined as the least amount of money kept in the checking account that is sufficient to meet the requirement. With some checking accounts, banks charge a fee if the account doesn't maintain a certain amount each day. Complete the following checking account goals.

Activity #2: Creating a Minimum Daily Balance Requirement Goals

In order to do the following exercise, you will need to research the best checking account option for your banking goals in order to fill in the required gaps.

1. Research Question: What is the daily balance minimum requirement?

Checking Account Type #1: _____ Monthly Fee: _____
Checking Account Type #2: _____ Monthly Fee: _____
Checking Account Type #3: _____ Monthly Fee: _____

2. Goal #1: I will maintain _____ to meet the minimum daily balance required.

_____
_____

3. Goal #2: If I don't maintain _____ to meet the minimum daily balance required, my account will be charged _____.

_____
_____

4. This extra fee will affect my budget. Write and then explain how the fee will affect your budget.

_____
_____
_____
_____

Remember that some institutions may close a checking account if it doesn't maintain the minimum daily balance requirement. Check with your institution to determine their policy on factors that lead to a closed checking account.

Nonsufficient Funds (NSF) Fees

Nonsufficient funds fees are assessed when a consumer authorizes a withdrawal when there is no actual money in the checking account. Consumers authorize withdrawals in many ways, which include writing a check or using their debit card. In some cases, the bank will cover the transaction by paying or sending it through; however, when this happens your account will become overdrawn and the account will incur a fee.

Whether the bank pays the transaction or rejects it, in this case the account bounces, your account will be assessed a fee. It is important that you understand the costs associated with incurring nonsufficient fees. Some banks charge a NSF fee of $34 for the transaction and additional fees per day or per week until the balance is paid. Check with your bank to determine what types of fees are assessed, how many, and the option of signing up for overdraft protection.

Activity #3: NSF Fees Research

Survey at least three financial institutions. In addition, also survey a credit union. What are the NSF fees? What are the charges for additional days? What is the bank's policy on overdraft protection? Use the following table as a guide.

Bank/Institution	Account Type	NSF Fees	Other Fees	Overdraft Protection?	Comments

This guide will help you establish plans for how to manage and/or prevent nonsufficient funds transactions. Establishing NSF goals will help you manage your cash flow and stay within your budgets. Before moving on to additional sections, begin to think about what types of goals are important for ensuring you don't overdraw your checking account. Write them down below.

Activity #4: Establishing NSF Goals

1. Research Question #1: What are my total necessity expenses by month?
_____
_____

2. Research Question #2: What are my recurring transactions? Which accounts have I set up that take money out? On what dates?

Account Type	Bill Amount	Schedule Payment Date	Pay Period

3. Research Question #3: During which pay period is my home budget most vulnerable? In essence, which pay period do I find myself having to transfer money from my savings account to my checking account to ensure I have money to cover the transaction?
_____
_____

4. Research Question #4: When did I forget to transfer money? What was the fee? How did it affect the home budget?
_____
_____
_____
_____

5. Goal #1: Ask about overdraft protection. Write the answer below.

_____
_____

6. Goal #2: Assess the recurring transactions. Which of the schedules may be possible to cancel? Consider canceling all of the transactions. Write your sentiments below.

_____
_____

7. Goal #3: Develop a relationship with your money. Establish a cash diet. Begin using the envelope system. Dedicate a bill to each envelope. Put cash in the envelope. Pay all bills using a cash-based system.

Envelope #1: _____   Pay Period: _____

_____
_____

Envelope #2: _____   Pay Period: _____

_____
_____

Envelope #3: _____   Pay Period: _____

_____
_____

Envelope #4: _____   Pay Period: _____

_____
_____

Envelope #5: _____   Pay Period: _____

_____
_____

Envelope #6: _____   Pay Period: _____

_____
_____

Use this system for discretionary and for some non-discretionary spending such as food, gasoline, rent/mortgage payment, clothes, fun money, eating out money, household cleaning supplies and giving. These are just eight items to start with. Later, consider using a cash diet for all of your expenses. This will help you to develop a relationship with your money and not with your credit card or your debit card.

Interest Rate

Checking accounts typically earn interest. The **interest** is the money the bank pays a depositor for funding the account. Free accounts usually don't earn interest. However, your checking account will typically be charged a monthly maintenance fee. Monthly maintenance fees can vary from $5 to $15 depending upon the type of account and the financial institution. It is much sounder budget-wise to get a free account without interest if you know for sure that you won't keep much money in the account.

Activity #5: Interest Rate/Monthly Fee Research

For this activity, research one or more institutions. Which accounts are free and without interest? Which accounts incur a monthly fee and interest? What is my budget for the monthly maintenance fee?

Institution	Type of Account	Free?	Monthly Fee	Assessed?	Pay Period	Rate of Interest	Daily? Weekly? Monthly?

Notes/Considerations
_____
_____
_____
_____
_____
_____

When considering a checking account, be sure to ask when the bank will charge the monthly fee. Prepare your home budget for the cost by developing a schedule. Use the following table to help you prepare your monthly budget for any changes.

Preparing the Home Budget for Monthly Bank Fee

Account	Monthly Fee	Assessed?	Pay Period	Budget Changes/Comments

ATM/Debit Cards

An ATM and/or debit card is typically offered with every checking account. An **ATM card** is a type of bank card issued by a financial institution that is used at an Automated Teller Machine (ATM) for the following transactions: deposits, withdrawals, and obtaining account information. A debit card is a type of bank card that provides access to the accountholder's banking account.

The debit card is used to make purchases without cash and withdraw money. The debit card is linked to a banking account from which the accountholder deposits and/or withdraws money. Debit cards are usually associated with checking accounts.

Today, prepaid debit cards are increasingly becoming the norm for individuals without a banking account, or "unbanked people." These are people who do not use banks or credit unions for reasons that may have something to do with their poor credit history. Card holders have the option of depositing their paychecks to their debit card as well as paying household expenses with the card.

Whether the debit card is linked to a banking institution or is a prepaid card, card holders will incur an ATM usage fee when transactions are conducted outside of the bank's and/or organization's network. Using an ATM machine that is not within a specific network will cause an accountholder to incur an institution fee and a machine fee. Fees typically range from $1.50 to $2.00 per transaction. These fees are important to consider when establishing and managing the household budget.

Activity #6: Survey of ATM Fee Charges In/Out of Network

Category	Assessed?	Pay Period	Budget Considerations
Monthly Fee			
NSF Fee			
ATM Fee (Network)			
ATM Fee (Out of Network)			
Other Fee			

The more knowledgeable you become about what to expect regarding fees the more involved you become with ensuring you don't go over your budget. Knowing when fees are typically charged to your account will help you to prepare your budget and manage the cash flow into and out of your house.

Opening

Once you have researched multiple checking accounts offered by multiple institutions, it is time now to open an account. To open a checking account, you will need to bring several things with you. Banks typically require some form of identification, a social security number, and a residential mailing address. The following categories of identification are required to open an account with a banking and/or credit union institution.

Category #1: Valid government-issued picture identification (primary)
- Driver's license
- State ID card
- Passport
- Military ID
- Resident alien ID

Category #2: Additional form of picture identification (secondary)

- Credit card
- Employee badge
- Student ID
- Union or trade ID
- Gun permit

In addition to these two major categories, prospective accountholders are required to have either a social security number or a tax identification number. A **Social Security number** (SSN) is a nine-digit number that is issued to U.S. citizens, permanent residents, and temporary residents. The number is issued under section 205(c)(2) of the Social Security Act. It helps the United States keep track of individuals. A social security number is typically given by an individual submitting an application, namely Form SS-5, Application for A Social Security Number Card.

A prospective accountholder must also supply information regarding a residential address as well as bring money to meet the opening deposit requirement.

Reading

Every bank account comes with an agreement that you must sign. The agreement outlines the terms and conditions of use, the steps the bank will take regarding breach, and your responsibilities.

When you sign the agreement, you provide the bank with a record of your signature and permission to pay money out of your account with respect to check writing and ATM/debit card withdrawals. Your signature is important because it helps to protect your account from identity fraud.

A standard agreement will outline the following legal conditions:
- The new account number
- The correct spelling of your name
- Your personal information, which includes date of birth, SSN, address, phone number, and place of employment
- The type of account you are opening
- How to contact the bank

The agreement also provides information about how the bank authorizes transactions. Review the agreement. It represents the primary guidance between you and the bank.

Depositing

Typically, for your account to remain active, you must deposit money. Some banks will close an account if there isn't activity over a period of time. There are common ways to deposit money to your account. You may deposit money by cash, check, and/or direct deposit.

You may also transfer money between accounts. In addition, money is added to your account when it accumulates interest. You can make a deposit at a local bank branch or by depositing money to your account via an Automated Teller Machine (ATM).

To make a deposit, you must know your account number and how much money you want to deposit. You must complete a deposit slip, which is a standard bank-specific document used to deposit checks and/or cash into your bank account. The process is simple. Use the following worksheet at home, as a guide, before completing the deposit slip. The worksheet prepares you for what to expect and helps you to gather your thoughts. You may use it or the deposit slip.

Activity #7: Deposit Slip Worksheet

Date of Deposit: _____ Bank: _____

Category	Dollars	Cents
Cash on hand		
Check#1		
Check #2		
Check #3		
Check #4		
Check #5		
Total of Cash and Coins		
Total of Check(s)		
Cash back		
Balance		

Be sure when completing the deposit slip that your cash back figure and the balance you calculate using the worksheet match the information on the slip.

In addition, always remember that when depositing checks, the bank may place a hold on one or more of your checks for verification purposes. This means that money may not be available for you until the hold expires. Check with your bank to determine what the hold policy is. Check also to determine if you can cash one or more checks because you have an account with the bank. If you can, cash the checks and deposit the money into the account.

Lastly, to prevent someone who has stolen your check from cashing it, write "for deposit only" on the back of the check. This will prevent the thief from gaining access to your funds by using the check.

Withdrawing

Withdrawing money from your account is simple as filling out a withdrawal slip or visiting an ATM. There are additional ways that you can withdraw money from your account. Below is a standard list of different types of withdrawals by you and/or by your bank.

- You can write a check to yourself or to another person and/or entity.
- You can make cash withdrawals through a teller.
- You can transfer money out of one account and deposit it into another account.
- The bank withdraws the monthly maintenance fee charged to your account.
- Purchases made through your debit card constitute as withdrawals.
- Recurring transactions created by automatic deductions are examples of withdrawals.

These are the common ways withdrawals are made on your account.

Check

A check is a type of form that requires you to fill in information specific to you and your checking account. What follows is a sample check form that you can expect to see and complete when making withdrawals from your account.

Figure: Sample Blank Check Form

```
┌─────────────────────────────────────────────────────────────┐
│ Your Name                                                    │
│ 1001[2]                                                      │
│ Address                                                      │
│ Phone Number [1]                                             │
│                                                    Date      │
│  _____ [3]                                         │
│                                                              │
│ Pay to the                                                   │
│ Order of_____  $_____   │
│                                                              │
│                                                              │
│ _____       Dollars  │
│                                                              │
│ Bull Banking [4]                                             │
│                                                              │
│ For _____          _____         │
│                                                              │
│ 3125[5]   709511135[6]   48925   0   1001[7]                 │
└─────────────────────────────────────────────────────────────┘
```

A pre-printed check form requires information about you, your account, the payment information, and to whom you are making the payment. Below is an explanation.

1. Your name, address, and phone number
2. Number of the individual check
3. Date of the check
4. Bank's name
5. Bank's identification number for electronic processing
6. Your account number for electronic processing
7. The individual check number for electronic processing

This is the standard information needed on a pre-printed check form. The last line to the right represents the place for your signature.

To gain practice with writing checks, complete the following activity. You want to pay your rent with a check instead of with a money order. You don't have much time this week. Therefore, with check number 1002, write out a check for your rent.

Activity #8: Fill out a Check

Your Name
1002
Address
Phone Number
Date
_____
Pay to the
Order of_____ $ _____
_____Dollars
Bull Banking
For _____   _____
3125   709511135 48925   0   1001

Keep a record of the checks you write and the reason you use them. At the end of this chapter is a worksheet you can use before writing a full check and also use as a method for keeping track of the checks you write.

Debit Card

The use of a debit card to withdraw money from your account requires you to establish a personal identification number, or PIN; and agree to the charge of a fee for any use at a non-network ATM. A debit card works similarly to a check, but the transaction is processed electronically. Debit cards withdraw money from your checking account. They are similar to credit cards in that they are accepted anywhere Visa or MasterCard is accepted. However, they are unlike credit cards in the sense that with a credit card you are borrowing money that you will need to repay at a later date.

Using a debit card requires the same discipline you need to have in writing checks. It is very easy to overdraw on your account if you don't have a plan for how you will spend your money. With this in mind, use the following worksheet to determine which bills and/or accounts would be better to pay with cash, debit card, or check (or money order).

Determining Payment Method Worksheet

Category	Amount	Cash	Debit Card	Check
Rent/Mortgage				
Electric				
Water				
Gas				
Food/Grocery				
Homeowner's Ins.				
Life Ins.				
Car Ins.				
Car Monthly				
Credit Card #1				
Credit Card #2				
Cable				
Toiletries				
Other: _____				
Other: _____				
Other: _____				

This worksheet will help you to prepare your budget as well as prepare for how you will expend money. This worksheet also will help you keep track of your spending in general.

ATM

Before withdrawing money from an Automated Teller Machine, review your bank's policy on standard fees charged for debit card use at a non-network terminal. Overdraft and ATM fees can hinder your progress of becoming more financially sound. When using a non-network ATM, you can expect to pay at minimum $3, which includes a fee from your bank as well as a fee from the third party; the fee is charged to use the ATM.

In addition, review the daily limits policy. Banks impose a daily limit on ATM withdrawals; if you go over this limit, your checking account will be charged. Therefore, it is important to keep track of all of your transactions to hedge against potential overdrafts on the account.

Automatic Deductions

An **automatic deduction** is defined as a process by which you set up money to be taken out of the account and directed to meet an obligation. For example, you can set up an automatic deduction for money to be withdrawn to pay your car loan, gym membership, school loans, and insurance. Using automatic deduction is easy because the money is taken out on a specific date and you always make sure that the money is in the account for this purpose.

However, automatic deductions can become a problem when you have too many scheduled transactions and you don't maintain a record of when the money will be withdrawn. Use the following worksheet to keep record of what monies will be taken out of your account based upon your pay period. You may add more accounts if you wish, but keep in mind that it is important to continue developing a relationship with your money. The more you let a thing or a person do the work for you, the more you stop working directly with your money. In other words, the more the computer or the electronic system does the work, instead of you using cash and doing it yourself, the less you become involved with your money.

Record of Automatic Deductions Scheduling Register

Category	Withdrawal Date	Amount	Pay Period	Cancellation

On this worksheet, record all of your past and future withdrawals. Be sure to record withdrawals where you have set up new automatic deductions. In addition, before creating an automatic deduction with a creditor, inquire about the company's policy concerning cancellations. Some companies require at least a 30- to 60-day notice before they will cancel an automatic deduction. Waiting too long to cancel will affect your budget and finance goals.

Withdrawal Slip

In the same way that you will need to use a deposit slip to add cash to your account via a bank teller, to withdraw money, you will need to complete a withdrawal slip. Standard withdrawal slips require information specific to you and your bank. For example, to withdraw money, you must know your name, account number, and how much money you want to withdraw. The bank requires that you sign a withdrawal slip exactly as your signature appears on the signature card.

Transfers

A **transfer** is defined as the process of withdrawing money from one account and putting it into another account at the same time. You can transfer money by using an ATM, by phone, in person, and through the Internet.

It is important to keep track of transfers made between your accounts because you must ensure that there is enough money in one or more of your accounts for automatic deductions. If you don't, then expect to be charged an overdraft fee and any related fee the bank charges. Use the following register to help keep track of all transfers. Before setting up a transfer, write it down in the register.

Record of Transfers and Scheduling Register

Account #1	Transfer Date	Amount	Account #2	Pay Period	Cancellation

Transfers and any type of withdrawals you make must coincide with your pay period or when you receive a consistent amount of income. This will help you to compare registers to ensure that you don't have too much money coming out of one pay period. Compare this record of transactions with those made through automatic deductions. You will find that both offer insight into how you are spending your money on overhead and personal expenses by pay period.

Managing the transactions that go in and out of your checking account is important within the scheme of personal financial management. That's why it is important to keep track of all account activities, both electronic and cash-based transactions. Use the worksheets as guides to help you manage your money.

THE SAVINGS ACCOUNT

The savings account is the most basic type of account offered by many banks. You deposit money into the account and the bank keeps it safe. You can take the money out when you need it. Deposits are insured by the FDIC for up to $100,000.

Banks pay interest on savings accounts. The rate is calculated as an **annual percentage yield** (APY), which is a finance term defined to mean a normalized representation of an interest rate that is based upon a compounding period per year. Simply, the APY is the rate paid to the depositor by a financial institution and is different from APR, or **annual percentage rate**, which means the rate the borrower pays to an institution.

Before opening an account with a bank, use the following research worksheet to determine which bank is most suitable for your personal finance management goals.

Survey of Savings Accounts Worksheet

Bank	Minimum Opening Deposit	Interest Rate/APY	Monthly Fee	Minimum Daily Balance

Knowing this information will help you set limits for how much you want to transfer into and out of this account. In addition, the most important automatic deduction you may want to set up is the one where you ensure that you pay yourself first. You should consider saving at least 15% of your pay per month, dedicating half each pay period. You can set up an automatic deduction from your checking account.

Once you receive your paycheck, a certain amount should be transferred into your savings account to go towards growing your emergency fund. Place this scheduled transaction on your automatic deductions register to keep track of monthly activities.

Types of Savings Accounts

A savings account offers unique advantages. It allows the accountholder to earn interest on the account, move money between accounts, and set up automatic withdrawals. An individual with a savings account has access to all banking branches within the network, online banking privileges, and overdraft protection options. However, with each savings account comes different criterion an accountholder must meet.

Money Market Savings

A standard money market savings account earns interest and often charges no fees if you maintain the minimum balance required in the account. Some money market savings accounts offer check-writing services, but there is a limit to the number of checks a depositor can write.

Certificate of Deposit

A certificate of deposit offered by a bank is a type of savings account. This type of account is called a time deposit. The CD earns a set rate of interest during the term the accountholder chooses. The term may be three months, six months, and up to 10 years. The interest on a certificate of deposit account is generally higher than a regular savings account due in part to an agreement between the accountholder and the bank to leave the money in the account for the set period of time. With a certificate of deposit there is an early withdrawal penalty. Deposits are insured up to $100,000 by the FDIC.

Individual Development Accounts

An **individual development account** (IDA) is defined as a type of account offered by community organizations to people with a lower income. The IDA is designed to help community members save money. An IDA is typically offered through a non-profit or government organization, but it is generally opened at a local bank. A deposit made by an IDA accountholder is matched by a deposit from a foundation, organization, or government agency.

An accountholder may use the funds to purchase a first home, pay for education and job training, and start a small business. For more information about individual development accounts, visit the organization's website. The address is located at the end of the chapter.

Karen learned the value of an IDA account while living in a homeless shelter facility. She found out how important it was to plan for the next transition. Without money, she wouldn't be able to make it beyond a month and might be forced to seek other means.

Case Study: Karen Saves for a House

Karen Lister is a recently paroled woman who spent 10 years in prison for robbery. While in prison, Karen completed job training coursework, her GED, and personal finance classes. Karen was paroled and released into a homeless shelter facility because she didn't have family to take her in. In the "Becoming a Productive Member" class, Karen learned for the first time about finances and the importance of creating and developing a savings plan. The program Karen was in offered an individual development account which matched her deposits dollar-for-dollar.

The IDA program is typically designed for low income individuals who want to establish a savings plan in order to purchase an asset such as a house; pay for education expenses; or start a small business. An asset provides both safety and financial security. These are some of the qualities of the program that prompted Karen to apply.

The matching dollars come from government agencies and local organizations invested in the community. Donors get a tax deduction for contributions to an IDA and they are also recognized for helping community members.

For her IDA, Karen selected a five-year plan, which she believed would be enough time to save and prepare for it mentally. A five-year plan would provide Karen with an opportunity to actually develop a savings plan, because the program would provide the structure she needed.

Before applying to the program, Karen had to meet certain eligibility requirements. They are as follows:

Income: Karen had to meet the maximum household income level requirement, which is approximately 200% below the federal poverty guidelines.

Earnings: All or part of Karen's savings had to derive from earned income. A paycheck is the most common source of earned income. However, if Karen received unemployment, welfare, disability, or social security, then she would qualify under this criterion.

Net Worth: Karen's IDA program requires that her current household assets combined cannot exceed $5,000.

Credit History: Since Karen was in prison for 10 years, she doesn't have a bad credit history. However, if Karen had serious debt problems, she wouldn't be able to qualify for the IDA program. Bad credit history and current debts make it harder for program participants to save money. Karen's IDA counselor informed her that if she had a bad credit history, then she would have to visit a credit counseling organization for help.

Because Karen met all of the eligibility requirements, she was able to enroll in the program and save at least 10% of her paycheck each pay period. By the end of her first year of saving money through an IDA account, Karen was able to save $500 by the end of the year. The sponsoring organization matched her deposits and Karen had $1,000 at the end of the year. The money in the account gave Karen hope that when she finished the program in five years, she would have at least $5,000 to put towards new home purchasing costs.

Although Karen didn't have a bad credit history, she enrolled in personal finance classes anyway, using a portion of her savings to pay for the classes. They qualified under the program's policy. Karen is still working hard to save money and meet her five-year goal. With discipline, patience, and determination, Karen will meet her goal.

BUSINESS PLANNER:

Small business entrepreneurs interested in developing a business banking relationship with a local branch must perform the necessary due diligence to ensure they make sound financial decisions. Not every business bank offers products that are beneficial for every part of the business. That's why it is important to establish business banking objectives with regard to managing monthly projected expenses, to signing up for overdraft protection, to using business debit cards, and to creating and monitoring transactions.

Use the following worksheet as a guide to direct your research of at least three major financial institutions. Compare their packages and benefits and determine which bank or credit union would be the best for your business.

FINANCIAL WELLNESS | 79

BUSINESS BANKING PRODUCTS RESEARCH

Institution	Bank #1	Bank #2	Bank #3	Notes and Comments
Minimum to open				
Monthly Service Fee				
Check Safekeeping Fee				
Image Statement Fee				
Check Return Fee				
Monthly Transactions Allowed				
Cash Deposit Limit				
Non-Bank ATM Inquiry or Transfer Fee				
Non-Bank ATM Withdrawal				
Overdraft Protection				
Business Online Services				

FINANCIAL WELLNESS | 81

CHAPTER KEY POINTS

Banking is defined as a process of depositing and withdrawing money from a bank. A **bank** is a type of financial institution and a financial intermediary that provides for the acceptance of customer deposits of which it channels through lending activities.

There are different types of banks. Banking activities are usually divided into multiple categories. For example, retail banking is typically for individuals and small businesses.

Underwriting is a process that large financial services providers use to determine the eligibility of customers that want to receive the institution's products. A **financial services provider** is typically a bank, an insurer, and/or an investment house.

The **checking account** is a standard product offered to each depositor. A checking account is protected by FDIC insurance, which is a type of insurance that guarantees the safety of deposits in banks that are members of the **Federal Deposit Insurance Corporation**.

An **automatic deduction** is defined as a process by which you set up money to be taken out of the account and directed to meet an obligation. For example, you can set up an automatic deduction for money to be withdrawn to pay your car loan, gym membership, school loans, and insurance.

A savings account offers unique advantages. It allows the accountholder to earn interest on the account, move money between accounts, and set up automatic withdrawals.

The IDA program is typically designed for low income individuals who want to establish a savings plan in order to purchase an asset such as a house; pay for education expenses; or start a small business. An asset provides both safety and financial security.

Chapter Key Terms

Annual percentage rate: term refers to the rate the borrower pays to an institution (loan).

Annual percentage yield: term refers to mean a normalized representation of an interest rate that is based upon a compounding period per year.

ATM: acronym stands for Automated Teller Machine.

ATM card: term refers to a type of bank card issued by a financial institution that is used at an Automated Teller Machine (ATM) for the following transactions: deposits, withdrawals, and obtaining account information.

Automatic deduction: term refers to a process by which you set up money to be taken out of the account and directed to meet an obligation.

Bank: term refers to a type of financial institution and a financial intermediary that provides for the acceptance of customer deposits of which it channels through lending activities.

Banking: term refers to a process of depositing and withdrawing money from a bank.

Business banking: term refers to the process by which institutions provide services to mid-market businesses.

Checking account: term refers to a standard product offered to each depositor.

Commercial bank: term refers to a general term used for normal banking.

Community bank: term refers to a locally-operated financial institution that provides community empowerment.

Community development bank: term refers to a regulated institution that provides financial services and typically credit to underserved markets and populations.

Corporate banking: term refers to a banking product tailored directly to larger business entities.

Credit union: term refers to a not-for-profit cooperative that is owned by the depositors.

Direct bank: term refers to a type of institution without any physical bank branches. It wholly operates on a network of computers. See *Internet-only Bank*.

Federal Deposit Insurance Corporation: term refers to a United States government corporation that operates as an independent agency.

FDIC: acronym stands for Federal Deposit Insurance Corporation.

Financial services provider: term refers to a bank, an insurer, and/or an investment house.

Individual development account: term refers to a type of account offered by community organizations to people with a lower income.

Interest: term refers to the money the bank pays a depositor for putting money into a checking account.

Internet-Only Bank: term refers to a type of institution without any physical bank branches. It wholly operates on a network of computers. See *Direct Bank*.

Investment bank: term refers to a type of financial institution that provides assistance to individuals, corporations, and governments by helping each raise capital through underwriting or by acting on the client's behalf as an agent in issuing securities.

Investment banking: term refers to the process by which financial and banking institutions enter the financial markets.

Minimum daily balance requirement: term refers to the least amount of money kept in the checking account that is sufficient to meet the requirement.

Monthly fee: term refers to a fee charged to a checking account and is defined as payment to the institution for managing it.

National Credit Union Administration: term refers to an independent federal agency that was created by the U.S. Congress for the purposes of regulating, chartering, and supervising federal credit unions.

NCUA: acronym stands for National Credit Union Administration.

Nonsufficient funds fee: term refers to a type of fee assessed when a consumer authorizes a withdrawal when there is no actual money in the checking account.

Offshore bank: term refers to a type of bank that is located in a non-U.S. jurisdiction.

Postal savings bank: term refers to a type of bank associated with a national postal system.

Private bank: term refers to a type of bank that requires a higher minimum deposit; this product is typically tailored to high net worth individuals.

Private banking: term refers to a banking product tailored directly to high net worth individuals and families where private banks provide wealth management services.

Retail banking: term refers to the process by which banks conduct business and execute transactions with consumers instead of corporations.

Savings bank: term refers to a type of bank that only accepts savings deposits.

Social security number: term refers to a nine-digit number that is issued to U.S. citizens, permanent residents, and temporary residents.

Transfer: term refers to the process of withdrawing money from one account and putting it into another account at the same time.

Underwriting: term refers to a process that large financial services providers use to determine the eligibility of customers that want to receive the institution's products.

GROUP WORK PROMPT

Write a paper on the topic of wealth management. Focus the discussion in the paper by comparing and contrasting three private banking institutions that offer asset management, commercial banking, investment banking, and securities services. Include an evaluation of J.P. Morgan Treasury Services product. Begin the discussion as a group in class. Follow it up with a 10-page paper with a partial bibliography.

HOMEWORK EXERCISE

For homework, compare and contrast three types of checking accounts. Construct a graph that provides an outline of the different types of accounts. Use it as a guide for structuring your thoughts. You may choose one institution or you may include within your discussion a survey of not more than three. Write a five-page paper on the topic and add a working bibliography.

ASSESSMENT

1. What is banking?

2. What are the types of banking? Provide an explanation of at least three.

3. What are nonsufficient funds transactions?

4. What are the elements of a pre-printed check form? Explain.

5. What is an individual development account?

Helpful Websites

IDA: Corporation for Enterprise Development
www.idanetwork.org

Chapter Forms

On the next pages are all of the forms discussed within this chapter. You may photocopy, scan, and print them out. Some forms you will need to complete the group work and the homework.

RECORD OF CHECKS REGISTER

Check Date	Pay to the Order of	For	Check #	Amount

BUSINESS BANKING PRODUCTS RESEARCH SHEET

	Bank #1	Bank #2	Bank #3	Notes and Comments
Minimum to open				
Monthly Service Fee				
Check Safekeeping Fee				
Image Statement Fee				
Check Return Fee				
Monthly Transactions Allowed				
Cash Deposit Limit				
Non-Bank ATM Inquiry or Transfer Fee				
Non-Bank ATM Withdrawal				
Overdraft Protection				
Business Online Services				

RECORD OF TRANSFERS AND SCHEDULING REGISTER

Account #1	Transfer Date	Amount	Account #2	Pay Period	Cancellation

RECORD OF AUTOMATIC DEDUCTIONS SCHEDULING REGISTER

Category	Withdrawal Date	Amount	Pay Period	Cancellation

Determining Payment method Worksheet

Category	Amount	Cash	Debit Card	Check
Rent/Mortgage				
Electric				
Water				
Gas				
Food/Grocery				
Homeowner's Ins.				
Life Ins.				
Car Ins.				
Car Monthly				
Credit Card #1				
Credit Card #2				
Cable				
Toiletries				
Other: _____				
Other: _____				
Other: _____				

CHAPTER 6

College Planning Tips

Learning Objectives

- Define college planning.
- List the types of college planning solutions.
- Complete planning worksheets.
- Develop cash flow objectives for industry.
- Review general admission requirements.
- Review information about types of loans.

WHAT IS COLLEGE PLANNING?

College Planning is defined as a process of preparing for academic work beyond the completion of secondary education. Prospective college students must be aware of the challenges they face in preparing to earn an education at the post-secondary level. One common challenge involves determining how to pay for college. Another challenge is determining what major to choose. Yet, another challenge involves choosing the type of college to attend. These are common issues that prospective college students will face as they plan the next chapters of their lives, which include succumbing to the demands of adulthood.

This chapter provides information about the college planning process, which includes understanding test preparation solutions. This chapter will provide insight into creating an education savings account as well as information about common federal student loan programs.

Parents and prospective college students will find this chapter helpful and practical, because it provides worksheets for the college student preparing to attend a college. This chapter also provides worksheets for the parent preparing a child for college. In other words, both the student and the parent can work together to determine the best solutions for their college planning needs.

Small business entrepreneurs that want to enter the college planning industry will find that it is saturated with different businesses offering both preparatory and long-term solutions to prospective college students. If you desire to enter this industry, be prepared to research businesses in your area that not only offer test preparation courses, but also letter writing services. Some companies have become official testing sites for the SAT, ACT, and TOEFL exam. In considering this industry, prepare the company by determining which type of structure you want for the business and by developing cash flow objectives that will ensure both short-term and long-term success.

TYPES OF COLLEGE PLANNING

There are different methods organizations and businesses use to help prospective college students. Businesses and organizations typically help parents and their children with exam and test preparation, offering additional solutions related to tutoring of writing. However, test preparation isn't the only method of college planning. Creating a college savings plan is equally important within the scheme of preparing the student to enter a post-secondary institution. This section provides guidance for how to begin the process of developing college savings objectives and also provides information about the different federal student loans programs.

Coverdell Education Savings Account

The **Coverdell Education Savings Account**, known by multiple variations, is a type of investment account that offers owners an opportunity to plan and save for college on behalf of their children. The purpose of the investment account is to encourage savings to offset future education expenses. These expenses may include costs of attendance for elementary, secondary, and college students. Owners of the Coverdell Education Savings Account are encouraged to design college planning objectives that reference costs associated with tuition, books, and uniforms. Tax information about the investment account can be found in section 530 of the Internal Revenue Code.

Concept Checker	*What is college planning?*

Tax Treatment
A Coverdell ESA offers tax advantages that are similar to a 529 plan, which is another type of investment vehicle. Deposits into a Coverdell account are not tax-deductible. However, money in a Coverdell ESA grows tax-deferred.

The proceeds from the account may be withdrawn tax-free, but only for qualified education expenses and only at a qualified institution. The term "qualified expenses" is applicable to primary and secondary schools as well as colleges and universities.

For tax information regarding education savings plans, review the following IRS guidance:
- Publication 970, Tax Benefits for Education
- Tax Topic 310, Coverdell Education Savings Accounts
- IRS Tax Tip 2007-48, Offset Education Costs

The IRS website offers information concerning distribution limits and the Hope and lifetime credit claims.

Differences on Limits

The Coverdell ESA differs from most 529 plans. The ESA has a lower maximum contribution limit per child. For example, the ESA allowed for parents to deposit up to $2,000 from 2002 to 2012. However, at the end of 2012, parents could only deposit $500 less than the previous maximum. With a 529 plan, there are generally no contribution limits.

A Coverdell ESA allows investments into stocks, bonds, and mutual funds. The rules for investment are the same for investments into IRAs. However, with a 529, investments are determined by state-run allocation programming objectives.

The balance in a Coverdell ESA is disbursed on qualified education expenses; the investment account allows disbursement for the beneficiary up to the age of 30 years old. If funds are not used, then the account can be given to another family member below this age to avoid tax penalties. However, with a 529 plan, there is no age limit.

A Coverdell ESA allows for the withdrawing of funds tax-free for qualified education expenses. A 529 plan does not. Lastly, the income level of a donor typically affects a Coverdell ESA contribution. This rule doesn't apply to 529 plans.

Similarities to 529

Monies donated to both a Coverdell ESA and a 529 plan are not considered the income of the child (beneficiary) when calculating federal financial aid eligibility. The owner of the account must be someone who is not the beneficiary; in this case, the parent is the owner. Because of this rule, this allows a prospective college student to apply for and receive financial aid to offset costs related to attendance.

The custodian who manages the ESA and the 529 plan can designate a new beneficiary without tax penalty. The new beneficiary must be an eligible family member of the previous beneficiary.

The 529 Education Savings Plan

The **529 plan** is a type of tax-advantaged investment vehicle that encourages saving for higher education expenses on behalf of a designated beneficiary. Rules that govern the 529 plan fall under section 529 of the Internal Revenue Code.

The 529 plan allows for out-of-state investment activity. However, there are significant tax advantages for investors who invest in a 529 plan within their state. For example, investing in a 529 plan within a state offers matching grant opportunities, protection from creditors, and other types of state exemptions.

A qualified distribution from a 529 plan is exempt from federal income tax.

Types

There are two types of 529 plans. The first type, **prepaid**, allows an investor to purchase tuition credits at the current rate and the credits are used in the future. In this respect, prepaid plan performance is based upon tuition inflation. A prepaid plan is administered by a state or a higher education institution.

On the other hand, the second type, **savings**, is based upon market performance of one or more of the underlying investments, usually mutual funds. Most 529 plans offer different asset-allocation options that are based upon the beneficiary's college age. A savings plan can only be administered by a state.

Use

Monies distributed from a 529 plan are typically used to cover the costs of tuition, fees, books, supplies, and equipment that are required for study. The money can only be used at an accredited college, university, and/or vocational school within the United States and at some select foreign institutions.

Money from a 529 plan is also used to cover room and board costs. The beneficiary must attend school at least half-time. Off-campus housing costs are only covered up to the amount required for on-campus room and board housing. These are costs that the student includes for federal financial aid purposes on the FAFSA.

A qualified education expense does not include a student loan or student loan interest.

Distributions from a 529 plan not used for qualified education expenses are subject to income tax and early withdrawal penalties. The following exceptions (to the tax treatment) apply:

- **The death of the designated beneficiary.** In this case, the distribution would go to another beneficiary or to the estate of the previous beneficiary.
- **The designated beneficiary becomes disabled.** Disabled, within this context, is defined as a person who cannot do any type of substantial gainful activity as a result of a physical and/or mental condition. The custodian must provide proof of a physician's determination regarding the beneficiary's condition, whether it will result in death or continue indefinitely.
- **The designated beneficiary receives another source of income.** Within this context, sources of income include qualified scholarship, veteran's educational assistance, education assistance provided by an employer, and non-taxable payments such as gifts or bequests.

Advantages

With a 529 plan, the principal amount continues to grow tax-deferred and distributions to a designated beneficiary are tax-exempt.

In addition, the donor maintains control of the account. In other words, the beneficiary has no inherent right to the funds. However, there is a drawback. A non-qualified withdrawal is subject to income tax and a penalty.

The continued investment activity of the account is handled by the plan and not by the donor. The plan's assets are managed by the state treasurer or an outside investment company.

The donor does not receive Form 1099 until the year of withdrawal(s).

The donor may change the options of a 529 plan every year or the account may be rolled over on behalf of the beneficiary.

A 529 plan has a low minimum contribution requirement, fees are lower than other investment vehicles, and there are no income or age limitations.

Lastly, the assets of a 529 plan are not counted for gross estate (estate tax) purposes. However, the 529 college savings plan is treated as an asset of the account owner, which is typically the parent.

Disadvantages

Not all investment vehicles are available through a 529 plan. With a 529 plan, donors can exchange and/or reallocate assets one time a year. Earnings withdrawn for a non-qualified expense will be subject to taxes and penalties.

Federal Grant & Loan Programming

The U.S. government provides different types of federal grant and loan options for student borrowers. A federal student loan is money you borrow from the federal government to pay for the costs of education. A student must repay the loan with interest. On the other hand, a federal grant is money that a student doesn't have to repay.

The following is a list of federal grant and loan programs. It provides insight into college planning for both parents and prospective students.

Federal Family Education Loan (FFEL) Program

Under the **Federal Family Education Loan FFEL) Program**, private lenders provide loans to students that are guaranteed by the government. Loan types include the following:

- Subsidized Federal Stafford Loans
- Unsubsidized Federal Stafford Loans
- FFEL PLUS Loans
- FFEL Consolidation Loans

Because of the passing of the Health Care and Education Reconciliation Act of 2010, federal student loans that fall under the FFEL Program are no longer provided by private lenders. Instead, the U.S. Department of Education manages all new student loan programs.

Federal Pell Grant

The **Federal Pell Grant** is a type of federal grant for undergraduate students that have financial need.

Federal Perkins Loan

The **Federal Perkins Loan** is a type of federal student loan for undergraduate and graduate students who demonstrate financial need. The loan is made by the recipient's school.

Federal Work Study

The **Federal Work Study** program is a type of federal student aid that provides part-time student employment to help pay for education expenses.

PLUS Loan

The **PLUS Loan** is a type of loan that is available to graduate students and also a parent of a dependent undergraduate student. The borrower must repay the loan with interest. Forbearance and deferment do not apply.

Private Loan

The **Private Loan** is a type of non-federal loan that is made by a lender to a borrower. The lender is typically a bank, credit union, state agency, or school.

Direct Loan

A **Direct Loan** is a type of federal student loan that is made through the William D. Ford Federal Direct Loan Program. Eligible students and parents borrow directly from the U.S. Department of Education at participating schools. There are multiple types of direct loans, which include the following:

- Direct Subsidized Loans
- Direct Unsubsidized Loans
- Direct PLUS Loans
- Direct Consolidation Loans

A **subsidized loan** is based on financial need. The government pays the interest on the loan while the borrower is in-school or while the loan is in grace or deferment status. On the other hand, with an **unsubsidized loan**, the borrower is responsible for both the principal and the interest. The interest on an unsubsidized loan continues to accrue from the date of disbursement and continues throughout the life of the loan.

A **Direct PLUS Loan** is a type of federal student loan where the borrower is fully responsible for paying both the principal and the interest. The U.S. Department of Education makes Direct PLUS Loans to graduate, professional, and parents of dependent undergraduate students.

Lastly, a **Direct Consolidation Loan** is a federal loan that allows a borrower to combine one or more federal student loans into one new loan. With this type of program, the borrower only has to make one monthly payment. A benefit of the Direct Consolidation Loan program is that a borrower is allowed loan extensions.

These are the education savings and loan programs that will help you create college planning objectives. If a loan is not feasible for you, then consider developing a savings plan. Research and consider multiple options before signing the federal government's master promissory note, which is a binding legal document. A federal student loan typically can't be discharged in bankruptcy.

As you continue to develop college planning objectives, use the worksheets that are included at the end of this chapter. They will help to guide your thinking about what to expect as a prospective college student.

BUSINESS PLANNER

Small business entrepreneurs wanting to enter the college planning industry have to determine which type of structure would be best for the business. This is expressly the goal that Davis had to confront when he was creating Davis College Test Prep.

Case Study:
Davis Chooses a Business Structure

Davis Browning is a test prep specialist. He has worked for various organizations such as College Board and Princeton Review, providing solutions as an education specialist for prospective college students. Today, Davis wants to enter the field of college planning as an entrepreneur. He hasn't decided on the best business structure, so he decides to conduct some research. The following sections represent the results of Davis's research. He weighs the pros and cons of choosing each type.

Sole Proprietorship

A **sole proprietorship** is a type of legal business structure where the owner of the business maintains complete control, makes all of the decisions, and earns all of the profits. With this type of structure, business expenses are deductible. It is easy to set up a sole proprietorship. On the other hand, with a sole proprietorship, the business owner is completely liable for all debts and lawsuits created against it. In addition, the business terminates when the owner dies and the tax rate for a sole proprietorship is significantly higher than other entities.

Davis continues to research.

Partnership

A **partnership** is a type of legal business structure where at least two parties come together to form a business, where both parties make the decisions, where the business expenses are deductible, and where each partner is taxed at an individual level and not as partners. However, with this type of structure, the partnership terminates on the death and/or withdrawal of any one of the partners. Each partner is totally liable for the business expenses and debts. Control of the partnership is difficult because each partner is legally allowed to bind the company. Lastly, each partner is liable for any agreement made by one or more partners.

A partnership doesn't sound like the best choice for Davis, so he continues to research.

Limited Liability Company (LLC)

A **limited liability company** is a type of legal business structure where either the owner or the manager has management authority. An LLC allows an unlimited number of shareholders. In terms of tax benefits, income or losses derived from the business can pass through to each member's returns. An LLC has the liability protection of a corporation with no responsibility for debts. On the other hand, there are disadvantages to creating an LLC, but there aren't many. For one, it is expensive to open an LLC than a partnership. There are rules that govern LLCs by state, so this means that a business owner would have to create multiple types of handbooks and reference state requirements. Control may be slightly difficult. The last issue with an LLC is that each member of the LLC must submit their consent to transfer any interest of the business to another person.

Davis believes that an LLC is the right choice, because the business structure provides him with the control he needs to maintain order for the business. Davis chooses to form an LLC and continues his research.

These are some of the types of business structures available for small business entrepreneurs, but they are not the only ones. Davis could have decided to form a corporation or a limited partnership, but it would have been too costly for his new business and harder to develop and maintain control mechanisms. Davis's choice of an LLC helps to protect him from personal liability.

When considering developing a solution to answer a problem, choose the type of business structure that would be best for your company. Consider the tax advantages that come with the structure as well as the liability protection.

Chapter Key Points

College Planning is defined as a process of preparing for academic work beyond the completion of secondary education. Prospective college students must be aware of the challenges they face in preparing to receive an education at the post-secondary level.

The **Coverdell Education Savings Account**, known by multiple variations, is a type of investment account that offers owners an opportunity to plan and save for college on behalf of their children. The purpose of the investment account is to encourage savings to offset future education expenses.

The **529 plan** is a type of tax-advantaged investment vehicle that encourages saving for higher education expenses on behalf of a designated beneficiary. Rules that govern the 529 plan fall under section 529 of the Internal Revenue Code.

The U.S. government provides different types of federal grant and loan options for student borrowers. A federal student loan is money you borrow from the federal government to pay for the costs of education. A student must repay the loan with interest. On the other hand, a federal grant is money that a student doesn't have to repay.

A **subsidized loan** is based on financial need. On the other hand, with an **unsubsidized loan**, the borrower is responsible for both the principal and the interest.

A **Direct Consolidation Loan** is a federal loan that allows a borrower to combine one or more federal student loans into one new loan.

Chapter Key Terms

529 Plan: term refers to a type of tax-advantaged investment vehicle that encourages saving for higher education expenses on behalf of a designated beneficiary.

College planning: term refers to a process of preparing for academic work beyond the completion of secondary education.

Coverdell Education Savings Account: term refers to a type of investment account that offers owners an opportunity to plan and save for college on behalf of their children.

Coverdell ESA: see *Coverdell Education Savings Account*.

Direct Consolidation Loan: term refers to a federal loan that allows a borrower to combine one or more federal student loans into one new loan.

Direct Loan: term refers to a type of federal student loan that is made through the William D. Ford Federal Direct Loan Program.

Direct PLUS Loan: term refers to a type of federal student loan where the borrower is fully responsible for paying both the principal and the interest.

ESA: see *Coverdell Education Savings Account*.

Federal Family Education Loan Program: term refers to a type of federal loan program where private lenders provide loans to students that are guaranteed by the government.

Federal Pell Grant: term refers to a type of federal grant for undergraduate students that have financial need.

Federal Perkins Loan: term refers to a type of federal student loan for undergraduate and graduate students who demonstrate financial need.

Federal Work Study: term refers to a type of federal student aid that provides part-time student employment to help pay for education expenses.

FFEL: see *Federal Family Education Loan Program*.

Limited liability company: term refers to a type of legal business structure where either the owner or the manager has management authority. An LLC allows an unlimited number of shareholders.

Partnership: term refers to a type of legal business structure where at least two parties come together to form a business, where both parties make the decisions, where the business expenses are deductible, and where each partner is taxed at an individual level and not as partners.

PLUS Loan: term refers to a type of loan that is available to graduate students and also a parent of a dependent undergraduate student.

Prepaid 529 Plan: term refers to an option where an investor is allowed to purchase tuition credits at the current rate and the credits are used in the future.

Private Loan: term refers to a type of non-federal loan that is made by a lender to a borrower. The lender is typically a bank, credit union, state agency, or school.

Savings 529 Plan: term refers to an option where the growth of donated funds is based upon the market performance of one or more of the underlying investments, usually mutual funds.

Sole proprietorship: term refers to a type of legal business structure where the owner of the business maintains complete control, makes all of the decisions, and earns all of the profits.

Subsidized loan: term refers to a type of federal student loan that is based on financial need.

Unsubsidized loan: term refers to a type of federal student loan where the borrower is responsible for both the principal and the interest.

Group Work Prompt

As a group, research additional education savings plan. Develop a case study for a parent of a prospective college student interested in attending Harvard University in ten years. How would you prepare the parent to save at least the first year's cost of education?

Develop an essay comparing multiple plans including the ones discussed in this chapter. Include within your discussion a reference to the cost of education and related expenses to attend Harvard University. Do not take into consideration tuition changes. Visit the Harvard websites and base your suggestions on current statistics.

Start the project in class and finish it as a group.

Homework Exercise

Pretend you are an international student located in China. You wish to come to California on a Visa. Prepare a paper outlining the requirements you would need to meet in order to accomplish the goal. Use one or more of the Chapter Forms for help. Attach a copy of the filled out form(s) with your essay.

Helpful Websites

Federal Student Aid: Glossary
http://studentaid.ed.gov/glossary#Federal_Perkins_Loan

Chapter Forms

On the next pages are all of the forms discussed within this chapter. You may photocopy, scan, and print them out. Some forms you will need to complete the group work and the homework.

Assessment

1. What is college planning?

_____
_____

2. What are examples of two education savings plans?

_____
_____

3. Based upon your group work exercise, name an additional education savings plan.

_____
_____

4. List examples of federal loan programs. Choose at least two. Provide a definition for each.

First Program

_____
_____
_____

Second Program

_____
_____
_____

HIGH SCHOOL REQUIREMENTS CHECKLIST

Subject	Years Required	Years Completed
History & Social Science		
English		
Math		
Laboratory Science		
Visual and Performing Arts		
College Preparatory Elective		

History & Social Science: includes U.S. history, civics, or American government, social science

English: includes college preparatory English, composition, literature

Math: includes Algebra I, Geometry, Algebra II, higher mathematics

Laboratory Science: includes biological science, physical science

Visual and Performing Arts: includes dance, drama, theater, music, or visual art

College Preparatory Elective:

_____

_____

TEST PREP PLANNING CRITERIA
(HIGH SCHOOL PROFICIENCY REQUIREMENTS)

Reading

Question Type	Number of Questions

Time Allotted:

Special Notes:

Writing

Question Type	Number of Questions

Time Allotted:

Special Notes:

Math

Question Type	Number of Questions

Time Allotted:
_____
_____

Special Notes:
_____
_____
_____
_____

Science

Question Type	Number of Questions

Time Allotted:
_____
_____

Special Notes:
_____
_____
_____
_____

Social Studies

Question Type	Number of Questions

Time Allotted:
_____
_____

Special Notes:
_____
_____
_____
_____

TEST PREP PLANNING CRITERIA (GED)

Language Arts, Writing

Question Type	Number of Questions

Time Allotted:

Special Notes:

Social Studies

Question Type	Number of Questions

Time Allotted:

Special Notes:

Science

Question Type	Number of Questions

Time Allotted:
_____
_____

Special Notes:
_____
_____
_____
_____

Language Arts, Reading

Question Type	Number of Questions

Time Allotted:
_____
_____

Special Notes:
_____
_____
_____
_____

Mathematics

Question Type	Number of Questions

Time Allotted:
_____
_____

Special Notes:
_____
_____
_____
_____

TEST SCORES OVERVIEW WORKSHEET (HIGH SCHOOL)

State: _____

Overall Score: _____

Writing Score: _____

English Language Arts Score: _____

Mathematics Score: _____

Reading Score: _____

Science Score: _____

Social Studies Score: _____

TEST SCORES OVERVIEW WORKSHEET (GED)

State: _____

Overall Score: _____

Language Arts, Writing Score:
_____

Social Studies Score: _____

Science Test Score: _____

Language Arts, Reading Score: _____

Mathematics Score: _____

State GED Certificate: _____

ACT Overall Score: _____

English Score: _____

Mathematics Score: _____

Reading Score: _____

Science Score: _____

Scores Sent:
Home_____School_____
Scores Sent:
Home_____School_____
Scores Sent:
Home_____School_____

SAT Overall Score:
_____

Critical Reading Score: _____

Math Score: _____

Writing Score: _____

Scores Sent:
Home_____School_____
Scores Sent:
Home_____School_____

HIGH SCHOOL ACADEMIC ADVISING CHECK

Course Number	Courses (For AP courses, place a star near the course.)	Credits Required/ Credits Completed	Grade	Fulfills College Requirement Y/N
		/		
		/		
		/		
		/		
		/		
		/		
		/		
		/		
		/		
		/		
		/		
		/		
		/		
		/		
		/		
		/		
TOTAL		/		

Note: See next page for questions.

Questions:
1. If a course doesn't fulfill a requirement for the college I want to attend, which course can I take to fulfill it?

College #1:
_____
_____

College #2:
_____
_____

College #3:
_____
_____

College #4:
_____
_____

2. Can I take the course as a dual registrant at a local community college?
        Yes_____No_____
        When is the course offered:
        Fall_____Spring_____Summer_____Other_____

College: _____
Course Number: _____Course Title: _____
Time: _____ Professor: _____
Department Contact: _____
Admissions & Registration Contact: _____

Notes (Advisor Suggestions):
_____
_____

3. Can I take the course at my high school?
    Year:
    Fall____Spring_____Summer_____

Notes (Advisor Suggestions):
_____
_____
_____
_____

ADMISSION REQUIREMENTS WORKSHEET

Category	Completed?	Notes
Application Fee		
Application Filing Period		
Fall Semester		
Spring Semester		
Summer Semester		
Term applied for		
Ordered transcripts		
College #1		
College #2		
College #3		
Financial Aid Application School code: _____ School code: _____ School code: _____ School code: _____	 _____ _____ _____ _____	
H.S. Graduation Test PSAT SAT ACT	_____ _____ _____ _____ _____	

Other: _____		
Admission Essay Scholarship Essay	_____ _____	
Letter of Recommendation		

ADMISSION REQUIREMENTS WORKSHEET (INTERNATIONAL STUDENT)

College _____

Application Filing Period
Fall: _____ Spring: _____ Summer: _____

Application Deadline _____

Letter of Recommendation
Recommender:
_____

Contact Information
Phone:
_____
Email:
_____
Postal:
_____

Tests

Test	Test Dates	School Code	Completed?
SAT			
ACT			
TOEFL			

Admission Essay
Finished_____ Need to Write_____ Need to Type_____
Need to Send_____ Sent_____

Exit Examination Scores

Test	Test Dates	Transcript Certified/Evaluated?	Notes

ADMISSION REQUIREMENTS WORKSHEET (INTERNATIONAL STUDENT) CONT'D

Statement of Financial Resources
Academic Program:
_____

Tuition and Fees:
_____

Expenses (College):
_____

Total Cost of Attendance:
_____

Category	1st Year	2nd Year	3rd Year	4th Year
Personal				
Savings				
Parents/Sponsor				
Scholarship/Loan				
Other Assets				
Total				

Sponsor Information:
_____
_____

Additional Documentation Checklist
Employment Letter: _____
Bank Statement: _____
Parent/Friend/Relative Letter: _____
Scholarship Award Letter: _____
Approved Personal Recommendation (Graduate): _____

Medical Insurance
Type: _____ Provider: _____

Admission Requirements Worksheet (International Student) Cont'd

Visa Applications (Completed?)
F1 Visa: _____
J1 Student Visa: _____
M1 Student Visa: _____
Green Card: _____

Department Major Admissions
Major:
_____
_____

Affected?
_____
_____

TAX & FINANCIAL INFORMATION CHECKLIST (FAFSA APPLICATIONS)

Category	Status	Need to do
Social Security card/driver's license/identification card		
W-2 forms; record of earned income		
Federal Income Tax Return		
Record of untaxed income Welfare benefits, Social Security benefits, TANF, ADC, military or clergy allowances		
Current bank statements; records of stocks, bonds, investments		
Alien registration number		

CHAPTER 7

Insurance

Learning Objectives

- Define insurance.
- List the types of insurance.
- Develop risk management objectives.
- Explain types of insurance policies.
- List types of health insurance.

WHAT IS INSURANCE?

Insurance is defined as the transfer of risk of a loss between one or more entities in exchange for payment. Insurance falls under the category of **risk management**, a term that refers to a process of identifying, assessing, and prioritizing risks. Risk managers use this process to coordinate the economic application of resources that help to minimize, monitor, and control the probability of future events. Risks assume many forms and typically derive from uncertainty, leading to legal liabilities, credit risk, project failures, accidents, and natural causes and disasters.

An **insurance carrier**, or company selling insurance, will insure one entity in exchange for a monthly premium. The insured is the person or organization purchasing the insurance policy; a person or organization becomes the policyholder in the transaction. The insurer, or insurance company, agrees to **indemnify**, or compensate, the insured in case of a personal loss. The policyholder receives a contract, which is considered the official **insurance policy**. The contract provides details concerning the circumstances upon which the insured will be financially compensated.

Small business entrepreneurs, particularly sole proprietors, must develop risk management objectives to hedge against the possibility of lawsuits and claims against personal assets. A sole proprietorship is a type of business entity where the business is owned and controlled by one person. There is no legal distinction between the business and the owner. The owner receives all profits that are also subject to taxation. The downside to this type of entity is that the sole proprietor must assume all responsibility for losses and debts. In other words, there is unlimited liability. Claims can be made against the personal assets of the individual owning the business.

In considering this type of business entity, small business entrepreneurs must develop risk management objectives that include purchasing insurance for products, property, professional services, workman's compensation, commercial auto, and miscellaneous (i.e., umbrella policies).

TYPES OF INSURANCE

There are over 80 categories of insurance. The most important types of insurance that consumers should consider include long-term care, short-term care, health, disability, life, and car or auto.

Long-Term Care Insurance

Long-term care insurance is a type of product sold in three countries: the United States, the United Kingdom, and Canada. This insurance product assumes the cost for individuals needing long-term care related to dressing, bathing, eating, and transferring (getting in and out of bed or a chair), and walking; the insurance also assumes the cost for continence issues. Individuals needing long-term care insurance are not sick in terms of health or in the traditional sense; instead, they need help with performing basic functions related to daily living.

Long-term care is not covered by traditional health insurance, or Medicare and Medicaid. Medicaid, as a government assistance product, provides some benefits of long-term care insurance which include coverage of medically necessary services for people with limited financial resources. For example, these are individuals who need the equivalent of nursing home care, but can also stay at home to receive the services offered by individual communities. In essence, Medicaid does not provide long-term care insurance for individuals who need to enter an assisted living facility.

Concept Checker	*What is insurance?*

For long-term care insurance, age is not a determining factor. In fact, long-term care policyholders range from 18 years old to 64 years old. The major drawback to this type of insurance product is the insurance is no longer available when there is a change in an individual's health.

Long-term care insurance usually covers home care, respite care, adult daycare, assisted living, nursing home services, hospice care, and Alzheimer's facility services.

Benefits

There are benefits to purchasing long-term care insurance. Individuals who want to purchase this type of insurance feel comfortable in not relying on children or related family members for support. Long-term care insurance usually helps with out-of-pocket expenses. The costs of care could easily deplete the financial resources of family members.

Long-term care insurance offers tax benefits. Paid premiums are typically eligible for an income tax deduction. The amount of deduction is dependent upon the age of the covered person.

Businesses that want to take a deduction for premiums must seek a qualified tax expert. Not every business can take the deduction. Corporations that pay premiums for their employees may take a 100% deduction, provided it is not included in the employee's taxable income.

Types of Policies

There are two major types of long-term care insurance policies: tax qualified and non-tax qualified.

Tax qualified (TQ) policies are the most common. A tax qualified policy is based on two different assumptions. The first assumption is the person requires services because he or she needs care for at least 90 days and is unable to perform two more daily living functions; the functions must fall under six categories, which include eating, dressing, bathing, transferring, toileting, and incontinence. The second assumption is the person requires services for at least 90 days and needs substantial assistance because of cognitive impairment. Tax qualified policies are not taxable. The policyholder's doctor must prescribe a plan of care.

Non-tax qualified (NTQ) policies require a medical necessity trigger. The policyholder's doctor in coordination with the insurance company may issue a statement that the patient needs care for any medical reason. In this case, the policy will pay. With an NTQ, the patient receives services for a daily living function such as walking; he or she is typically unable to perform at least one daily living function. Individuals receiving services under a non-tax qualified policy may receive a large tax bill for benefits.

Non-tax qualified policies are typically not for sale, primarily because policyholders want to pursue eligibility for tax deductions. Tax-qualified policies are often restrictive in nature and stipulate when the policyholder can receive benefits. Most benefits are reimbursable and group plans may not be tax qualified or guaranteed renewable.

Rates

Long-term care insurance rates are determined by six factors: age, daily benefit, length of benefit, elimination period, inflation protection, and health rating. The health rating of an individual falls under three sub-categories: preferred, standard, and sub-standard.

Insurance companies typically offer policies to couples who may consist of spouses and two people living in a committed relationship. Premiums are typically paid annually, semi-annually, quarterly, or monthly.

There are additional options that come with many plans. Some of these options include spousal survivorship, restoration of benefits and return of premium, and non-forfeiture.

The purchase of long-term care insurance is not ideal for individuals receiving Medicaid benefits, individuals with limited assets who can't afford the premiums, or individuals receiving Social Security benefits, especially if this is your only source of income.

Short-Term Care in Contrast

Short-term care insurance, typically referred to as short-term recovery care, is a cost-effective plan that provides inexpensive coverage for events that result in a recovery. This type of insurance product is ideal for patients requiring confinement in a convalescent facility. It should be a part of any retirement protection planning objective.

Short-term care insurance can be used in conjunction with any long-term care product, which allows for the lowering of premiums and accessing of broader services. A short-term care policy will help to cover out-of-pocket expenses during an elimination period and pay out cash benefits on an indemnity basis.

A short-term care policy allows individuals to remain in control of their finances, their assets, and their choice of facility.

Health Insurance

Health insurance is a type of insurance product that hedges against the risk of incurring medical expenses particularly among individuals. Health insurance companies estimate the risk of health care and expenses necessary to run a health system and base the results upon a targeted group. With these estimates, the insurance company develops a finance structure that includes a monthly premium to ensure that money will be available to pay health care benefits that are outlined within the insurance agreement. Benefits are administered by a government agency, private business, and/or not-for-profit entity.

Contract

A **health insurance policy** is a contract between an insurance provider and an individual. The insurance provider may represent an employer or a community organization. The individual may include the spouse of an insured. The contract is typically renewable and may be lifelong.

Lifelong insurance contracts typically fall under private insurance policies. The contract can also be mandatory for citizens of a country. The types of health insurance services are outlined in a member contract, or "Evidence of Coverage" (private insurance) or national health policy (public insurance).

Coverage and ERISA

Health insurance is covered by an employer-sponsored, self-funded ERISA plan. The Employee Retirement Income Security Act of 1974 is a federal law that establishes minimum standards for pension plans administered in the private industry. The law does not require companies to establish a pension plan.

However, if a company establishes a pension plan, there are guidelines that the company must follow. The law doesn't specify the amount of money a participant of a company plan must be paid. Instead, ERISA requires companies to provide information about plan features which include funding, set minimum standards for participation, require accountability, and give participants the right to sue for breach of fiduciary duties and sue for benefits.

Obligations

Policyholders of a health insurance plan are obligated to follow certain guidelines that range from the payment of a premium to the payment of the deductible. The **premium** under a health insurance plan is the amount the policyholder pays to the sponsoring organization to purchase coverage. The sponsoring organization is typically the employer. The **deductible** is the amount the policyholder pays out-of-pocket; the individual must pay this expense before the health insurance company will pay its share.

Concept Checker	*What is health insurance?*

The **co-payment** is the amount the policyholder pays out of pocket before the health insurance company pays for a particular doctor's visit; a co-payment is typically paid each time and before the insured receives a particular service. The **co-insurance** is a fixed amount the insurer would have to pay over and above the co-payment. For example, an insurer might be required to pay 20% of the cost of an elective surgery, while the company pays the remainder. For **exclusions**, this means that not all services are covered and the insured would be expected to pay the cost of services that are not covered under the health insurance plan.

There are **coverage limits**. Policyholders of a health insurance plan may be expected to pay for excess charges that are over and above the maximum payment specified within the health plan. Some insurance plans have both annual maximums and lifetime coverage maximums. Once a policyholder reaches a maximum, then he or she would be responsible for paying all remaining costs.

Insured policyholders are required to receive **prior authorization or certification** before receiving certain medical services. When obtaining the authorization, the insured is obligated to pay for the service.

Lastly, insured policyholders typically seek out services through **in-network providers** who have developed an agreement with the health insurance company to accept rates that are discounted from the normal charges of out-of-network providers.

When considering a health insurance plan, research your company's options as well as the variety of benefits the plan offers. Use the following worksheet as a guide for determining which plan is best for you and your family.

Disability Insurance

Disability insurance, often referred to as **DI** or **disability income insurance**, is a type of insurance that insures the beneficiary's earned income against a particular type of risk. The risk is that the disability hinders the worker from completing core functions of a particular job. For example, a disability linked to a psychological disorder will prevent a worker from focusing or maintaining composure on a job. An illness, injury, or condition could also be a contributing factor that hinders the capacity of a worker. Disability income usually takes the form of paid sick leave, short-term disability benefits, or long-term disability benefits.

There are different types of disability insurance. The following represents a brief list.

Individual disability insurance

This type of insurance is for individuals whose employers do not provide benefits and individuals who are self-employed. Coverage varies between companies and occupations as well as between states and countries. Premiums under this plan are higher when the policy provides for more monthly benefits. Premiums also tend to be higher for policies that offer a broader term of a disability.

When determining if how much disability insurance you will need, consider using a disability insurance calculator. The following worksheet will help you determine how much disability insurance you might need as well as help you determine any disability insurance gaps.

High-Limit Disability Insurance

High-limit disability insurance will help to maintain an individual's disability benefits at 65% of income. This type of coverage is usually supplemental to a standard plan. Benefits under this plan can range from $2,000 to $100,000 per month.

Key-Person Disability Insurance

Key-person disability insurance provides protection for a company. The insurance protects the company from financial hardship due to a loss of a key employee; the loss of this type of employee is often due to a disability. The company typically uses the benefits to hire a temporary employee, provided the key employee's condition is short-term. When the condition is permanent, benefits from this insurance product are used to defray costs, which within this context typically include hiring a replacement, recruitment, training, startup, revenue loss, and salary funding and continuation.

Richard discovered the importance of purchasing key-person disability insurance when he lost his Director of Center Programming.

Case Study:
Richard Purchases Key-Person Disability Insurance

Richard Smith is a small business owner who has maintained excellent cash flow objectives. He operates a business consulting firm that nets about five million a year. He has over 15 employees and runs the company as the chairman of the board. Recently, Richard experienced a business setback. One of his key people, Jack Wolford, Director of Center Programming, recently took another job in another state, leaving Richard with the struggle of finding a replacement.

Jack had worked for the company for more than 25 years. He was valuable in every sense of the word. Richard never thought that he would lose one of his middle management team members. He had only planned for the exit of an executive member.

Because of the loss of Jack, Richard found it difficult to sustain adequate cash flow in 25 years. Jack's expertise and responsibilities included bringing in education revenue in the forms of teaching, textbooks, and professional consulting to businesses and universities.

To make sure that this never happened again, Richard decided for the first-time to purchase key-person disability insurance. He used the following questionnaire to guide his research efforts.

Key-Person Disability Insurance Questionnaire

1. What contingencies are in place for when a key employee becomes disabled or leaves the company?
2. What time frame is available to the company to locate and train a replacement?
3. What will be the compensation for the new employee?
4. In terms of percentage, how much revenue will be attributable to the new employee?
5. Will the loss of the key person directly correlate to the loss of the company's clients?
6. What are the benefits of a key-man disability insurance policy?
7. What payout options are available?
8. What are additional costs the company must meet to make the change?

This questionnaire only serves as a guide for preparing companies to research this type of product. Richard found the questionnaire helpful and purchased a policy that provided his company with the opportunity to receive a lump sum payout in case of a future change with key personnel of the company. This lump sum payout would help Richard's company locate and train a new employee and assume much of the costs related to the loss of revenue.

There are additional types of disability insurance that Richard might find informative. They include the following three categories.

Business Overhead Expense Disability Insurance

Business overhead expense (BOE) disability insurance reimburses a business when the owner suffers a disability. Reimbursement is for costs related to overhead expenses. Eligible benefits of the insurance include rent/mortgage payments, leasing costs, utilities, laundry/maintenance, accounting/billing, property tax, and related monthly expenses.

National Social Insurance Programs

National social insurance programs include Social Security, which is separated into two parts: Social Security Disability Insurance (SSDI) and Supplemental Security Income (SSI). The benefits derived from these programs are enough to hedge against the risk of poverty.

Worker's Compensation

Worker's compensation is a type of **employer-supplied disability insurance**. This type of insurance is the second largest form of disability insurance provided by employers whose employees suffer an on-the-job injury.

There are additional types of disability insurance plans, which include veteran's benefits and plans that offer basic coverage. Research this topic on various websites to determine the best plan for you and your family.

Concept Checker	*What are the types of disability insurance?*

Life Insurance

Life insurance is a contract between two parties: the insurer and the insurance policyholder. Within this context, the insurer promises to pay a sum of money (benefits) to a designated **beneficiary** upon the death of the insured person. There are triggers that fall under this type of contract. A terminal illness or a critical illness can trigger payment. For a life insurance policy, the policyholder pays a premium and related expenses (funeral) may be included in the benefits.

Life insurance contracts fall under two major categories: protection and investment. Under **protection policies**, the beneficiary receives a lump sum payment. This is typical of term insurance. With an investment policy, the goal is to facilitate the growth of capital by paying regular or single premiums. Common forms of **investment policies** include whole life, universal life, and variable life policies.

Life insurance is typically divided into classes and sub-classes. The two basic classes are temporary and permanent. The sub-classes are term, universal, whole life, and endowment life insurance.

Term Insurance

Term insurance provides coverage for a specific term. This type of policy does not accumulate a cash value. The premium buys protection in the event of a death. When considering purchasing term insurance, the following three factors are important:

- Face amount (protection or death benefit)
- Premium (cost to insured)
- Term (length of coverage)

Use these three factors as bases for determining life insurance planning objectives.

There are three common types of term insurance: level, annual renewable, and mortgage insurance. With a **level term** policy, the premium is fixed for at least a year. The terms are five years, ten years, fifteen years, twenty years, twenty-five years, thirty years, and thirty-five years. This type of term insurance is commonly used for long-term planning because premiums remain constant every year. When the term ends, some policies can be renewed or converted.

With an **annual renewable term**, the policy is for one-year only. The insurance company usually guarantees that it will issue a policy that is equal in value to the previous one; the premium will be set according to the applicant's age at the time of application.

With **mortgage life insurance**, there is a level premium and declining face value. The face on this type of insurance typically equals the amount of the mortgage on the policyholder's property. Should the applicant die, the outstanding amount will be paid.

It is important to note that term life insurance policies may end before the insured dies. If the insured dies before the term is up, then the beneficiary will receive a payout. However, if the insured does not die, then the beneficiary does not receive anything.

Permanent Life Insurance

Permanent life insurance is active until the policy matures, provided the owner continues to pay the premium. This type of insurance product accumulates a cash value and reduces the risk to the insurance company and the insurance risk. For example, a policy with a million dollar face value can be expensive to a policyholder over 65 years old. However, with this policy, an owner can access the cash value by withdrawing money or borrowing it. The owner can also surrender the policy and receive the surrender value. With this in mind, there are four types of permanent life insurance policies: whole life, universal life, limited pay, and endowment.

Whole Life Insurance

Whole life coverage policies provide death benefits for a level premium. The premium is much higher than a term insurance policy. The insurance contract stipulates that a policyholder can access the cash value reserve; it can be accessed at any time through policy loans. The income is received as tax free. The policy loan is available until the death of the insured. If there are any unpaid loans on the books, then the insurance company subtracts the loan amount from the death benefit and pays the remainder to the beneficiary designated on the policy.

Universal Life Insurance

Universal life insurance (UL) policies offer the flexibility of a premium payment. The potential for growth of the cash value is also one benefit of the product. There are several types of universal life insurance policies. One type is *interest sensitive*. Another type is *variable universal life* (VUL). Additional types include *guaranteed death benefit* and *equity indexed universal life insurance*. Universal life insurance policies carry a cash value. The premiums paid increase the cash value; however, the cost of insurance reduces the cash value. Interest is paid at a rate specified by the insurance company, which increases the cash value. The surrender value of this type of policy is the amount payable after surrender charges. A **surrender charge** is a fee that the life insurance policyholder must pay upon cancelling the policy. The fee covers the costs related to keeping the insurance policy on the insurance company's books.

Limited pay policies, or **limited-pay life insurance**, require premiums be paid over a specific period. After the period ends, no additional premiums are required. Pay periods include ten-year and twenty-year. The premiums are paid out at the age of 65.

Endowment Life Insurance

With **endowment life insurance policies** the cumulative cash value equals the death benefit of the insured at a certain age. This age is known as the endowment age. An endowment policy is considered relatively more expensive than whole life or universal life policies. The premiums per pay period are shortened; however, the endowment date is earlier. Endowment insurance is paid out when the insured lives or dies and after a specific period or specific age called the endowment age.

Limited Life Insurance

Accidental death is a type of **limited life insurance** plan where the insurance covers the insured should the policyholder die as a result of an accident. Accidents under the policy typically include injury; but this type of policy does not cover death from health problems or suicide. Limited life insurance policies are typically less expensive than other life insurance policies, because they only cover accidents.

Concept Checker	*What is permanent life insurance?*

Car Insurance

Car insurance, commonly referred to as **vehicle insurance**, is a type of insurance purchased for cars, trucks, motorcycles, and related road vehicles. The primary purpose of car insurance is to provide financial protection in the event of a traffic collision that contributes to the physical damage of a vehicle or the bodily injury of a passenger. The insurance also protects against liability should such a problem arise.

Coverage Level

Vehicle insurance covers the insured party in terms of medical payments; the insured vehicle if physical damage exists; third parties which include car, people, property damage, and bodily injury; third party related to fire and theft; injuries resulting from a passenger riding in the insured vehicle; car rental costs; and towing costs.

Each vehicle insurance policy is different. Therefore, it is important to research the topic to determine the best policy for you and your budget.

Premium Charges

The charges of a vehicle insurance premium is based upon multiple factors, which include government mandates, gender, age, driving history, marital status, vehicle classification, distance, and credit ratings.

Regulations set by the government dictate the premiums that insurance companies can charge to an insured. However, when the government doesn't mandate the sum of a premium, the insurance company typically calculates the payment using actuary principles that are based upon statistical data.

Teenage drivers without a driving record will usually be charged higher premiums. A driving record includes references to incidences of running red lights and speeding. Premiums are subject to rise within this context. Accidents affect premiums.

Premium charges are also based upon an applicant's credit rating. Insurance companies are using credit ratings to determine risk. A driver with a good credit rating will pay lower insurance premiums. The assumption here is that the driver is financially stable and more responsible. However, drivers with a lower credit score can expect to pay a higher premium.

There is also another type of car insurance: **auto repair insurance**. This type of insurance is available throughout the United States. The insurance covers the wear and tear of the vehicle. Some insurance products will cover mechanical breakdowns, or necessary repairs for breakable parts needing to be fixed or replaced, and related issues.

BUSINESS PLANNER

For the small business entrepreneur, there are different types of business insurance products available. Business insurance policies typically cover any risk that the business faces. Rates and coverage limits may vary.

General Liability Insurance

General liability insurance protects a small business from third-party claims for bodily injury. A lawsuit may arise as a result of an injury, an accident, or because of negligence. Claims that are covered include bodily injury, personal injury, property damage, and false advertisement. The insurance provider typically covers expenses that include those that result from the use of legal representation. General liability insurance doesn't cover punitive damages.

Product Liability Insurance

Companies that make, sell, or distribute products will be held liable for its safety. This type of insurance covers those claims that arise from the use of a defective product, provided that the product causes injury and/or harm. Coverage is based upon the type of product. For example, pharmaceutical companies are exposed to higher product liability risks.

Professional Liability Insurance

This type of insurance is known as "errors and omissions insurance." Businesses that provide professional services purchase this insurance product. Coverage includes malpractice, errors, and negligence. Doctors typically carry this type of policy.

Property Insurance

This type of policy is typically offered as a commercial product. It is available for businesses that are located in non-standard commercial buildings. Coverage includes loss and damage to commercial property due to fire, theft, smoke, vandalism, wind, hail, and related events. Company property is defined as buildings, equipment, business interruptions, loss of income, money, and business documents. Home-based businesses can purchase the same type of coverage through their home owner's policy.

Workman's Compensation Insurance

Businesses that hire employees should purchase workman's compensation insurance. If one or more employees are injured on the job, the policy will cover medical expenses and loss of income. When an employee suffers a permanent disability, the policy will provide benefits until the employee reaches the age of retirement. Most business owners do not provide coverage for themselves; they typically purchase personal liability insurance.

Commercial Auto Insurance

Commercial auto insurance is a type of policy typically used for company vehicles used in the normal course of business. Coverage includes personal injury and property damage. Commercial auto insurance covers the business for loss due to an accident.

Umbrella Policies

Small business owners can also purchase an umbrella policy. This type of policy is inexpensive, but the business owner must purchase up to the maximum limit.

Chapter Key Points

Insurance is defined as the transfer of risk of a loss between one or more entities in exchange for payment. Insurance falls under the category of **risk management**, a term that refers to a process of identifying, assessing, and prioritizing risks.

Small business entrepreneurs, particularly sole proprietors, must develop risk management objectives to hedge against the possibility of lawsuits and claims against personal assets.

Long-term care insurance is a type of product sold in three countries: the United States, the United Kingdom, and Canada. This insurance product assumes the cost for individuals needing long-term care related to dressing, bathing, eating, transferring (getting in and out of bed or a chair), and walking. It also covers incontinence issues.

There are two major types of long-term care insurance policies: tax qualified and non-tax qualified.

Health insurance is a type of insurance product that hedges against the risk of incurring medical expenses particularly among individuals.

A **health insurance policy** is a contract between an insurance provider and an individual.

Disability insurance, often referred to as **DI** or **disability income insurance**, is a type of insurance that insures the beneficiary's earned income against a particular type of risk.

Key-person disability insurance provides protection for a company in the event of a loss of a key person due to disability or resignation.

Business overhead expense (BOE) disability insurance reimburses a business when the owner suffers a disability. Reimbursement is for costs related to overhead expenses.

Worker's compensation is a type of **employer-supplied disability insurance**.

Life insurance is a contract between two parties: the insurer and the insurance policyholder.

Term insurance provides coverage for a specific term. This type of policy does not accumulate a cash value.

Permanent life insurance is active until the policy matures, provided the owner continues to pay the premium. This type of insurance product accumulates a cash value and reduces the risk to the insurance company and the insurance risk.

Car insurance, commonly referred to as **vehicle insurance**, is a type of insurance purchased for cars, trucks, motorcycles, and related road vehicles.

Chapter Key Terms

Accidental death: term refers to a type of limited life insurance where the insurance covers the insured should the policyholder die as a result of an accident.

Annual renewable term: term refers to a type of term insurance policy where it is only for one year.

Beneficiary: term refers to a person who receives benefits after the death of an insured policyholder.

BOE: acronym stands for business overhead expense.

Business overhead expense disability insurance: term refers to type of disability insurance that reimburses a business when the owner suffers a disability.

Car insurance: term refers to a type of insurance purchased for cars, trucks, motorcycles, and related road vehicles.

Co-insurance: term refers to a fixed amount the insurer would have to pay over and above the co-payment.

Co-payment: term refers to the amount the policyholder pays out of pocket before the health insurance company pays for a particular doctor's visit; a co-payment is typically paid each time and before the insured receives a particular service.

Commercial auto insurance: term refers to a type of business for company vehicles used in the normal course of business.

Deductible: term refers to the amount the policyholder pays out-of-pocket; the individual must pay this expense before the health insurance will pay its share.

DI: acronym stands for disability insurance.

Disability income insurance: term is synonymous with disability insurance. See **disability insurance**.

Disability insurance: term refers to type of insurance that insures the beneficiary's earned income against a particular type of risk.

Employer-supplied disability insurance: term is synonymous with worker's compensation.

Endowment life insurance policies: term refers to the cumulative cash value and how it equals the death benefit of the insured at a certain age, which is called the endowment age.

ERISA: acronym stands for Employee Retirement Income Security Act of 1974.

Exclusions: term refers to services that are not covered under an insurance policy.

General liability insurance: term refers to a type of business insurance that covers the business when a claim or lawsuit arises.

Health insurance: term refers to type of insurance product that hedge against the risk of incurring medical expenses particularly among individuals.

Health insurance policy: term refers to contract between an insurance provider and an individual.

High-limit disability insurance: term refers to type of disability insurance that will help to maintain an individual's disability benefits at 65% of income.

Indemnify: term refers to compensation from the insurance provider to the provider for a qualified event.

Individual disability insurance: term refers to type of insurance for individuals whose employers do not provide benefits and individuals who are self-employed.

Insurance: term refers to the transfer of risk of loss between one or more entities in exchange for payment.

Insurance carrier: term refers to a company selling insurance.

Insurance policy: term refers to an official contract issued by the insurance carrier to the policyholder, or insured.

Insured: term refers to the policyholder of an insurance contract.

Key-person disability insurance: term refers to type of disability insurance that protects the company from financial hardship due to a loss of a key employee; the loss of this type of employee is often due to a disability.

Level term: term refers to a type of term insurance policy that is fixed for at least a year.

Life insurance: term refers to type of contract between two parties: the insurer and the insurance policyholder.

Limited-pay life insurance: term refers to a type of permanent life insurance that requires premiums to be paid over a specific period.

Long-term care insurance: term refers to a type of insurance product that provides benefits for individuals needing long-term care related to dressing, bathing, eating, continence issues, transferring (getting in and out of bed or a chair), and walking.

Mortgage life insurance: term refers to the declining face value of this type of product.

National social insurance programs: term refers to public social disability programs such as Social Security Disability Insurance (SSDI) and Supplemental Security Income (SSI).

Non-tax qualified policy: term refers to type of long-term care policy where the policy and the receipt of care are taxable.

NTQ: acronym stands for non-tax qualified.

Permanent life insurance: term refers to a type of insurance product that accumulates a cash value and reduces risk.

Premium: term refers to the amount the policyholder pays to the sponsoring organization to purchase coverage.

Prior authorization: term refers to the obligation of the insured to request permission to receive certain medical services.

Short-term care insurance: term refers to type of insurance product that can be used with a long-term care insurance product; the policy provides for help with out-of-pocket expenses.

Product liability insurance: term refers to a type of business insurance that covers those claims that arise from the use of a defective product, provided that the product causes injury and/or harm.

Professional liability insurance: term refers to a type of business insurance known as "errors and omissions insurance."

Property insurance: term refers to a type of business insurance offered as a commercial product.

Protection policies: term refers to a type of life insurance contract where the beneficiary receives a lump sum payment.

Risk management: term refers to a process of identifying, assessing, and prioritizing risks.

SSDI: acronym stands for Social Security Disability Insurance.

SSI: acronym stands for Supplemental Security Income.

Surrender charge: term refers to a fee charged to the life insurance policyholder for cancelling the insurance policy; the fee covers costs related to keeping the insurance policy on the insurance company's books.

Tax-qualified policy: term refers to type of long-term care policy where the policy and the receipt of care are not taxable.

Term insurance: term refers to a type of policy that does not accumulate a cash value.

TQ: acronym stands for tax-qualified.

UL: acronym stands for universal life insurance.

Universal life insurance: term refers to type of permanent life insurance that offers flexibility and growth of cash value as a benefit.

Vehicle insurance: see **car insurance**.

Whole life coverage: term refers to a type of permanent life insurance that provides death benefits for a level premium.

Worker's compensation: term refers to type of employer-supplied disability insurance.

Workman's compensation insurance: term refers to a type of business insurance that covers medical expenses and loss of income for an injured employee.

GROUP WORK PROMPT

Research multiple companies that provide life insurance. Develop an essay comparing and contrasting the three life insurance companies. Provide information about each company's policy benefits and the rates. Take notes in class and finish the project as a group at home. Be sure that each of your names is on the first page of the essay document.

HOMEWORK EXERCISE

For homework, research the life insurance products offered by Voya. Review the company information, which includes the management structure as well as the public disclosures. Provide answers for the following.

1. What are the individual life insurance plans?
___
___

2. Explain one of the children plans?
___
___

3. What are the key benefits of one of the children plans?
___
___
___
___

4. What are the product features of one of the children plans?
___
___
___
___

5. What is the Voya TermSmart Plan?
___
___
___
___

6. What are the key benefits of the Voya TermSmart Plan?
___
___
___
___

7. What are the product features of the Voya TermSmart Plan?

8. What is the Voya Single Premium Immediate Annuity?

9. What are the key benefits of the Voya Single Premium Immediate Annuity?

10. What are the product features of the Voya Single Premium Immediate Annuity?

Assessment

1. What is insurance?
   _____
   _____

2. What are the types of insurance?
   _____
   _____

3. What are the benefits of long-term care insurance?
   _____
   _____

4. Long-term care insurance is sold in which countries?
   a. United States
   b. United Kingdom
   c. Canada
   d. All of the above

5. What are the types of long-term care insurance policies?
   _____
   _____

6. What is health insurance?
   _____
   _____

7. What is ERISA?
   _____
   _____

8. What is disability insurance?
   _____
   _____

9. What are the different types of disability insurance? List at least three types.
   _____
   _____

10. What type of key-person disability insurance did Richard Smith choose for his company? Why was it necessary?
    _____
    _____

11. What is life insurance?
_____
_____

12. What is term insurance?
_____
_____

13. What is permanent life insurance? List the four types.
_____
_____
_____
_____

14. **True or False.** Whole life coverage is a type of permanent life insurance.

15. What is car insurance?
_____
_____

16. What are examples of business insurance? List and define one type.
_____
_____

Helpful Websites

Forbes.com: 13 Types of Insurance a Small Business Owner Should Have
http://www.forbes.com/sites/thesba/2012/01/19/13-types-of-insurance-a-small-business-owner-should-have/

SBA.gov: Types of Business Insurance
http://www.sba.gov/content/types-business-insurance

Department of Labor: The Employee Retirement Income Security Act (ERISA)
http://www.dol.gov/compliance/laws/comp-erisa.htm

Blue Cross and Blue Shield: What to Consider when Choosing a Health Insurance Plan
http://www.bluecrossmn.com/Page/mn/en_US/what-to-consider-when-choosing-a-plan

Money-Zine: Disability Insurance Calculator
http://www.money-zine.com/Calculators/Insurance-Calculators/Disability-Insurance-Calculator/

Term Life Insurance FAQs
http://www.accuquote.com/learning-center/term-life-insurance-faqs.cfm

Chapter Forms

On the next pages are all of the forms discussed within this chapter. You may Photocopy, scan, and print them out. Some forms you will need to complete the group work and the homework.

Health Insurance Research & Planning Worksheet

Date:
_____

Health Insurance Company:
_____

Contact Information:
_____
_____

1. What type of coverage do I need? Short-term? Long-term?
_____
_____

2. What is basic coverage? What is comprehensive coverage?
_____
_____

3. Will my doctor and/or hospital be covered with the plan?
_____
_____

4. Does the plan's network require a referral?
_____
_____

5. Will the health plan cover me while traveling?
_____
_____

6. What services are important to me? Will the plan cover those services?
_____
_____

7. Will the plan cover my family? What is the limit?
_____
_____

8. Will the plan cover preexisting medical conditions? What is the limit?
_____
_____

9. Will the plan work with a health savings account? What is the limit?
_____
_____

10. Will prescription drugs be covered?
_____
_____

Notes and Considerations
_____
_____
_____
_____

Use this worksheet to help you focus and meet your insurance planning objectives.

DISABILITY INSURANCE CALCULATION WORKSHEET

Monthly Income: _____

Other Sources of Income: _____

Total Gross Monthly Income (Pre-tax): _____

Estimated Tax (% of Gross Monthly Income): _____

BALANCE (Gross Monthly Income – Tax %): _____

Essential Monthly Expenses:
    Monthly housing (mortgage, rent, insurance, taxes): _____

    Utilities (telephone, electricity, gas, oil, cable TV, internet):_____
    Food: _____
    Transportation (car payments, gasoline, insurance): _____
    Education (tuition, books, supplies): _____
    Healthcare (out of pocket expenses, insurance premiums): _____
    Debt Payments (credit cards, other debt): _____
    Other (dependent care, life insurance premiums): _____

    Total Essential Monthly Expenses: _____

BALANCE (Monthly Income – Essential Expenses): _____

Existing Disability Insurance Benefits
    Group Long-Term Disability (employer): _____
    Social Security Disability: _____
    Other Disability Income Sources: _____
        Total Disability Income: _____

Disability Income Gap:
Essential Monthly Expenses – Total Disability Income: _____

Determining how much disability insurance you will need will help to hedge against emergencies related to the disability and will also help to fill the disability income gap.

KEY-PERSON DISABILITY INSURANCE QUESTIONNAIRE

1. What contingencies are in place for when a key employee becomes disabled or leaves the company?

2. What time frame is available to the company to locate and train a replacement?

3. What will be the compensation for the new employee?

4. In terms of percentage, how much revenue will be attributable to new employee?

5. Will the loss of the key person directly correlate to the loss of the company's clients?

6. What are the benefits of a key-man disability insurance policy?

7. What payout options are available?

8. What are additional costs the company must meet to make the change?

CHAPTER 8

Mortgage Mechanics

Learning Objectives

- Define mortgage.
- List the types of mortgages.
- Define amortization and negative amortization.
- Calculate a fixed rate mortgage.
- Develop a mortgage note contract.

WHAT IS A MORTGAGE?

The word mortgage is commonly used to refer to *mortgage loan*. A **mortgage**, or mortgage loan, is a loan that is secured by real property. The mortgage lender holds a **mortgage note**, which provides evidence of the existence of a loan. The mortgage note officially represents the promissory note where the borrower signs a written promise to repay a specified sum of money; the promise also includes an agreement by the borrower to pay the interest, which is calculated at a specific rate for a specific length of time. A mortgage note essentially specifies the amount of debt, rate of interest, and borrower's obligation to the loan.

The mortgage note places an encumbrance on the property. An **encumbrance** is a right of the lender (or creditor) on real property; through the existence of the mortgage note, the mortgage lender can place a lien on the property. In simple terms, encumbrances may include security interests, liens, servitudes (i.e., easements), restrictions, and encroachments. The encumbrance does not prohibit the passing of title; however, it does diminish the value of the property. Encumbrances may be financial or non-financial; they typically affect the title (i.e., lien).

Mortgage loans involve multiple features. Mortgage loans vary by the size of the loan, loan maturity, interest rate, payment method, and related characteristics that obligate the borrower. First-time home buyers are cautioned to research this topic and enroll in homebuyer readiness training workshops before considering the purchase of a home. Homebuyer workshops typically offer training in creating a budget, contacting creditors and disputing errors on the credit report, managing earnings and cash flow, reviewing fair housing laws, and purchasing a home.

Small business owners interested in real estate investing have a unique advantage because mortgage notes can be used as investment tools. Mortgage notes offer investors a stream of revenue and they are typically traded on the market. Although mortgage notes provide opportunities for companies and individual real estate investors, no goal can be accomplished without a strategic capital and asset management plan. Without the capital to purchase notes, **mortgage note buyers** (investing companies) will fail to see their goals accomplished. To best understand the definition of mortgage is to understand the different types.

Types of Mortgage Loans

There are different types of mortgage loans. Mortgage loans are used worldwide and are subject to local regulation and federal requirements. All mortgage loans specify the following:

- **Interest:** The interest on a mortgage loan may be fixed or variable. The interest on a loan may change at pre-defined periods. It may also be higher or lower.
- **Term:** The term of a mortgage loan is usually set at a maximum time period. The maximum period represents a number of years. Some mortgage loans may offer amortization or negative amortization depending upon the loan product.
- **Payment Frequency:** The payment amount for a mortgage loan is directly correlated to the payment frequency. Amounts are set by period and may change. The borrower may request that the payment amount increase or decrease.
- **Prepayment:** Some mortgage lenders prohibit prepayment of a portion or even all the loan. Lenders often will assess a prepayment penalty against the borrower.

These features are foundational to most mortgage loans, but they do not represent the complete structure of a mortgage loan contract. Research the field. Download and review sample home mortgage loan contracts to get a comprehensive view of what to expect when purchasing a home.

Amortized Loans

Amortization is the process by which the principal of the loan decreases over the life of the loan. Each time the borrower pays the loan, a portion of the payment is applied to the principal and another payment applied towards the interest. Some loans require fully repayment of the outstanding balance by a certain date. Some mortgage loans may offer negative amortization. With **negative amortization**, also referred to as deferred interest or graduated payment mortgage, the loan payment is less than the charged interest; with this method, the outstanding balance on the mortgage loan increases. With this in mind, there are two types of amortized loans:

- Fixed rate mortgage (FRM)
- Adjustable-rate mortgage (ARM)

Fixed Rate Mortgage

A fixed rate mortgage is a fully amortizing mortgage loan. The interest rate on the note remains the same until the end of the loan. With this type of loan, the interest rate doesn't adjust or float. The payment amount and the duration of the loan are both fixed. However, there are **ancillary costs**. Ancillary costs within this context refer to costs associated with property taxes and insurance. But the principal and the interest on this type of loan do not change.

As you research multiple loans, consider using a fixed-rate mortgage calculator typically offered online for free. Type in the keyword "fixed rate mortgage calculator" to locate a suitable resource. Use the **Fixed Rate Mortgage Calculations Worksheet** at the end of this chapter to help keep track of your research.

Adjustable-Rate Mortgage

An adjustable-rate mortgage is synonymous with *floating rate* or *variable rate*. In simple terms, adjustable-rate refers to any debt instrument that does not have a fixed rate of interest. The debt instruments include loans, bonds, mortgages, and credit. With an adjustable-rate mortgage, the interest rate on the loan begins with a fixed rate for a period of time, but it will periodically increase or decrease based upon the market index.

The interest rate risk is transferred from the lender to the borrower. **Interest rate risk** is defined as the value of an investment and how it contributes to the change in the absolute level of interest rates; these changes usually affect securities. These types of mortgages are commonly used when the borrower finds it difficult to obtain funding, especially fixed rate funding, due to credit problems. Borrowers with credit problems like Tom often find it difficult to manage their finances when the rate on their mortgage loans is variable.

Negative Amortized Loans

Although popular, negative amortization loans have attracted criticism. For example, negative amortized loans begin with what is called a teaser rate; it is an introductory interest rate. Consumers often are unaware of the dangers of teaser rates where only one-percent of the loan amount is paid each year. Some negative amortized loans contain clauses that stipulate the payment will not increase more than a specific percentage. However, consumers are unaware that there are exceptions. The payment may not increase for a specific period or if the balance grows beyond a specific percentage.

Negative amortized loans make it harder for consumers to manage payment objectives. For example, the term payment shock is applicable to a class of borrowers that are required to make different payments each month. **Payment shock** affects a consumer when the monthly mortgage payment continues to jump from month to month. This potentially makes the mortgage payment unaffordable. Let's examine the differences between a fixed rate amortized mortgage and a negative amortized mortgage.

Negative amortized loans make it difficult for consumers to set consistent payment objectives. Because the interest rate can increase and cause the loan balance to grow, consumers will find that their mortgage loan is more harmful than beneficial. It is important to read the fine print within mortgage loan contracts. Use the **Terms of Repayment Worksheet** at the end of this chapter to help you understand some of the fine print in a mortgage loan contract.

Case Study: Tom's Problems with an Adjustable-Rate Mortgage

Tom has a lot of student loan debts. When he graduated with a bachelor's degree in business, he didn't know that one day he would become his own case study. As an avid saver, Tom has managed to build a two-year emergency fund and a sound retirement account. He has investments in stocks and often takes risks. His greatest risk was in purchasing two homes that he converted into rental income properties.

For one home, Tom qualified for a fixed-rate mortgage. This made it easy for him to develop a sound cash flow management plan. However, the other home has a variable rate mortgage that often fluctuates.

The rate on Tom's mortgage began at 2.5%. This is the **LIBOR rate**, or the average interest rate calculated by leading banks in London. The acronym **LIBOR** stands for the London Interbank Offered Rate. The LIBOR rate is calculated using ten different currencies and for 15 borrowing periods.

Tom's rate also included an additional interest rate of 3.5%. The total rate of interest for Tom's loan was 6% and this was for six months. The LIBOR rate for Tom's mortgage loan changed for the next six months and rose to 4%, which resulted in Tom paying 7.5%. With this type of mortgage loan, Tom's borrowing costs increased, which made it difficult for Tom to develop a consistent cash management plan.

To prevent this type of problem from happening to you, consider using an adjustable-rate mortgage calculator. Use the **Adjustable-Rate Mortgage Research Worksheet** at the end of this chapter as a guide for asking the mortgage lender what you can expect for your loan. Research multiple lenders and compare your results before applying for a loan.

Mortgage Rate Type Comparison

Mortgage Type	Defined
30-year fixed rate, fully amortized	The payment doesn't jump from month to month. This is also for a 15-year fixed rate, fully amortized loan products.
5-year adjustable-rate amortized mortgage	Payments remain stable for five years. Then the payment may increase or decrease after the five years. A new rate is introduced.
10-year interest only mortgage, recasted to 20-year amortized schedule	This loan product is based upon 10 years of interest-only payments. The consumer could see a payment increase up to approximately $600. This assumption is based upon a mortgage loan balance of more than $300,000.
Negative amortized mortgage	The consumer can expect a payment jump after the five-year mark OR payment jump when the balance grows to approximately 15% higher than the original loan amount. This assumption is based upon the type of loan product. With this type of mortgage, the payment will increase and the consumer will be required to make a *full interest plus the principal* payment. The payment could increase more because of interest rate changes.
First month free	In this context, the borrower could skip the first month's payment. But the payment will be added to the principal and the lender will charge compounded interest on the amount for many years.

Business Planner

Small business entrepreneurs in the business of real estate investing are entering the mortgage note buying industry. Mortgage notes offer investors a consistent sum of payments over a specific period of time. Mortgage notes are traded on the **secondary market**, which is a financial market that allows for the buying and selling of previously issued financial instruments such as stocks, bonds, options, and futures. An example of a secondary market is when a mortgage bank sells a loan to an investor such as Fannie Mae and Freddie Mac.

Mortgage notes are typically sold and bought as part of a **mortgage-backed security** (MBS), which is a type of asset-based security. An MBS has a claim on the cash flows that result from mortgage loans. This process is called **securitization**, or the process of pooling together types of contractual debt. Types include residential mortgages, commercial mortgages, auto loans, and credit card debt obligations. The debt is pooled together and sold as bonds, pass-through securities, and collateralized mortgage obligations (CMOs).

There are risks associated with purchasing mortgage notes. Those risks include credit risk, interest rate risk, and prepayment risk. Mortgage note buyers must have the capital to purchase a mortgage note and have enough capital to hedge against multiple risks.

Small business entrepreneurs must take an inventory of capital reserves to determine the costs related to buying mortgage notes. Considerations must include reference to foreclosure proceedings. Researching the chain of title is costly and foreclosing parties must produce evidence of ownership of the debt. Without this, you could pay for a mortgage note and not receive it.

Research sample mortgage documents to get an idea of what to expect. Make sure for each note you plan to purchase that you understand what each section means. Use the **Mortgage Note Contract Planning Worksheet** at the end of this chapter as a way to develop plans for each contract clause.

Chapter Key Points

The word mortgage is commonly used to refer to *mortgage loan*. A **mortgage**, or mortgage loan, is a loan that is secured by real property. The mortgage lender holds a **mortgage note**, which provides evidence of the existence of a loan.

The mortgage note places an encumbrance on the property. An **encumbrance** is a right of the lender (or creditor) on real property; through the existence of the mortgage note, the mortgage lender can place a lien on the property.

Mortgage loans vary by the size of the loan, loan maturity, interest rate, payment method, and related characteristics that obligate the borrower. First-time home buyers are cautioned to research this topic and enroll in homebuyer readiness training workshops before considering purchasing a home.

Amortization is the process by which the principal of the loan decreases over the life of the loan. Each time the borrower pays the loan, a portion of the payment is applied to the principal and another payment applied towards the interest.

With **negative amortization**, also referred to as deferred interest or graduate payment mortgage, the loan payment is less than the charged interest; with this method, the outstanding balance on the mortgage loan increases.

A fixed rate mortgage is a fully amortizing mortgage loan.

An adjustable-rate mortgage is synonymous with *floating rate* or *variable rate*. In simple terms, adjustable-rate refers to any debt instrument that does not have a fixed rate of interest.

Interest rate risk is defined as the value of an investment and how it contributes to the change in the absolute level of interest rates; these changes usually affect securities.

Payment shock affects a consumer when the monthly mortgage payment continues to jump from month to month.

Small business entrepreneurs in the business of real estate investing are entering the mortgage note buying industry. Mortgage notes offer investors a consistent sum of payments over a specific period of time. Mortgage notes are traded on the **secondary market**, which is a financial market that allows for the buying and selling of previously issued financial instruments such as stocks, bonds, options, and futures.

Chapter Key Terms

Adjustable-rate mortgage: term refers to a debt instrument that does not have a fixed rate of interest.

Amortization: term refers to the process of the principal of a mortgage loan decreasing over the life of the loan.

Ancillary costs: term refers to costs associated with property taxes and insurance.

Encumbrance: term refers to the right of the lender on real property.

Fixed rate mortgage: term refers to a fully amortizing loan where the interest rate on the loan remains the same.

Interest: term refers to the percentage of payment added to the principal on a mortgage loan.

Interest rate risk: term refers to the value of an investment and how it contributes to the change in the absolute level of interest rates; these changes usually affect securities.

LIBOR: acronym stands for London Interbank Offered Rate. See LIBOR rate.

LIBOR rate: term refers to the average interest rate calculated by leading banks in London.

Mortgage: term refers to a mortgage loan secured by real property.

Mortgage-backed security: term refers to a type of asset-based security.

Mortgage note: term that refers to the evidence of the existence of a mortgage loan.

Mortgage note buyers: term refers to companies and investors who purchase mortgage notes.

Negative amortization: term refers to where the loan payment is less than the charged interest; the outstanding balance on the mortgage loan increases.

Payment shock: term refers to when the monthly mortgage payment continues to jump from month to month making the mortgage unaffordable.

Prepayment: term refers to the prepayment of the principal of a mortgage loan.

Securitization: term refers to the process of pooling together types of contractual debt.

Secondary market: term refers to a financial market that allows for the buying and selling of previously issued financial instruments.

Term: term refers to the period of time for repayment of a mortgage loan.

Group Work Prompt

Using this chapter as a guide, construct a sample mortgage contract. You may research preferred contract clauses. You may start this project in class and finish it as a group at home.

Homework Exercise

Research listed properties through Realtor.com. Visit a local lender. Interview a loan officer. Use the Terms of Repayment Worksheet to complete the homework. Enter your results on the sheet.

Assessment

1. What is a mortgage?
___
___

2. What are the types of mortgages?
___
___

3. **True or False**. The interest on a loan may be fixed or variable.

4. All mortgage loans specify which of the following:
a. Interest
b. Term
c. Payment frequency
d. All of the following

5. What is the difference between amortization and negative amortization?
___
___

6. What is payment shock?
___
___

Helpful Websites

Onecle: Sample Business Contracts
http://contracts.onecle.com/

Sample Mortgage Contract
http://www.luxuryhomesandproperties.com/forms/mortgage.htm

Chapter Forms

On the next pages are all of the forms discussed within this chapter. You may photocopy, scan, and print them out. Some forms you will need to complete the group work and the homework.

Fixed Rate Mortgage Calculations Worksheet

Location	Home Price	Down Payment	Loan Term	Interest Rate	Payment

ADJUSTABLE-RATE MORTGAGE RESEARCH WORKSHEET

Date: _____

Loan Type: _____

Lender: _____

Contact Information: _____
_____
_____

Loan Amount: _____

Initial Interest Rate: _____

Number of Months: _____

What is the **Absolute Minimum Rate** for Term of Loan?
_____

What is the **Absolute Maximum Rate** for Term of Loan?
_____

Number of Months **before** Rate Adjusts: _____
Number of Months **between** Adjusting of Rate: _____
Over the life of the loan, will rate **increase, decrease, or stay the same**?
_____

What is the **assumed rate adjustment** (%)? _____

Notes and Special Considerations
_____
_____
_____

TERMS OF REPAYMENT WORKSHEET

Amount of Principal: _____

Interest Rate: _____

Interest Adjustment Date: _____

Interest Rate Calculated?
Annually: _____ Semi-annually: _____

When will the Principal and Interest Payments be required?
Weekly: _____ Bi-weekly: _____ Monthly: _____

What day of the week will the installment payments come due:
_____

What are the Principal and Interest payments?
_____

Maturity Date:
_____

Are annual prepayments of principal allowed?
_____

When can the prepayment be made?

Anniversary of Interest Adjustment Date: _____
Anytime during the year up to/including Interest Adjustment Date: _____
Percentage of principal can Mortgagor/Borrower prepay: _____

Can Mortgagor/Borrower prepay any amount not prepaid in the previous year?
_____

Is prepayment of entire principal allowed?
_____

Will the Mortgagee/Lender include a power of sale clause*?
_____

*The power of sale clause within a mortgage contract permits the lender to sell the mortgaged property if the mortgagor/borrower defaults.

Mortgage Note Contract Planning Worksheet

Borrower's Promise to Pay
_____
_____

Interest
_____
_____

Payments
_____
_____

Time and Place of Payments
_____
_____

Amount of Monthly Payments
_____
_____

Borrower's Right to Prepay
_____
_____

Loan Charges
_____
_____

Borrower's Failure to Pay
_____
_____

Late Charge for Overdue Payments
_____
_____

Default
_____
_____

Notice of Default
_____
_____

No Waiver by Note Holder
_____
_____

Payment of Note Holder's Costs and Expenses
_____
_____

Giving of Notices
_____
_____

Obligations of Persons under Note
_____
_____

Waivers
_____
_____

Uniform Secured Note
_____
_____

CHAPTER 9

Home Buyer Basics

Learning Objectives

- Define first-time homebuyer.
- List the types of homebuyers.
- Complete questionnaire.
- Review types of mortgages for first-time home buyers.
- Review and list mortgage loan closing documents.

WHAT IS A FIRST-TIME HOME BUYER?

A **first-time home buyer** is defined as an individual who is purchasing a principal residence for the first time. This is the type of person who has never been listed on a deed as the owner of real estate. Purchasing a home involves many factors from understanding real estate lingo and choosing a home to negotiating a sound deal and paying into escrow. Prospective homeowners should familiarize themselves with various websites that offer information about house-hunting tips, realtor principles, home inspection procedures, and mortgage basics. Prospective homeowners who have had a long history of renting should not enter the home buying market without first educating themselves. It is a different world that requires a sound understanding of principles and procedures. It is not for the faint at heart.

With this in mind, this chapter provides information regarding the fundamentals of first-time home buyer ownership. Highlights of this chapter include information about loan pre-approval, house hunting, negotiating, insurance, tax benefits, and closing procedures. For a comprehensive view of information about the different types of mortgages, review "Mortgage Mechanics."

Individual real estate investors that wish to enter the home buying market have multiple options, from purchasing older homes to purchasing distressed properties and converting them into income-producers. Small business owners must familiarize themselves with sample agreements typically used within the industry. Within this context, the task of a real estate investor is double. If the investor wants to rent out the property, then he or she becomes a landlord to the tenant. The property is income-producing, but also laden with responsibilities that require sound management techniques and sustainable cash flow. It is important for the real estate investor to conduct a thorough analysis of a property, giving attention to its potential as well as the negative drawbacks that might contribute to future problems.

Nevertheless, whether the first-time homebuyer is an individual or an investor, it is important to become a knowledgeable consumer.

TYPES OF FIRST-TIME HOME BUYERS

Types of first-time home buyers are directly related to the type of loan. A first-time home buyer loan offers many benefits, but also restrictions. First-time home buyer loans are mortgages that lenders and government agencies tailor specifically for people buying their first home. Loans under this category often require the consumer to make a low down payment. The interest is reduced. There are limited fees. Prospective homeowners may have the option of deferring payments.

Loans of this type are administered at the federal level by the **Federal Housing Administration** (FHA). The FHA is a United States government agency that insures loans made by banks and private lenders for the purposes of home building and home buying. The FHA was created as part of the National Housing Act of 1934. The goals of the agency are to improve housing standards, provide home financing through insurance of mortgage loans, and stabilize the mortgage market.

First-time home buyer loans insured by FHA offer easier qualifying guidelines, which include higher debt ratios, lower credit scores, limited down payments, and reduced closing costs and fees. These are the benefits of receiving this type of loan. However, there are negative consequences. For example, there is a limit on the cost of the property. There are also loan limits; first-time home buyers rarely receive a FHA loan for an expensive property. In addition, the major drawback to this type of loan is the home you purchase must become your primary place of residence. You can't use it as an investment property. There are other drawbacks related to selling the property; if you sell the home too soon after purchasing it, then you could lose some of the loan benefits. Lastly, you may not be able to refinance the loan at a later date or change the terms of the debt. It is important to research and perform your due diligence before entering the market.

MORTGAGE BASICS

The chapter titled "Mortgage Mechanics" provides information about the different types of mortgages available to prospective homeowners. However, within this chapter, it is important to highlight the different mortgage types to qualify the discussion for the first-time home buyer.

Fixed-Rate Mortgage

If a first-time home buyer qualifies for a fixed-rate mortgage, then he or she can expect their monthly principal and interest payment to stay the same for the entirety of the loan. This type of mortgage provides stability. If the interest rate goes up, this won't affect the homeowner. However, there is a drawback. If the interest rate goes down, then the rate would stay the same. You would have to refinance the debt in order to receive the benefit of a lower interest rate.

The ARM

If a first-time home buyer qualifies for an adjustable-rate mortgage (ARM), then he or she can expect their monthly principal and interest payment to change after the introductory period, which is typically set at five years. During the introductory period, the interest rate remains fixed, which makes it easier for the homebuyer to plan cash flow each month. However, after the introductory period, the interest rate will go up, which will affect the monthly principal and result in the homebuyer experiencing payment shock, a term discussed in "Mortgage Mechanics." This type of increase will negatively impact your ability to manage monthly payments.

To guard against payment shock, before signing an agreement, discuss with the mortgage lender what the cap will be on an adjustable-rate mortgage. In other words, there are two kinds of rate caps: adjustment cap and lifetime cap. A **rate cap** is defined as the limit on how much the interest rate can change; the rate could change during a particular adjustment period or the rate could change over the entire term of the loan.

An **adjustment cap** limits how much the rate can go up or down within a single adjustment period. Loans with this type of cap help to limit how much your loan payment can change when subject to adjusting procedures. On the other hand, a **lifetime cap** establishes a maximum and a minimum interest rate throughout the term of the loan. With this type of cap, the monthly payment could still increase, which may result in you experiencing payment shock. This type of cap would make it difficult for the first-time home buyer to pay the mortgage on time, because interest rates would rise and cause the monthly payment to increase also. In some cases, your monthly payment could double. Use the **First-Time Home Buyer Mortgage Questionnaire** at the end of this chapter when discussing loan options with multiple lenders.

Interest-Only Mortgage (I/O)

If a first-time home buyer qualifies for an interest-only mortgage, then he or she can expect to make an interest-only payment for a set period in the first years of the loan. An **interest-only mortgage** can be adjustable-rate or fixed rate. The first years of the loan are typically representative of ten years where the borrower delays paying the principal and only makes the interest payment. When the interest-only period ends, the total monthly payment would increase significantly because the borrower would have to begin making the principal payment along with the interest.

A drawback to this type of mortgage is if the borrower doesn't make principal payments during the interest-only payment period, then this would affect the unpaid loan principal. In fact, there wouldn't be a reduction and for the remaining years of the loan, the unpaid principal would have to be paid back. This is on top of the interest. For a first-time home buyer, this change would cause significant payment shock.

Therefore, it is important to consider how change to the monthly payment will affect your cash flow and cash management objectives. Consider also the fact that when only paying the interest, you have not paid the principal, which means you have not built equity in your home. Unless the value of your home goes up, the only equity you would have in your home is the sum of the down payment. If the market value of your home goes down, you would undoubtedly lose some or all of the down payment.

Keep all of these ideas in mind when considering the best mortgage option for your budget.

Calculating Income and Debt

Before considering a home loan, take inventory of your finances. Throughout this book you will find content about cash flow planning and resolving credit issues. Therefore, a discussion about finances is never enough. You must know what you have in order to know what you can do. Your personal finances reflect you: how you think and your habits. In essence, your personal finances reflect your belief system. What you earn and what you owe will determine how much of a risk a lender is willing to assume when considering your goals for homeownership.

Income Considerations

You must present evidence of gross monthly income. This type of income includes both regular and recurring income. Prospective first-time home buyers that cannot provide documents evidencing income will not qualify for a loan. Evidence includes paycheck stub and tax returns. This is the standard. Of course, there are exceptions to the standard. Lenders will consider unearned income in the forms of alimony and lottery payoffs when determining your ability to repay a mortgage loan. In addition, if you have income-producing properties such as real estate and stocks, income generated from these assets will be used in calculating your total income.

Debt Obligations

Lenders rarely approve loans where the debt exceeds or overloads income. Calculate all of your monthly debt obligations. Obligations include credit cards, installment and revolving loans, car loans, and related personal debts. If you have an ongoing obligation such as alimony and/or child support, this must be considered also. When calculating debt in terms of total monthly expenditures, use only the monthly minimum payment figure. This will give you an idea of what you expend every month in terms of debt.

Monthly Overhead

When planning to qualify for a mortgage loan, consider other factors related to total monthly housing expense. All of your monthly housing expenses, which will include a sum of payments for taxes, insurance, loan principal and interest, should not exceed more than 30% of your gross monthly income. Estimate your tax and insurance expenses to be about 15%. The remainder will be put towards the principal and interest payments.

Keep in mind that lenders will not approve mortgage loans where the total monthly housing expense combined with debt obligations exceeds 36% because the application will be in danger of not meeting underwriting guidelines. In other words, there is more flexibility in in the 30% versus the thirty-six percent. There is even greater flexibility in 25% to twenty-eight percent.

When determining if you can afford the home price you want, use a finance calculator available on multiple websites to help guide your goal of meeting the lender's qualifications. Use the **First-Time Home Buyer Affordability Finance Questionnaire** at the end of this chapter to calculate your potential to repay the mortgage loan based upon your income and current debt obligations. It provides insight into how to approach the lender and maintain a record of research before applying for a mortgage loan.

It is beneficial for first-time home buyers who need to calculate how much their total monthly housing payment will be in contrast to their gross monthly income.

Susan used one of the finance calculators to determine her ability to repay a mortgage loan. She realized that saving for a higher down payment would help her to appear less of a risk with the lender.

Case Study: Susan Uses a Finance Calculator

Susan is a first-time home buyer. Susan lives in San Diego. She just graduated with a bachelor's degree in business administration from the University of San Diego. She is ready to enter the home buying market. She wants a house or condo for no more than $100,000, which is hard to find in the San Diego market. Susan's gross income from her new job as a business analyst will be about $30,000, give or take.

She has about $20,000 to put towards a down payment on the home. She saved the money from working summer jobs over five years. Susan uses a finance calculator to calculate the minimum down payment she would need to meet the lender's requirement as well as the estimated costs.

Using her future gross income of $30,000, current monthly debt of $300 not including estimated student loan payments, down payment estimate of $20,000, and mortgage rate of 5.625%, Susan was able to gain insight into her current situation. Here are the results:

Results of Susan's Mortgage Finance Calculations

Category	Amount
Maximum House Price Qualify for	$92,973
Estimated Monthly Payment	$600

Loan Amount Qualified for	$75,230
Down Payment Needed	$17,743
Estimated Closing Costs	$2,257
Estimated Principal Interest	$433
Estimated Taxes	$97
Estimated Hazard Insurance	$39
Estimated Private Mortgage Insurance	$31

The estimated monthly payment leaves much room for Susan to meet her debt obligations of $300 and estimated student loan debt, which may range from $250 to $500. In addition, a down payment of approximately $20,000 will help to decrease Susan's loan obligation significantly. The house price she qualifies for is within her current means. Susan's total monthly costs would be approximately $1,200, without the student loan debt estimate. Susan's estimated gross monthly income would be $2,500.

This leaves Susan with approximately $1,300 for related overhead expenses. This program would work well for Susan if she qualifies for a fixed-rate mortgage. However, if Susan only qualifies for an adjustable-rate mortgage, where the interest rate will change after five years, Susan may experience payment shock unless her income increases also.

Susan's current dilemma is finding a house or condo in San Diego for under $100,000.

Getting Pre-Approved

Getting pre-approved for a mortgage loan before searching for a home is the first step you need to take after performing the calculations. In other words, Susan's next step would be to search for a lender and submit an application for preapproval. Susan would need to provide evidence of employment, proof of gross monthly income earnings, source of down payment, and proof of related financial circumstances including current debt obligations. Therefore, Susan organizes the home mortgage loan paperwork before submitting an application for pre-approval. Below are the standard documents you would need to submit an application:

- W2 earning statements or 1099 DIV income statements for the last 2 years
- Federal tax returns for the last 2 years

- Bank statements for the last few months. The balance on the statement needs to be greater than or equal to the amount need for the down payment.
- Recent paycheck stubs
- Proof of other income (i.e., tips, Social Security payments, etc.)
- Proof of investment income

You may be required to submit additional documents as evidence of your ability to repay the debt.

It is important to note that a **pre-approval letter** is different from a **pre-qualification letter**. With the latter, the first-time home buyer just enters financial information and the letter is sent automatically without the process of in-depth verification. However, with a pre-approval letter, the mortgage broker or lender verifies all of the information on the application. Getting pre-approved is much more time-consuming, but it carries more weight. Here is a sample letter that Susan will receive when she applies for pre-approval.

Sample Pre-Approval Letter

December 11, 2012

Susan Jones
1736 State Street #403A
San Diego, CA 92101

RE: Pre-Approval Letter

Dear Ms. Jones,

Congratulations! Based upon the information you provided in your letter, you have been pre-approved for a home mortgage loan, within the following parameters:

- Property: 123 El Cajon Drive, San Diego, CA 92143
- Sale Price: $92,973
- Loan Amount: $75,230
- Term of Loan: 30 years at best rate

You must obtain final approval. In order to obtain final approval, you must meet the following conditions:

- Satisfactory Purchase Agreement
- Sufficient Appraisal for the purchased property
- Marketable Title to the property

Please note that we cannot underwrite your loan and give official approval before we officially fund the property. Please be aware that this is not a commitment to lend. You are also not required to obtain a loan because you have received this letter. In addition, no fees were charged by us to you in providing this letter.

If you have any questions, please feel free to call me at the number below.

Sincerely,

Karlie Sims
Loan Officer
Ellis Financial Group, Inc.
Ph: 800-234-8262
CA DRE License No: 99999999
NMLS No. 6542222

As you can see, a financial institution will estimate their ability to fund a property based upon the verifiable criteria you include within an application.

In contrast, with a pre-qualification, the lending company hasn't verified the data. In this case, Susan enters information online into multiple boxes, and the company sends a letter by email or fax indicating that the prospective borrower has been pre-qualified for a home mortgage loan. Here is a sample pre-qualification letter.

CARR Mortgage Company

Susan Jones is prequalified for a residential loan in the amount of $100,000 for the property located at 123 El Cajon Drive, San Diego, CA 92143. This qualification is based upon a 30-year conventional mortgage at 5.75% interest with total taxes not to exceed $5,250.

Based upon the information received during the time of application, along with credit and income verification received by CARR Mortgage Company, the applicant meets the requirements for a conventional loan at the terms stated above.

CARR Mortgage Company has reviewed cash assets and reserves of the applicant and finds that the applicant does possess sufficient funds necessary to close the transaction.

This pre-qualification letter does not constitute loan approval or commitment to rate, fees, or term. Any misrepresentation in the loan application or adverse change in the applicant's financial condition may void this pre-qualification letter. Poor credit standards would also void this pre-qualification letter.

This pre-qualification letter does not intend to confer any rights or privileges upon any third parties including, but not limited to, sellers of real property.

A completed loan file with an acceptable appraisal must be provided for underwriting review and before a loan decision can be made.

If you have any question or need more information, please don't hesitate to call.

Sincerely,

Your Home Mortgage Consultant

As you can see the pre-qualification letter is similar to a standard form letter. With the pre-approval letter, the lending group provides official contact information and references particular documents necessary to complete the process. The pre-approval letter also provides licensing information so Susan can verify the company and the loan officer.

There are additional benefits to receiving a pre-approval letter. You will know how much money you qualify for, depending upon your income. In addition, with a pre-approval letter, you'll have more leverage with the seller when it is time to negotiate. The real estate agent will work hard to help close a deal; the pre-approval letter motivates a realtor. Lastly, the lender will recalculate your maximum mortgage amount if your financial situation changes. These are some ideas to keep in mind as you begin the process of purchasing your home.

Reviewing the Real Estate Purchase Agreement

When negotiating with the seller, it is important to consider the price and the offer. A seller that overprices a home will turn off prospective buyers. Similarly, making an offer that is far below the asking price will alienate the seller. Therefore, asking and selling prices should be based upon the market prices of comparable homes.

In addition, it is important to respect each side's priorities. Don't push too hard and be willing to compromise on a few sensitive issues. A seller that is not willing to decrease the sales price may budge on the transaction costs. Approach the negotiations process with the goal of meeting in the middle, resolving difficulties, and seeking advice from countless experts familiar with real estate transactions.

The advice from experienced realtors and attorneys will come in handy when it comes to the real estate purchase agreement. Terms and conditions that permeate this type of agreement will undoubtedly provide for a complex process. This type of agreement will require a prospective home buyer to review the document closely before signing it. The legal jargon is complicated and if the terms and conditions don't sit well with you, it would be best to consider walking away from the deal.

With any typical real estate purchase agreement, there are standard clauses that you, the seller, and the lender must agree on. The following represent some clauses to consider and plan for as you begin the process of signing the contract and closing the deal. The main question to consider when constructing these clauses is this: *Who is responsible?*

- Cutoff dates for inspections. Approvals of the inspection reports.
- Repairs needed to be resolved as a result of inspection results.
- Representations/warranties regarding the condition of the property.
- Purchase of home warranty plan.
- Closing of escrow.

After the inspection, the buyer will want the seller to resolve any issues regarding the condition of the home. In addition, the buyer can order one or more inspections, but the seller isn't obligated to make repairs or modifications as a result of the inspection report. The inspection report, essentially, is a negotiation document.

The purchase agreement should provide guidance concerning who will be responsible for resolving major problems. The agreement should reference representations and warranties. Does the seller warrant that the condition of the roof, central heating, and cooling system are in good condition? Or do these items need repair? Is the buyer purchasing the home "as is"? Reference to these items should be in the contract.

The most important date to keep in mind is the escrow closing date. When the property changes hands, the seller must move out completely. Buyers usually pick up the keys to the property on the day escrow closes. All of these issues should be fully expressed within the real estate purchase agreement to prevent confusion and conflict.

Closing the Mortgage Loan

Even though you have signed the purchase agreement and the lender has approved your loan, you have no rights to the property until legal title is transferred to you and the loan is officially closed. When it is time to close a mortgage loan, the following will happen:

- Buyer signs the mortgage loan documents.
- Seller executes the deed to the property.
- Lender collects and disburses funds.
- Closing agent records the necessary instruments to ensure legal ownership of the property.

Be sure that the lender and the seller of the property provide a firm closing date. Settlement or closing must take place before the loan commitment from the lender expires. The settlement date must also reference the lender's and seller's commitment to satisfy any problems with the property and provide adequate time to complete them. With this in mind, there are standard documents required for closing a loan.

- **Title Insurance Policy:** The title company will research legal records to ensure that the buyer receives clear title, or ownership, to the property. In order for the buyer to own the property outright, there cannot be claims, or liens, against the property.

- **Homeowner's Insurance:** The lender requires the buyer to purchase homeowner's insurance on the property. The policy must cover the value of the property and the contents in the case of a fire or storm. Buyer must have this policy at the time of closing.

- **Termite Inspection and Certification:** Properties must be inspected for termites. The report is required for FHA and VA loans.

- **Survey or Plot Plan:** The lending company may require a survey of the property. A survey typically includes an assessment of the property boundaries, location of improvements, easements for utilities, and encroachments on the boundaries such as fences or buildings.

- **Water and Sewer Certification:** Properties are typically served by public water and sewer facilities. If this is not the case, the buyer will need to secure local government certification of any private water source and sanitary sewer facility.

- **Flood Insurance:** Properties located near a designated, defined flood plain will require flood insurance. Lenders will require the buyer to keep the insurance for the life of the loan.

- **Certificate of Occupancy or Building Code Compliance Letter:** Properties under new construction will require a certificate of occupancy. The builder of the property will obtain the certificate. The buyer must ensure that the ordering of an inspection and the payment of required repairs must be borne by the lender and spelled out in the real estate purchase agreement.

These are some of the first-level documents necessary to close the loan. Additional documents include the following:

- **Settlement Statement – HUD-1 Form:** This form is required by federal law and it is prepared by the closing agent. Both the seller and the buyer sign the form. The form details the sale of the transaction, which references the sale price, amount of financing, loan fees and charges, proration of real estate taxes, and amounts due by the seller and the buyer to third-party agents.

- **Truth-in-Lending Statement (TIL):** This form is also required by federal law. If there are corrected changes to your TIL, the lender must provide a copy to the buyer.

- **Mortgage Note:** The mortgage note is evidence of the buyer's indebtedness to the lender and represents a promise to pay. It outlines the amount and the terms of the loan. It also references penalties for loan default.

- **Mortgage or Deed of Trust:** The mortgage or deed of trust represents a security instrument that the lender can use as a claim against the borrower's home if he or she fails to adhere to the terms of the mortgage note. The document gives the lender the right to take the property by foreclosure. The mortgage or deed of trust will become a matter of public record. It provides public notice of the lender's claim on the property.

There are a number of additional, but miscellaneous documents such as a Statement of Intent to Occupy and related institutional forms. All documents must be signed at the time of closing to ensure the buyer's right to ownership.

BUSINESS PLANNER

Small business owners and individual real estate investors interested in purchasing distressed properties need to be aware of the ramifications associated with leveraging and renting them. A **distressed property** is one that falls under three categories: short sale, bank purchase, and foreclosure auction.

With a **short sale**, the owner still owns the property. The bank will usually take less than what the owner owes on the property to satisfy the debt. The owner must sell the property and all proceeds of the sale go towards meeting the debt obligation. Short sales are contingent upon the approval of the bank. A short sale typically requires a *Short Sale Addendum*; with this addendum, the seller must obtain consent from creditors, permitting a reduction in the closing costs in order to close the transaction. With short sales, the lender will require changes to agreements. Therefore, buyers must be prepared to deal with such demands, especially to the changes of terms.

When purchasing a property directly through the bank, the bank has already foreclosed on the property and now owns it. On the bank's books, it is a **real estate owned property**, or REO. In some cases, the owner of the property will sign a *deed in lieu of foreclosure*, which means the owner signs over right to the property. An REO property is typically sold using forms and procedures developed by the lender.

Lastly, with a foreclosure, the property is auctioned and the proceeds of the sale go to the owner, who is now the bank.

The most important thing to consider in purchasing distressed properties is to make sure that there is a clear title to the property. In other words, make sure there are no claims against the property from third parties. In addition, as a real estate investor, conduct a thorough assessment of the property, giving attention to its condition. Foreclosed homes are typically sold "as is." Therefore, ask yourself this question: Do you have the budget to repair the home and bring it to a marketable condition? Obtain a pre-inspection report before purchasing the home.

When searching for properties, familiarize yourself with the area. What is the rental market? What are some comparable properties for which you can base your own pricing objectives? Will you get a sufficient return on your money? It is important to consider the income-producing potential of each property.

Knowing the state of your accounts will help to guide you as you research properties. Without a sound assessment of your current cash flow, you may find that you do not have the capital to sustain the property until you get a renter. Within the current market, it might be harder to sell it. Therefore, assess your current financial situation to ensure that you can maintain the property and that it won't eat up your resources significantly.

Chapter Key Points

A **first-time home buyer** is defined as an individual who is purchasing a principal residence for the first time. This is the type of person who has never been listed on a deed as the owner of real estate.

Individual real estate investors that wish to enter the home buying market have multiple options, from purchasing older homes to purchasing distressed properties and converting them into income-producers.

Types of first-time home buyers are directly related to the type of loan. A first-time home buyer loan offers many benefits, but also restrictions. First-time home buyer loans are mortgages that lenders and government agencies tailor specifically for people buying their first home.

First-time home buyer loans insured by FHA offer easier qualifying guidelines, which include higher debt ratios, lower credit scores, limited down payments, and reduced closing costs and fees. These are the benefits of receiving this type of loan. However, there are negative consequences.

A **rate cap** is defined as the limit on how much the interest rate can change; the rate could change during a particular adjustment period or the rate could change over the entire term of the loan.

An **adjustment cap** limits how much the rate can go up or down within a single adjustment period. Loans with this type of cap help to limit how much your loan payment can change when subject to adjusting procedures. On the other hand, a **lifetime cap** establishes a maximum and a minimum interest rate throughout the term of the loan. With this type of cap, the monthly payment could still increase, which may result in you experiencing payment shock.

If a first-time home buyer qualifies for an interest-only mortgage, then he or she can expect to make an interest-only payment for a set period in the first years of the loan. An **interest-only mortgage** can be adjustable-rate or fixed rate.

You must present evidence of gross monthly income. This type of income includes both regular and recurring income. Prospective first-time home buyers that cannot provide documents evidencing income will not qualify for a loan.

Lenders rarely approve loans where the debt exceeds or overloads income.

It is important to note that a **pre-approval letter** is different from a **pre-qualification letter**.

When negotiating with the seller, it is important to consider the price and the offer. A seller that overprices a home will turn off prospective buyers. Similarly, making an offer that is far below the asking price will alienate the seller.

Even though you have signed the purchase agreement and the lender has approved your loan, you have no rights to the property until legal title is transferred to you and the loan is officially closed.

Small business owners and individual real estate investors interested in purchasing distressed properties need to be aware of the ramifications associated with leveraging and renting them. A **distressed property** is one that falls under three categories: short sale, bank purchase, and foreclosure auction.

Chapter Key Terms

Adjustment cap: term refers to the limit of how much the rate can go up or down within a single adjustment period.

Deed in lieu of foreclosure: term refers to a type of document signed by the owner of a property, selling right to the property to the bank.

Distressed property: term refers to three types of properties that fall under short sale, bank purchase, and foreclosure auction.

Federal Housing Administration: term refers to a federal agency whose goals are to improve housing standards, provide home financing through insurance of mortgage loans, and stabilize the mortgage market.

FHA: acronym stands for Federal Housing Administration.

First-time home buyer: term refers to an individual who is purchasing a principal residence for the first time.

HUD-1 Form: See *Settlement Statement*.

Interest-only mortgage: term refers to where the borrower delays paying the principal and only makes the interest payment.

Lifetime cap: term refers to the establishment of a maximum and a minimum interest rate throughout the term of a loan.

Pre-approval letter: term refers to a document that reflects the lender's process in verifying an applicant's financial information to determine eligibility for a mortgage loan.

Pre-qualification letter: term refers to a document sent by a financial institution that has processed the applicant's information without the process of in-depth verification.

Rate cap: term refers to the limit on how much the interest rate can change.

Real estate owned property: term refers to a type of property owned by a bank.

REO: acronym stands for real estate owned.

Settlement Statement: term refers to a type of document prepared by a closing agent; the document details the sale of the transaction, which references the sale price, amount of financing, loan fees and charges, proration of real estate taxes, and amounts due by the seller and the buyer to third-party agents.

Short sale: term refers to the process where the bank takes less than what is owed on a property to satisfy the defaulted borrower's debt obligation to the bank.

TIL: acronym stands for Truth in Lending.

Truth in Lending Statement (TIL): term refers to a type of form that reflects corrected changes.

GROUP WORK PROMPT

Visit the Department of Housing and Urban Development website at HUD.gov. Once there, click on the tab "Homeowner Help." Review the material on the site and answer the questions below. You may start this project in-class and finish at home.

1. What are some tips to avoid foreclosure? List at least three.
_____
_____
_____
_____

2. What are some ways to avoid foreclosure scams? Refer to the video on the site.
_____
_____
_____
_____

3. Where is an FHA Homeownership Center in your area?
_____
_____
_____
_____

4. What are examples of a list of programs that may help you avoid foreclosure?
_____
_____
_____
_____

Homework Exercise

For homework, pretend that you want to purchase a home. Answer the following questions:

- What is your gross monthly income?
- What are your current debts?
- What is your price range?
- Do you have credit problems?
- What do you have for a down payment?
- Do you want a new home or a distressed property?
- Do you have an earnest money deposit?

After you have answered these questions, then use multiple mortgage finance calculators. You may access a mortgage finance calculator by typing in as a keyword "mortgage finance calculator" or you may visit one of multiple realtor websites such as Realtor.com. Use the results as a guideline for planning purposes.

Develop a plan for purchasing a home as a first-time homebuyer. Organize the required documents as if you were submitting them to a lender. Review a sample real estate purchase agreement downloadable from the internet. See if you can fill out the agreement as much as you can.

Assessment

1. What is a first-time home buyer?

2. What are examples of loan closing documents?

3. **True or False**. A new home is a type of distressed property.

4. What is the difference between a pre-approval letter and a pre-qualification letter?

5. What is an interest-only mortgage?

Helpful Websites

HUD: Common Questions from First-Time Homebuyers
http://www.hud.gov/buying/comq.cfm

Bank of America: Understanding Your Mortgage Options
https://www.bankofamerica.com/home-loans/mortgage/finding-the-right-loan/understanding-mortgage-options.go

Organize Your Mortgage Loan Paperwork
http://www.myfico.com/loancenter/mortgage/step1/organizepaperwork.aspx

Closing Your Mortgage Loan
http://mortgage-x.com/brochure/closing.htm

How to Take Advantage of Warren Buffet's #1 Investment Idea
http://www.businessinsider.com/warren-buffett-buying-distressed-houses-2012-3?op=1

Chapter Forms

On the next pages are all of the forms discussed within this chapter. You may photocopy, scan, and print them out. Some forms you will need to complete the group work and the homework.

First-Time Home Buyer Mortgage Questionnaire

Date: _____

Lender: _____

Mortgage Type: (Based upon pre-approval and/or pre-qualification)

Fixed-Rate: _____

Projected Principal: _____
Projected Interest Rate: _____
Loan Term: _____

Adjustable Rate: _____

Introductory Period: _____

Introductory Principal: _____
Introductory Interest Rate: _____

Rate Cap:
Adjustment Cap: New Principal: _____ New Interest: _____
Lifetime Cap: New Principal: _____ New Interest: _____

Interest-Only Mortgage (I/O):

Fixed-Rate? _____ *Adjustable-Rate?* _____
Payment Period: _____
Interest Payment: _____
Monthly Principal: Year: _____ Total: _____

Notes and Considerations
_____
_____
_____
_____

First-Time Home Buyer Affordability Finance Worksheet

Date: _____

Lender: _____

Gross Income:

Yearly_____Monthly_____Weekly_____

Monthly Debt Payments: Monthly _____Weekly_____

Current Down Payment (Saved): _____

Mortgage Rate (%): _____

Closing Costs (%): _____

Minimum Down Payment (%): _____

Property Tax Rate (%): _____

Hazard Insurance Rate (%): _____

Private Mortgage Insurance Rate (PMI) (%): _____

Housing Expense-to-Income Ratio (%): _____

Long-Term Debt-to-Income Ratio (%): _____

Notes and Considerations
_____
_____
_____
_____

CHAPTER 10

Credit and the Pitfalls of Borrowing Money

Learning Objectives

- Define debt.
- List the types of debt.
- Record number of payday loans.
- Review different types of business debt.
- Review problems associated with business and personal debt.

WHAT IS DEBT?

A **debt** represents an obligation that involves two parties: a debtor and a creditor. The obligation, or debt, is created when the creditor agrees to loan assets to the creditor. The creditor grants the debt under the assumption that the debtor has the ability to repay. Repayment is typically subject to terms that include the attachment of interest to the loaned principle. Parties to a debt instrument must agree on how the debt will be repaid, whether the debt will be repaid in money (i.e., currency), goods, or services.

Parties must also outline if the debt will be repaid in increments over a period of time. Criteria for the loaned amount and repayment terms are typically outlined within a loan agreement which may represent a promissory note.

Within some business contexts, debt is used as a financing instrument, which allows companies purchasing power. Under these circumstances, debt is used one tool for meeting corporate finance strategies. This is important to know for small business entrepreneurs that desire to use debt for leveraging purposes.

TYPES OF DEBT

There are different types of debt specific to both personal and corporate finance.

There is consumer debt, which involves multiple categories. On the other hand, there is debt that companies use to leverage purchasing power. See the table *Comparison of Personal and Business Debt* for an outline of the different categories and sub-categories of debt. Multiple debt instruments typically fall under one or more of these categories.

Comparison of Personal and Business Debt

Consumer Debt	Business Debt
Secured Debt Unsecured Debt Revolving Debt Installment Debt	Secured Debt Unsecured Debt Private Debt Public Debt Syndicated Debt Bilateral Debt

CONSUMER DEBT

Consumer debt may be secured, unsecured, revolving, and/or installment. The most common types of consumer debt are credit card debt, payday loans, and related alternative financing instruments.

Secured Debt

This is debt secured by collateral. This type of debt reduces risks associated with lending. An example of secured debt would be a mortgage. In this context, the house is considered collateral. The collateral is used towards the debt. If a homeowner with a mortgage defaults on the repayment of the debt, the bank can seize the house, sell it, and apply the proceeds from the sale to the debt. In most cases, the homeowner would still be obligated to arrange to pay for any difference (i.e., outstanding balances) in order to satisfy the obligation with the bank or lending institution.

Concept Checker	*What is debt?*

Unsecured Debt

This is debt where collateral is unnecessary. Simply, it is debt uncollateralized. Under this category, if a debtor defaults and chooses the bankruptcy route, then the unsecured creditor will have a general claim on the assets. This can only happen after the secured creditors have satisfied their claim to specific pledged assets (i.e., house, land, property). Unsecured loans are often referred to as signature loans and/or personal loans. These types of loans typically are used for the following:

- Computers
- Home Improvement
- Vacation
- Emergency Expenses

Lending institutions use credit as a major factor for administering these loans. They rely on the creditworthiness of the borrower and on the borrower's promise to pay. Because the administration of unsecured loans involves greater risk, interest rates tend to be higher. In this case, creditors don't have the collateral, or assurance, that the borrower will pay. Therefore, creditors tend to send delinquent accounts to collections.

Revolving Debt

A revolving debt account is one in which the lender doesn't require the borrower to pay the outstanding balance in full every month. The borrower can make a minimum payment, which typically represents a percentage amount of the outstanding balance. Although the borrower is only obligated to pay the minimum amount to satisfy the lending conditions, the borrower will not be penalized for paying an amount that exceeds the minimum. The remaining balance on this type of account rolls over, or revolves, to the next month and is added to that balance. Interest is charged and also added to the balance. An example of a revolving debt is a credit card.

The downside to revolving debt is that if you don't pay the outstanding balance in full, you will undoubtedly continue to carry a big balance that will drive up your payments and make the debt somewhat unmanageable.

Installment Debt

In contrast, with an installment debt, the consumer pays a set amount each month. Installment loans can be used for both unsecured debt and secured debt. Examples of consumer installment debt include car loans, boat loans, student loans, private (unsecured) loans, and mortgage loans. The downside to installment debt is that consumers cannot make charges against the account until it is repaid in full.

Comparison of Personal and Corporate Debt

Alternative Financing

Alternative financing is typically provided by commercial organizations that are outside the traditional outlets of banking and lending. These are non-bank financial institutions that tailor their products for low-income individuals and for individuals with credit problems.

The products these companies offer fall under the term "microfinance," where small businesses and micro-entrepreneurs lack access to traditional banking services because of the high transaction costs, lack of collateral and sufficient cash flow, and credit problems. Alternative financing includes the following:

- Payday Loans
- Rent-to-Own Agreements
- Pawnshops
- Refund Anticipation Loans

- Sub-prime Mortgage Loans
- Car Title Loans
- Non-Bank Check Cashing
- Money Orders
- Money Transfers
- Small Business Micro-Loans

Payday Loans are fast becoming the preferred method for lending money to individuals with marginal credit ratings. Applicants receive these loans and begin a cycle that keeps them at a level where they never learn how to repair their credit because they position themselves "outside" of traditional services. In other words, while they continue to pursue a payday loan, they never pursue working on their credit. Therefore, their credit reports reflect inactivity and their credit scores never increase.

> **Three Main Types of Unsecured Loans for Bad Credit:**
> 1. Inventory Loans
> 2. Renovation and/or Expansion Loans
> 3. Temporary Cash Flow Loans

QUICK EXERCISE

Starting and continuing the payday loan cycle will only hinder your ability to work on your credit. Review your records. List the total number of payday loans you have received from when you started. Use the following worksheet as a guide. The important thing to remember here is that sometimes viewing the information on the page is helpful for determining when something is no longer beneficial.

Use the **Payday Loan Accumulation Worksheet** at the end of this chapter to chart the number of payday loans you have received within a week or any given month. Be honest. If you are not able to locate and list all of your payday loans, then chances are you have lost control over your money. If you have more than one payday loan, then chances are you have lost control over your money. If you have even one payday loan, because one is one too many, then chances are you have lost control over your money. More of your earned dollars are being put towards the satisfaction of this debt.

BUSINESS DEBT

Business debt is typically used for financing purposes. Companies use debt to finance its operations, to finance mergers, and to leverage assets. There are different types of business debt, which include the following:

- Secured Debt
- Unsecured Debt
- Private Debt
- Public Debt
- Syndicated Debt
- Bilateral Debt
- Other related types

Creditors typically have recourse to the debtor's assets when the debt is **secured**. Within this context, assets are proprietary; creditors typically have recourse ahead of general claims. On the other hand, when the debt is **unsecured**, creditors do not have legal recourse to the assets; they rely on the borrower's promise to pay. They will typically have to pursue legal action for defaulting borrowers.

Private debt is simply money that individuals and businesses owe within a given country. It is a loan given by a private entity and guaranteed by the official sector. Private debt consists of bank-loan obligations and it is typically used for underserved financing industries where small and middle-market companies need funding for commercial projects and real estate investments.

Public debt is government debt. It is synonymously with "national debt." Public or government debt may also refer to the debt of a state or province and local government (i.e., municipal). Public debt is typically used to finance government operations. A government usually borrows money by issuing securities, bonds, and bills. Therefore, government debt can represent internal debt or external debt. With internal debt, a government owes money to lenders within its own country. With external debt, a government owes money to foreign lenders. There are further sub-categories; public debt may represent short-term, medium term, or long-term. The broader definition of public debt includes multiple categories of government liabilities such as future pension payments.

Syndicated loans (debt) are granted to companies that wish to borrow millions of dollars, which incurs more risk. Within this context, the loan agreement consists of a syndicate of banks that each put forward a portion of the principal. In essence, the loan is provided by a group of lenders. However, it is structured, arranged, and administered by multiple commercial and/or investment banks.

In contrast, **bilateral debt** is a type of international debt where one country owes another country's money. There are different types of bilateral debt: foreign aid and export credits. Foreign aid represents bilateral development assistance; it is a traditional loan that helps governments to meet their development goals. Development goals include health care, education, agriculture, and infrastructure spending. With export credits, governments may allow a developing country to purchase the exports of another country and may defer payment for the goods. Within this context, export credit agencies guarantee payment.

Business debt involves multiple sub-categories such as business debt restructuring and bad debt deduction. Research this topic further to determine the information applicable to your business.

BUSINESS PLANNER

More and more small businesses are using credit cards to finance operations and overhead expenses. This has become the standard in small business entrepreneurship. Although this is true, there has been a new trend that requires owners to sign over a personal guarantee. With a personal guarantee on file with the creditor, if the consumer defaults on a loan agreement, then the creditor can report a business debt on the personal credit report. Now all things business has an impact on the personal. This is the case of John, a small business owner.

Case Study:
John's Business Debt Affects Personal Credit

John is in the business of government contracting. John also offers professional solutions where he provides business, technical, and financial management consulting. John receives revenue from both of these businesses.

John recently received a government contract through one of the armed services. The contract was for a little under $10,000. John was excited at the prospect of providing solutions for the federal agency. As John began to fill the contract, he ran into problems with cash. He decided to apply for a small business card. He reasoned that because of his good credit he wouldn't have a problem with fulfilling the contract. On the professional consulting side of the business, John was finding more success with multiple customers. He gained more lucrative contracts and payments were on-time. Enter a problem.

John was able to use money from prior contracts and the small business credit card to fill the contract. Fulfilling the contract took much of his business reserves. All would be well if one of the customers on the professional side of the business didn't refuse to submit the last payment, which would add a significant amount to John's reserves and give him the ability to repay the credit card balance. Because the customer refused to pay John for his efforts and because John no longer had the reserve cash to pay the small business credit card, John defaulted on the agreement. The credit was for $15,000 and John didn't have the full balance or even the minimum payment to meet the obligation. When John defaulted, the credit card company threatened to report the delinquency to all three credit reporting agencies.

This is perfectly legal. Lenders want to report this delinquency on your personal credit report because they feel you would be so determined to resolve it; lenders know that with a negative item on your report it would be hard to get a mortgage, an auto loan, a student loan, or other credit cards. Small business lenders review a consumer's credit report; if they discover a delinquency, they will likely offer the consumer higher interest rates or worse, not offer credit at all.

Going forward, there are several ways to address this problem. There are some consequences that every consumer and small business owner needs to be aware of before mixing business with personal. Use the **Resolving Business Debt Planning Worksheet** at the end of this chapter while you plan to repair your business debt and your credit report.

Chapter Key Points

A **debt** represents an obligation that involves two parties: a debtor and a creditor. The obligation, or debt, is created when the creditor agrees to loan assets to the creditor.

Consumer debt may be secured, unsecured, revolving, and/or installment.

Secured debt reduces risks associated with lending.

Unsecured debt is debt uncollateralized.

A revolving debt account is one in which the lender doesn't require the borrower to pay the outstanding balance in full every month. The borrower can make a minimum payment, which typically represents a percentage amount of the outstanding balance.

Alternative financing is typically provided by commercial organizations that are outside the traditional outlets of banking and lending. These are non-bank financial institutions that tailor their products for low-income individuals and for individuals with credit problems.

Private debt is simply money that individuals and businesses owe within a given country.

Public debt is government debt.

Syndicated loans (debt) are granted to companies that wish to borrow millions of dollars, which incurs more risk. Within this context, the loan agreement consists of a syndicate of banks that each put forward a portion of the principal.

Chapter Key Terms

Alternative financing: term refers to non-bank financial products such as payday loans, rent-to-own agreements, sub-prime mortgage loans, car title loans, refund anticipation loans, and non-bank check cashing.

Bilateral debt: term refers to a type of international debt.

Debt: term refers to an obligation involving two parties: a debtor and a creditor.

Consumer debt: term refers to multiple categories such as secured, unsecured, revolving, and installment.

Installment debt: term refers to an account where the consumer pays a set amount each month.

National debt: See "Public debt."

Private debt: term refers to money that individuals and businesses owe within a given country. It is a loan given by a private entity.

Public debt: term refers to government debt.

Revolving debt: term refers to an account in which the lender doesn't require the borrower to repay the outstanding balance in full every month.

Secured debt: term refers to debt secured by collateral.

Syndicated loan: term refers to debt granted to companies that wish to borrow millions of dollars with greater risk to the lender.

Unsecured debt: term refers to debt uncollateralized.

GROUP WORK PROMPT

It is increasingly becoming difficult for consumers to resolve their credit problems, because consumers are looking to fill their needs through alternative means. This tendency to substitute one answer to a problem for another and never confront the problem head on is hindering consumers from understanding the importance of financial management and realizing their life goals.

For your task, you will review a sample credit report that you can download from the Internet. Use the keyword "sample credit report" to locate a printable version. You will review the report and answer the following questions. You will have to research to find some answers. You may start this project in-class and finish it as a group at home.

1. What is a public record?

_____

_____

2. What is a credit report?

_____

_____

3. What is a negative item? What is an example of a negative item?

_____

_____

4. What is a collection account?

_____

_____

5. How can a consumer dispute an item? What is the process?

_____

_____

_____

6. What are accounts in good standing?

_____

_____

7. What are the different account types?

_____

_____

8. What are the steps for a consumer who wants to close an account?

9. What is an inquiry?

10. What are the different types of inquiries?

11. What are inquiries allowed under the Fair Credit Reporting Act (FCRA)?

12. What are the steps for a consumer to submit a personal statement?

13. What is the contact information for at least one credit reporting agency?

FINANCIAL WELLNESS | 225

HOMEWORK EXERCISE

It is time to evaluate the payday loan contract in all of its glory. In order to repair your debt, you must become familiar with contract terminology. The payday loan contract offers insight into the annual percentage rate, the finance charge, the amount financed, and the total number of payments. All of these terms seem easy to understand. However, what happens when you miss one payment. You are considered in default of the contract.

Since many people don't always read the fine print, they are blindsided by the fees. They never read the language upon which the fees are based. With this in mind, for homework, review your payday loan contract. If you have never applied for a payday loan, you can still do this exercise. Download a document off the internet using the keywords "payday loan contract." Select any one of the results to do the following exercise.

1. What is the security interest?
_____
_____

2. What is the late payment?
_____
_____

3. What is the method of payment?
_____
_____
_____
_____

4. What are the returned check charges?
_____
_____

5. What is the prepayment?
_____
_____

6. When does the consumer default?
_____
_____

7. What is the lender's right when the consumer defaults?
_____
_____

8. What is the waiver?
_____
_____

9. When will the institution report the default to the consumer's credit report?
_____
_____

10. What does "joint and several" mean within the context of a payday loan contract?
_____
_____

11. What is governing law?
_____
_____

12. What is assignment?
_____
_____

Assessment

1. **True or False**. A debt represents an obligation that involves two parties: a debtor and a creditor.

2. What are the different types of debt? Provide a brief definition.

_____
_____
_____
_____
_____
_____
_____

3. Consumer debt includes:
   a. Secured Debt
   b. Syndicated Loan
   c. Temporary Cash Flow
   d. All of the above.

4. John gave a personal guarantee for a small business credit card. Because one of his clients refuses to pay, John must default on his credit card agreement. The credit card company is threatening to submit the delinquent information to John's personal credit card account. The delinquent amount on John's small business credit card is $35,000. John only has $2,000 in his business reserves. He has approximately $1,000 in his personal reserves. John's mortgage is due; his mortgage is $2,250. What are some options for John? He wants to pay the credit card, but not become homeless in the process. He also wants to ensure that he protects his personal credit as well. Suggest to John some ways he could accomplish these goals.

_____
_____
_____
_____
_____
_____

Chapter Forms

On the next pages are all of the forms discussed within this chapter. You may photocopy, scan, and print them out. Some forms you will need to complete the group work and the homework.

Helpful Websites

Consolidated Credit Counseling Services, Inc.
http://www.consolidatedcredit.org/

Investopedia
http://www.investopedia.com

Sample Payday Loan Contract
http://www.wdfi.org/_resources/indexed/site/wca/consumer_credit/SamplePaydayLoanContract.pdf

Syndicated Loan
http://en.wikipedia.org/wiki/Syndicated_loan

Credit.com Article: A Small Business Owner's Debt Bleeds Over Into His Personal Credit
http://www.credit.com/rs/vol1.jsp

True Credit Sample Credit Report
http://tui.transunion.com/pdf/learnCenter/Reading_Your_Report.pdf

Southeastern Louisiana University: Understanding Debt
http://www.selu.edu/acad_research/programs/cse/finance/debt/index.html

Schwab MoneyWise: Understanding Debt
http://www.schwabmoneywise.com/public/moneywise/life_events/starting_out/understanding_debt

Schwab MoneyWise: Organize Your Financial Life
http://www.schwabmoneywise.com/public/moneywise/life_events/starting_out/organize_your_financial_life

FDIC Consumer News PDF: You Can Organize and Simplify Your Financial Life: A How-To Guide
http://www.fdic.gov/consumers/consumer/news/cnwin1011/Win1011BW.pdf

Dummies.com: How to Organize Your Financial Records
http://www.dummies.com/how-to/content/how-to-organize-your-financial-records.html

Federal Trade Commission: Credit Repair: How to Help Yourself with Sample Dispute Letter
http://www.ftc.gov/bcp/edu/pubs/consumer/credit/cre13.shtm

PAYDAY LOAN ACCUMULATION WORKSHEET

Application Date	Institution	Amount	Pay Period	Reason

RESOLVING BUSINESS DEBT PLANNING WORKSHEET

1. How much money do you have in your personal reserves? Have you allocated it to anything?

Going forward, there are several ways to address this problem. There are some consequences that every consumer and small business owner needs to be aware of before mixing business with personal. Use the **Resolving Business Debt Planning Worksheet** at the end of this chapter while you plan to repair your business debt and your credit report.

2. How much money do you have in your business reserves? Have you allocated it to anything?

3. Determine how much you can take from each to pay down the business debt. What are those amounts?

4. Call the lender. Check to see if the lender will take a minimum payment. If yes, what is that minimum payment?

5. If the lender takes the minimum payment, will the lender consider the account past due?

6. Call the lender. Ask if the lender will allow the business account to be converted from a transactional account to a revolving account. If yes, what are the terms?

7. If the account can be converted, what is the outstanding balance? What is the payment arrangement? Will the lender allow the account to remain in good standing?

8. Do you have a revolving credit card without an outstanding balance?

9. What is the cash advance requirement? What are the standard terms?
___
___

10. Can you take out a cash advance against the card?
___
___

11. Will the cash advance be enough to satisfy the debt, make the minimum, and/or satisfy a significant chunk of the debt?
___
___

12. If this applies, what steps will you take to collect from a delinquent client?
___
___

CHAPTER 11

Understanding Bankruptcy

Learning Objectives

- Define bankruptcy.
- List the types of bankruptcy.
- Define chapter 7 bankruptcy.
- List the fee and eligibility requirements of bankruptcy chapters.

WHAT IS BANKRUPTCY?

Bankruptcy is a legal status representative of a person or organization that cannot repay the debt or debts he, she, or it owes to a creditor. Bankruptcy is typically imposed by a court order for some jurisdictions and is often initiated by the debtor. Bankruptcy is not synonymous with insolvency.

The United States Constitution through Article 1, Section 8, authorizes Congress to enact laws regarding the subject of bankruptcy. With the tenets of this legislation in mind, Congress enacted the Bankruptcy Code in 1978, which stipulates the criteria for administering the process. The process, or procedural aspects, of bankruptcy are governed and monitored by the Federal Rules of Bankruptcy Procedure, or the **Bankruptcy Rules**. The Bankruptcy Code and Bankruptcy Rules maintain legal procedures for dealing with the debt problems of individuals and businesses.

There are 90 bankruptcy districts across the United States, with a bankruptcy court located within each judicial district. Some states have more than one district. Each court has an officiating judge responsible for applying the law of bankruptcy according to the Bankruptcy Code and the corresponding rules. The United States bankruptcy judge is the official judicial officer; he or she determines the eligibility of a filer and whether or not the debt or debts should be discharged.

Although the bankruptcy process is entirely administrative, it is typically conducted outside of the courthouse. Exceptions apply. The process for filings under chapters 7, 11, and 13 is typically administered by a trustee. Therefore, the debtor is typically not involved with the bankruptcy judge.

Small business owners struggling with cash flow and on the brink of insolvency may elect to pursue bankruptcy options appropriate for their financial condition. However, other options exist primarily for small business owners. Debt restructuring is one such option that allows a company in financial distress to renegotiate delinquent debts for the purpose of improving and/or restoring liquidity. This option allows the company to rehabilitate itself while continue to manage operations.

Bankruptcy offers many options, but as you plan to regain your life, let the option of seeking bankruptcy be your very last. For the time it will take for the bankruptcy status to go off your credit report, you could have solved the problem on your own. Keep this in mind as you continue to develop personal financial and budgeting goals.

Concept Checker	*What is bankruptcy?*

TYPES OF BANKRUPTCY

There are different types of bankruptcy options. The following represents a list of the major types:

- Chapter 7
- Chapter 11
- Chapter 13

Each of these options is discussed below and on the following pages.

Concept Checker	*What are the types of bankruptcy?*

CHAPTER 7

Chapter 7 bankruptcy is typically referred to as a "no-asset" case. The debtor usually has no assets subject to liquidation. With Chapter 7, the assets of a case filer are usually liquidated by a court-supervised procedure. With this option, the bankruptcy trustee assumes full right over the assets of the debtor's estate. The trustee reduces the assets to cash and distributes amounts to creditors. There are exceptions. A debtor may retain the right to certain exempt property.

In this type of case, there may be a creditor with an unsecured claim. This type of creditor will only receive a distribution from the sale of the debtor's assets provided the case is an asset case. The creditor, in this case, must file a proof of claim with the bankruptcy court.

When the debtor is an individual, he or she can receive a discharge of debts that releases him or her from personal liability, provided that the case item is a dischargeable debt. The debtor will receive a discharge of debts a few months after the petition is filed.

Eligibility

To qualify for Chapter 7 relief, a debtor may be an individual, partnership, corporation, or other type of business entity. Relief is available regardless of the amount of the petitioner's debts and regardless of the solvency or insolvency of the company. If an individual debtor filed a bankruptcy petition and failed to appear before the court and/or comply with the orders of the court, or the debtor voluntarily dismissed the case, and if these actions happened during the preceding 180 days, the debtor cannot file under Chapter 7. In addition, debtors must seek and receive credit counseling from an approved credit counseling agency before filing for Chapter 7 bankruptcy protection.

The purpose of bankruptcy is to give the debtor a fresh start. The debtor would have no liability for discharged debts. But the option of a discharged debt under Chapter 7 is only available to individual debtors and not partnerships or corporations. Even though a debtor may receive a discharge of debts under Chapter 7, not every debt is eligible for discharge. A bankruptcy discharge cannot extinguish a lien on a property.

The following **forms** are specific to **Chapter 7** bankruptcy filings:

B9A (Official Form 9A): Chapter 7 Individual or Joint Debtor No Asset Case
B9B (Official Form 9B): Chapter 7 Corporation/Partnership No Asset Case
B9C (Official Form 9C): Chapter 7 Corporation/Partnership Asset Case

Each form provides guidelines and explanations for filing. A creditor can file a proof of claim (Form B10), outlining the amount of debt owed. There are additional types of claims that may apply to Chapter 7 filings or related filings. These types are predicated upon whether the debtor has assets and whether the creditor can attach a claim to those assets. Review the proof of claim form for more information about the different types of claims available to creditors.

How it Works

The debtor files a petition with the bankruptcy court. The debtor must file a case with the bankruptcy court serving the area; in the case of a business, the debtor must file the case where the business is organized, and/or where the principal business is located, and/or the location of principal assets. After filing the petition, the debtor must file with the court the following information and/or documents:

- Schedule of assets and liabilities
- Schedule of current income and expenditures
- Statement of financial affairs
- Schedule of executor contracts and unexpired leases

The debtor must also provide to the trustee assigned to the bankruptcy case a copy of the tax return and/or transcripts of the most recent tax year. The debtor must also submit copies of tax returns filed during the case.

Individual debtors that have consumer debts will be subject to additional document filing requirements which include receiving and/or doing the following:

- Receiving a certificate of credit counseling
- Receiving a copy of a debt repayment plan developed through credit counseling
- Providing evidence of payment from employers (received 60 days prior to filing)
- Providing a statement of monthly net income
- Providing proof of anticipated increase in income or expenses after filing
- Providing evidence of a record of interest the debtor has in federal/state qualified education and/or tuition accounts

A husband or wife may file a joint petition or file individually. However, a husband or wife are subject to the filing requirements individually and must submit all documentation required for a bankruptcy case to be heard. All official forms are available on the U.S. Court's website at:
www.us.courts.gov/bkforms/index.html

Petitioners cannot obtain forms through the court.

Fees

Filing a petition for bankruptcy is subject to three types of fees, normally payable to the clerk upon filing. The court charges the following fees:

- $245: case filing fee
- $46: miscellaneous administrative fee
- $15: trustee charge

Fees are typically paid to the clerk. However, there are exceptions; some petitioners can request to pay in installments, which is limited to four and the final installment paid not later than 120 days after filing the petition. For joint petitions, one filing fee, one administrative fee, and one trustee fee is charged. Failure to pay the required fees may result in the case being dismissed. In cases where the debtor's income is less than 150% of the poverty level, the court may waive the requirement of fees to be paid.

Required Documents

To complete the petition, the debtor must provide information concerning creditors and the amount and nature of all claims; source and frequency of debtor's income; list of debtor's property; and list of debtor's monthly living expenses, which include references to food, clothing, shelter, utilities, taxes, transportation, and medical.

Exempt Property

The bankruptcy court allows debtors to file a schedule of exempt property. In this case, the debtor may be able to protect some property from the claims of creditors because the type of property may be exempt under federal bankruptcy laws or under the laws of the state in which the debtor lives. Whether or not the debtor can file a schedule of exempt property may be subject to state law. Therefore, the debtor can choose between a federal package or a state package of exemptions under the law. It is important to consult an experienced bankruptcy attorney to determine the best approach.

Collection Implications

Filing a Chapter 7 bankruptcy petition automatically stops, or stays, collection actions against the debtor and/or the debtor's property. As long as the stay is in effect, creditors can't initiate and/or continue lawsuits nor can they initiate wage garnishments or even make demanding phone calls.

Meeting

After the petition is filed, between 21 and 40 days the case trustee will hold a meeting at a location that does not have a regular U.S. trustee or bankruptcy administrative staffing. The meeting will typically be held no more than 60 days after the order of relief at which time the trustee will put the debtor under oath. Both the trustee and the creditors may ask questions, which means that the debtor must appear to answer questions as required by law. It is important for the debtor to cooperate with the trustee and provide all necessary financial records or documents to support claims of financial hardship and inability to repay debts.

To complete the order of relief, the court allows the debtor to convert the Chapter 7 case to a case under Chapter 11, Chapter 12, or Chapter 13, provided that the debtor is eligible under one of the three options.

CHAPTER 11

Chapter 11 bankruptcy is referred to as "reorganization" and is specific to commercial enterprises that continue operating a business, repaying creditors concurrently through a court-approved plan of reorganization. The debtor filing for Chapter 11 relief has the right to file a plan of reorganization for the first 120 days after filing the case. The debtor must then provide the creditors with a disclosure statement. The statement must contain information to enable creditors to evaluate the plan. The court ultimately approves or disapproves of the plan of reorganization.

Under the plan, the debtor can reduce debts by repaying a portion of the obligations and discharging other parts. The debtor will be allowed to terminate some contracts and leases, recover assets, and rescale its operations to meet profitability objectives.

Debtors under this plan normally emerge with a reduced debt load and a reorganized business.

Eligibility
Commercial enterprises are eligible to file Chapter 11 bankruptcy.

How it Works
A chapter 11 petition is filed with the bankruptcy court serving the area where the debtor has a place of residence. The petition may be voluntary, which is filed by the debtor. However, a petition may be involuntary, in which case the petition is filed by the creditors of the debtor.

Voluntary petitions must adhere to a specified format. Form 1 of the Official Forms prescribes the format for all chapter 11 petitions. The form is prescribed by the Judicial Conference of the United States. The debtor must also file with the court the following:

- Schedule of assets and liabilities
- Schedule of current income and expenditures
- Schedule of executor contracts and unexpired leases
- Statement of financial affairs

Individual debtors must also file additional documents and proof of the following:

- Certificate of credit counseling
- Copy of debt repayment plan received through credit counseling
- Evidence of payment from employers
- Statement of monthly net income
- Anticipated increase of income or expenses
- Record of interests in federal/state qualified education or tuition accounts

All documents are available on the U.S. Court's website.

Fees
Fees are charged to file for Chapter 11 relief. Fees fall under two categories: case filing fee ($1,000) and miscellaneous administrate fee ($46). Fees are paid to the clerk of the court upon filing. With the permission of the court, fees may be paid in installments, which is limited to four and the final installment paid not later than 120 days after the filing of the petition. Failure to pay the required fees may result in the case being dismissed.

Required Documents
The voluntary petition will include information concerning the debtor's name, social security number, tax identification number, place of residence, location of principal assets (business), the debtor's plan or intention to file a plan, and a

request of relief. With an involuntary case, the debtor assumes an additional identity as "debtor in possession." The debtor, in this case, keeps possession and control of assets while going through the process of reorganization under Chapter 11. All of this happens without the appointment of a trustee.

A debtor will remain as a debtor in possession until the plan of reorganization is confirmed, the debtor's case is dismissed, or the case is converted to Chapter 7 or Chapter 11. The debtor will also remain a debtor in possession until the appointment of a Chapter 11 trustee. The debtor can still operate the business and perform similar functions that are specific to a trustee.

A debtor must file a written disclosure statement and a plan of reorganization with the court. The disclosure statement is a type of document that contains information concerning the assets, liabilities, and business affairs of the debtor. The information must be sufficient for the creditor to determine the validity of the debtor's plan of reorganization.

In small business cases, the debtor may be required to file a separate disclosure statement if the court determines that enough information is contained in the reorganization plan. The contents of the plan contain a classification of claims; and the contents must specify how each class of claims will be treated under the reorganization plan.

Filers of Chapter 11 are subject to multiple requirements that include considerations of a creditor's objection as well as dismissal of the case because of an unconfirmed reorganization plan.

CHAPTER 13

Chapter 13 bankruptcy is designed for individuals with a regular source of income. Chapter 13 is different from Chapter 7, because the debtor may keep some assets. Chapter 13 refers to the adjustment of debts of an individual with regular income. It is often preferable to Chapter 7 bankruptcy. For example, with Chapter 13, the individual can keep a valuable asset such as a house, but must make payments to the creditor.

In addition, with Chapter 13, the debtor can propose a plan to repay creditors over a time period that ranges from three to five years. Debtors that do not qualify for Chapter 7 relief and that also have consumer debts may qualify under Chapter 13. To determine qualification, debtors must attend a confirmation hearing where the court will either approve or disapprove the debtor's request for consideration.

Although Chapter 7 petitioners immediately receive a discharge of debts, the debtor under Chapter 13 must complete payments under the plan before the discharge will be effective. However, the debtor receives protection from lawsuits, garnishments, and related creditor actions.

Eligibility

Individuals eligible for Chapter 13 bankruptcy include self-employed persons and owners of an unincorporated business. There is a limit to eligibility.

Unsecured debts cannot exceed $360,475; in other words, the total of all debts must be less than this figure. With this in mind, corporations and partnerships cannot file for Chapter 13 relief.

Concept Checker	*What is Chapter 11 bankruptcy?*

There are additional restrictions. Debtors cannot file for Chapter 13 relief if a prior bankruptcy petition was dismissed for failure to appear in court and/or comply with orders; or if the debtor voluntarily dismissed the case after creditors sought relief. The cutoff period is the preceding 180 days prior to the bankruptcy petition.

How it Works
Debtor files a Chapter 13 petition with the bankruptcy court that serves the area where the debtor has a place of residence. The debtor must file with the court the following:

- Schedules of assets and liabilities
- Schedule of current income and expenditures
- Schedule of executor contracts and unexpired leases
- Statement of financial affairs
- Certificate of credit counseling
- Copy of debt repayment plan developed through credit counseling
- Evidence of payment from employers
- Statement of monthly net income
- Evidence of anticipated increase in income or expenses
- Record of interest in federal or state qualified education or tuition accounts

In addition to the above documents, the debtor must also provide a copy of a tax return or transcripts for the most recent tax year. If the debtor files tax returns during the case, he or she must also submit copies of the documents. Filing forms are available only on the U.S. Courts website.

Fees
Similar to the previous policies on bankruptcy filings, there are fees charged for Chapter 13 bankruptcy protection. The court charges a case filing fee ($235) and a miscellaneous administrative fee ($46). Fees may be paid in installments, limited to four; the final payment must be paid no later than the first 120 days after the case filing.

Required Documents
The debtor must supply information about the following:

- List of all creditors and amounts owed
- Source and amount of debtor's income, referencing frequency
- List of debtor's property
- List of debtor's monthly living expenses

When listing the monthly expenses, give attention to amounts for categories under food, clothing, shelter, utilities, taxes, transportation, and medical.

Special Considerations

It is important to note that filing the petition under Chapter 13 causes collection actions to stop automatically. In addition, the trustee assigned to the case collects and disburses all payments to the creditors. Chapter 13 offers stay provisions for co-debtors; in other words, creditors cannot seek to collect a debt from an individual who is also a co-debtor; this applies to consumer debt.

Petitioners may use Chapter 13 to stop foreclosure actions. The automatic stay stops foreclosure proceedings when the petitioner files. However, there are some exceptions. If the mortgage company completes the foreclosure sale under state law, and this happens before the petitioner files for Chapter 13, then the debtor may lose the home. The debtor may also lose the home if mortgage payments are not made in a timely manner according to the debt repayment plan.

Meetings

The debtor must attend all meetings held by the trustee. The trustee and the creditors attending the meeting will ask the debtor questions regarding current financial affairs and the proposed terms of the plan. Problems are typically resolved at the meeting.

To receive distributions from the bankruptcy estate, creditors must file their claims with the court within a specific period, typically within 90 days after the meeting. Once the meeting with the creditors is complete, the debtor, the creditor, and the trustee must attend court to discuss the Chapter 13 debt repayment plan. After the plan is confirmed, the debtor must ensure that the plan will succeed and begin the process of executing it.

During this process, the debtor cannot incur new debt. In addition, if the debtor fails to make payments as agreed, the bankruptcy court will then have two options. The court can dismiss the case or convert it to a liquidation case under Chapter 7. The court can also convert the case for a debtor's failure to pay what are called domestic support obligations which include child support and alimony.

The Discharge

Chapter 13 bankruptcy cases are complex. Debtors should consult legal counsel before considering this option. Debtors are entitled to a Chapter 13 discharge under the following conditions:

- The debtor certifies that he or she has met domestic support obligations, if applicable

- The debtor has not received a discharge in a prior case filed within two years (Chapter 13) and four years for chapter 7, 11, and 12 cases
- The debtor has completed an approved financial management course

The court will enter the discharge only if there are no related pending proceedings. The discharge releases the debtor from all debts and creditors can no longer initiate and/or continue legal actions, provided that all conditions have been met that were outlined in the debt repayment plan.

Hardship Discharge

Chapter 13 bankruptcy allows for a **hardship discharge**. When circumstances exist that may prevent the debtor from completing the plan, the debtor may request that the court grant a hardship discharge. Conditions apply and are related to circumstances that are out of the control of the debtor. A discharge is available if the creditors have received as much as they can and the modification of the plan is impossible. A hardship discharge does not apply to debts that are non-dischargeable in a common Chapter 7 case.

BUSINESS PLANNER

Small business owners struggling with debt and considering bankruptcy may choose to pursue other options that will allow for the business to continue. Debt restructuring is one such plan that offers benefits to business owners. This option allows the business owner time to rehabilitate the business and earn profits. This is what John decided to do for his business.

Case Study:
John Develops a Debt Restructuring Plan

John is in the auto repair business. He has been in business for over 25 years and has faithfully paid his creditors. However, during the current recession, John began to lose revenue and was tempted to close because of the emotional and psychological distress. John decided against it. He is a fighter and believes in not walking away from a battle.

John did some research and consulted an expert in debt restructuring. He began to develop a general debt restructuring plan that would help him to pay a lower interest rate. He submitted requests to his lenders asking for an extension of the loan period. John also wanted to pay the remainder debt later. This would allow him to create revenue potential and earn significant profits.

There are two types of debt restructuring plans: general debt restructuring and troubled debt restructuring. In the first case, the creditor doesn't incur a loss. The accrued interest is reduced. In the latter, the creditor incurs loss. The value of the collateral takes a dip, which affects the debtor's relationship with the creditor.

When considering debt restructuring for your business, use **Debt Restructuring Planning Questionnaire** at the end of the chapter to guide you.

Chapter Key Points

Bankruptcy is a legal status representative of a person or organization that cannot repay the debt or debts he, she, or it owes to a creditor. Bankruptcy is typically imposed by a court order for some jurisdictions and is often initiated by the debtor. Bankruptcy is not synonymous with insolvency.

Chapter 7 bankruptcy is typically referred to as a "no-asset" case. The debtor usually has no assets subject to liquidation.

To qualify for Chapter 7 relief, a debtor may be an individual, partnership, corporation, or other type of business entity. Relief is available regardless of the amount of the debtor's debts and regardless of the solvency or insolvency of the company.

To complete the petition for Chapter 7 relief, the debtor must provide information concerning creditors and the amount and nature of all claims; source and frequency of debtor's income; list of debtor's property; and list of debtor's monthly living expenses, which include references to food, clothing, shelter, utilities, taxes, transportation, and medical.

Chapter 11 bankruptcy is referred to as "reorganization" and is specific to commercial enterprises that continue operating a business, repaying creditors concurrently through a court-approved plan or reorganization.

Chapter 13 bankruptcy is designed for individuals with a regular source of income. Chapter 13 is different from Chapter 7, because the debtor may keep some assets. Chapter 13 refers to the adjustment of debts of an individual with regular income. It is often preferable to Chapter 7 bankruptcy.

Chapter 13 bankruptcy allows for a **hardship discharge**. When circumstances exist that may prevent the debtor from completing the plan, the debtor may request that the court grant a hardship discharge.

Chapter Key Terms

Bankruptcy: term refers to the legal status representative of a person or organization that cannot repay the debt or debts he, she, or it owes to a creditor.

Bankruptcy Rules: term refers to the process, or procedural aspects, of bankruptcy and how they are governed and monitored by the Federal Rules of Bankruptcy Procedure.

Chapter 7: term that refers to a type of bankruptcy for no asset cases.

Chapter 11: term that refers to a type of bankruptcy that is specific to commercial enterprises that want to undergo reorganization while continuing to operate the business and repaying creditors through a court-approved plan.

Chapter 13: term that refers to a type of bankruptcy that is designed for individuals with a regular source of income.

Group Work Prompt

Review the U.S. Courts government website. Develop an essay comparing and contrasting three types of bankruptcy. Reference the processes, eligibility requirements, and forms. Begin the project in-class and finish it as a group at home.

Homework Exercise

Review the chapter case study. Create a debt repayment plan for John's auto repair business by answering the questions of the questionnaire. To gain insight into the assignment, research auto repair businesses and research the field. Visit multiple websites to help you design a plan.

Helpful Websites

United States Courts: Bankruptcy Basics
http://www.uscourts.gov/FederalCourts/Bankruptcy.aspx

Chapter Forms

On the next pages are all of the forms discussed within this chapter. You may photocopy, scan, and print them out. Some forms you will need to complete the group work and the homework.

Assessment

1. What is bankruptcy?

2. What are the different types of bankruptcy? List all five.

3. What are the benefits of Chapter 7 bankruptcy?

4. What is the process for a Chapter 11 bankruptcy?

5. What documents are required for a Chapter 11 bankruptcy?

6. Explain Chapter 13 bankruptcy.

7. What are the required fees for a Chapter 13 bankruptcy?

8. Who must attend the meeting of a Chapter 13 bankruptcy?
_____
_____
_____
_____

9. What is a hardship discharge?
_____
_____
_____

Debt Restructuring Planning Questionnaire

1. What is the quantity of existing assets?

2. What is the value of existing assets?

3. What are possible liquidation scenarios?

4. What is the viability of current business operations?

5. What are the current debtor-creditor issues?

6. What are the current outstanding loans?

7. What are the current commercial transactions?

8. What is the potential for developing new equity?

9. What is the potential for receiving capital injections?

10. What are the current cash flows?

11. What are the company's plans for debt restructuring?

12. How will sustainable debt be restructured?

13. What will be the terms and conditions of the debt restructuring plan?

14. Who or what company will formalize the debt restructuring plan?

CHAPTER 12

Credit Repair Tips

Learning Objectives

- Define credit repair.
- List types of credit repair options.
- Evaluate credit report.
- Dispute information.
- Develop a debt repayment plan
- Calculate disposable income.
- Create a business savings plan.

WHAT IS CREDIT REPAIR?

Credit repair is the process of fixing bad credit. This process includes ordering a credit report, disputing inaccuracies, establishing a sound budget, and repaying obligations. Victims of identity theft will have to develop a strategic plan for repairing their credit. This plan will include contacting law enforcement officials, writing a personal statement for the credit report file, contacting financial institutions, and continuing to be proactive in making sure that errors are reported and corrected.

Small business owners must be doubly concerned about credit repair. Most lending institutions are now requiring that small business owners sign a personal guarantee. If a business owner defaults on a loan, then the lending institution can report the default to not only the business credit report, but also to the owner's personal credit report. Now the task becomes difficult because just as there are multiple credit reporting agencies, there are also multiple business credit reporting agencies and organizations that evaluate the creditworthiness of a small business owner.

> **Credit repair does not necessarily mean restoring financial health.**

It is simply much easier to design personal financial goals that will allow you to manage both earnings and opportunities for establishing credit. In other words, it is better to design goals where you pursue quality versus quantity. Working with one credit card is quality. Working with multiple cards is quantity. Debt eats at your resources. Keep this in mind as you travel through this chapter. Pick up tips that will help you to design a strategic plan for managing your personal finances.

Types of Credit Repair

There are different types of credit repair options. Companies and organizations offer credit repair solutions, assuming that consumers are too afraid to confront the problem. Organizations believe that consumers lack the ability to evaluate their credit reports and design a solution. They also believe that the task is too cumbersome. But confronting issues with credit and personal finances are two tasks that are achievable. By creating a plan, you can pass this course. Of course, although the completion of such a goal is possible, credit repair companies expect you to still need them. With this in mind, there are three standard credit repair options that are common today.

- DIY: Do It Yourself
- Credit Repair Companies
- Credit Counseling

All three options require you to do some research. In other words, whether you do it yourself or choose an agency, you will have to do something. You can't just hand off your debt to someone and ask the company to fix it. You must develop a relationship with your problem in order to understand it and fix it.

Concept Checker	*What is credit repair?*

DIY: Disputing Inaccurate Information

Repairing your own credit is simple as ordering a credit report, studying it for mistakes and errors, and then disputing the inaccurate information. Sometimes the information is outdated. In addition, sometimes the information on the credit report reads that you have missed a payment. If you know that you haven't missed a payment, then you have cause to begin the disputing process. Always remember that you will likely find the same error on one report also on another. Therefore, you would have to pull three credit reports to determine if the error is on all reports.

Strategy #1: Evaluating

When viewing your report(s), here are some issues to consider:

- Give attention to the area of the report that displays information about your "account history." Here you will find information about your payment history as well as information about whether an account was sent to collections.

- In addition, evaluate the "Recent Balance" on the report. Compare the report's recent balance with your credit statement. If they don't match up, then dispute the issue.

- If you determine that one of your accounts requires a personal statement, evaluate the account first. What is wrong with it? Then create a letter that best reflects the problem and your justification.

- Review your personal information. Evaluate any information that appears to be different from what you know to be true.

By evaluating the report, you are now beginning to develop a relationship with your credit. Long gone are the days where you just swiped the card, got the receipt, and threw it in the trash. Now you have serious issues to confront concerning your debt and you must design a strategy that will ensure success.

Strategy #2: Disputing

Credit reporting agencies provide opportunities for consumers to dispute information free of charge. In order to dispute information on your report, you must request a recent report. **Disputing** is the process of submitting a request to a credit reporting agency to investigate an error and/or an inaccuracy.

The Fair Credit Reporting Act (FCRA) allows consumers to receive a free annual report. Each of the consumer reporting agencies—Equifax, Experian, and TransUnion—offers access to a free report through AnnualCreditReport.com. Consumers may order a report by calling 1-877-322-8228. You may also request a free annual report via mail:

>Annual Credit Report Request Service
>P.O. Box 105281
>Atlanta, GA 30348-5281

The FCRA also allows consumers to receive a free credit report due to an "adverse action." If an application for credit, insurance, or employment was denied, you can order a free report. Organizations must send you a notice with the company's name, address, and phone number and information about the credit reporting agency used.

Disputes Contact Information

	Experian	TransUnion	Equifax
Website	experian.com	transunion.com	equifax.com
Dispute Contact	1-888-397-3742	1-800-916-8800	1-800-685-1111
Online Dispute	experian.com/disputes	dispute.transunion.com	ai.equifax.com/CreditInvestigation/
Mail Dispute	Experian P.O. Box 2002 Allen, TX 75013-0036	TransUnion Consumer Solutions P.O. Box 2000 Chester, PA 19022-2000	Equifax Information Services, LLC P.O. Box 740256 Atlanta, GA 30374

Lastly, consumers who are unemployed (but searching for employment within 60 days); who are on welfare; and who are victims of identity theft are also entitled to a free report.

In situations where you no longer are eligible to receive a free credit report, you may purchase a report through one of the agencies. One or more of the credit reporting companies may charge you up to $11 for a copy of your credit report. To purchase a copy, contact or visit the site of one of the agencies within the table.

All three agencies offer online dispute assistance. Consumers can create an account and initiate a dispute. With every initiated dispute, the credit reporting agency contacts the data provider or information source to verify the reported information. The source of information has up to 30 days, but may not exceed 45 days to verify the data. If the source fails to return a response within the required timeframe, then the credit reporting agency will remove the information from the report. However, if the source verifies that the information is accurate, then it will remain on the credit report. This is standard practice. Receiving the results for online credit disputes tends to be faster than a notification requested by mail. However, you can submit a dispute by mail.

Disputing the information on a credit report is labor-intensive, but rewarding. Janey went through the process of evaluating and disputing information on her report. She learned the value of confronting a problem and enduring it until it was resolved.

Case Study:
Janey Disputes Inaccuracies on her Credit Report

Janey is 45 years old and is on the brink of losing her job. She has worked as a postal clerk for twenty-five years and has been faithful to her job. Now that the government is threatening to close some post office branches, Janey feels compelled to evaluate her financial situation. She realizes that she doesn't have an emergency fund. Her retirement account is low. Her life insurance is non-existent. And she has a second mortgage on her home. She basically can't borrow any money and if she loses her job, she would be hard-pressed to get even a payday loan, which is out of the question. Janey feels stuck and discouraged.

Throughout the process of evaluating her financial situation, Janey requests a credit report from TransUnion. She orders a free annual report, evaluates the information, and notices a few inaccuracies regarding her credit card balance, her mortgage payment history, and her personal contact information.

Janey researches credit repair tips on the web and is happy to see that the Federal Trade Commission offers tips for how to dispute errors. The FTC website advises consumers to provide copies of documents when initiating a dispute. Janey then visits the TransUnion website. She reads the information, locates the disputes contact information, and begins the process of creating a file that she will later mail to the agency. Janey also locates a sample disputes letter of the FTC website.

Janey locates the following items:
  Credit Card Statement
  Mortgage Payment Receipts
  Driver's License

Janey makes copies of the items and the credit report. Next, Janey creates a letter. See Figure: Janey's Letter to TransUnion. After Janey composed the letter, she mails it with the enclosures to the TransUnion disputes address. She sends the letter by certified mail, return receipt requested.

The credit reporting company investigates Janey's dispute and finds that the credit card information is correct, but that the mortgage information is incorrect. The information regarding the credit card remains on file. TransUnion corrects the mortgage information. Although it appears that Janey is headed down the right path, she learns that she has become the victim of identity theft. Someone with the name Janey Collins has been stealing her identity in Dallas, Texas. Now Janey must evaluate all of her reports and begin the process of repairing her credit. As Janey begins this path, she considers a few agencies she believes might be able to help her repair her credit.

Janey's Letter to TransUnion

November 25, 2011

TransUnion
Consumer Solutions
P.O. Box 2000
Chester, PA
19022-2000

RE: Dispute, Credit File #1238569257*

Dear Consumer Relations,

My name is Janey Collins. I have recently ordered a credit report through TransUnion. In evaluating the report, I noticed three inaccuracies for which I would like to dispute. I am writing to dispute the following items:

Credit Card Balance
The recent balance on my credit, as of November 1, 2011, is not $542. It is $342. In addition, my highest balance was not $783. It was approximately $689. My card is with American Express.

Mortgage Payment History
My mortgage is with Wells Fargo. I have had this mortgage for 15 years. The date opened is incorrect. The account was not opened until 1986. On the report, you have 1996.

Personal Contact Information
On the report you have 7326 Neuhoff Drive, Dallas, Texas 75249 as a place of residence. I never lived at this location. I've been living in Las Vegas, Nevada for 20+ years.

I am requesting that the first two items be corrected and the last item be removed from my credit report. I have enclosed a copy of a recent credit report and circled the items I am disputing.

Enclosed also are copies of my mortgage papers and my driver's license. Please resolve these inaccuracies.

Sincerely,
Janey Collins

Enclosures
Copy of personal credit report
Copy of driver's license
Copy of credit card statement

The credit file number is not real.

CREDIT REPAIR COMPANIES

Credit repair companies represent another type of credit repair option. These companies help you fix your credit. They use tactics such as the following:

Credit problems? No problem!"
"We can remove bankruptcies, judgments, liens, and bad loans from your credit file forever!"
"We can erase your bad credit — 100% guaranteed."
"Create a new credit identity — legally."

Companies that use this type of marketing strategy are often part of a larger scam to get your money. It is cheaper and simpler to do it yourself, because there is no quick fix to repairing your credit. You must create a debt repayment plan that affords you the opportunity to look at how much total debt you have and what percentage of your income you can put towards paying off the debt. When contemplating a debt repayment plan, you must know the following factors:

- Your total income
- Your necessity expense
- Your disposable income
- Your total debt
- Your total payoff (for each creditor)
- Your percentage of payment

Without an understanding of these key factors, you will not be successful in creating a long-term, sustainable and effective plan.

To better help you create a plan for outlining and repaying your debt, you will need to know how much debt you have. But first, let's begin this process by helping you calculate your disposable income and later the percentage of payments you can make to each creditor.

Calculating Debt and Repayment Worksheet

1. What is your total income?

Fixed Income Source #1: _____
Fixed Income Source #2: _____
Variable Income Source #1: _____
Variable Income Source #2: _____
Other Source of Income #1: _____
Other Source of Income #2: _____

2. What is your necessity expense?

Housing: _____
Utilities:
      Electricity: _____
      Water: _____
      Gas: _____
      Phone _____
      Trash: _____
      Cable: _____
      Food: _____
Transportation:
      Car Payment: _____
      Bus Fare: _____
      Gas and Oil: _____
      Repairs/Tires: _____
      Car Insurance: _____
Insurance:
      Health: _____
      Life: _____
      Home: _____
Retirement Funding: _____

3. What is your disposable income?

Subtract your necessity expense from your total income. This is your disposable income. You will use this total to determine the percentage of payments you will make to each creditor.

_____

4. List all of your creditors. You will perform calculations for each creditor.

_____
_____
_____
_____

5. **What is the total payoff amount for each creditor?**

Creditor	Total Payoff Amount

6. **Calculate the total payoff amount for all creditors. What is your total debt?**

_____

7. **For each creditor, calculate the payment amount using the following Dave Ramsey "Pro Rata Debt" payment calculation formula.**

Total Payoff Amount **divided by** Total Debt Amount = **Percent**
Percent **multiplied by** Disposable Income = **Payment.**

This formula has been adapted from Dave Ramsey's "Financial Peace University Workbook." All rights reserved.

Dave Ramsey Pro Rata Debt List (Form 11)

Item	Total New Payoff Payment	Total Debt	Percent	Disposable Income
_____	_____ /	_____ =	_____ x	_____

= Payment_____

On a separate sheet of paper, create this table to list your debt and calculate what the new payment would be for your debt repayment plan.

Credit Counseling

Credit Counseling companies offer solutions to help you fix your credit. Within this context, the purpose of a credit counselor is to evaluate your income, your bills, and your credit. Next, a credit counselor estimates how much it will cost for you to pay off your debt by helping you create a budget. Counselors will often contact your creditors on your behalf and develop a repayment plan for high-balance, high-interest accounts. It is important to note that credit counseling companies cannot require fees upfront.

The Credit Repair Organizations Act requires both credit repair and credit counseling companies to give you a copy of the "Consumer Credit File Rights Under State and Federal Law." Companies must give you this document before you sign a contract. Companies must also give you a written contract outlining your rights and obligations and the terms and conditions.

Under the statute, credit repair and credit counseling companies cannot do the following:

- Make a false claim about the services it provides
- Request an upfront free before services are performed
- Perform services without your signature on a written contract
- Complete any services within the three-day waiting period

These four conditions must be met before a credit repair and/or credit counseling company can perform any services.

Before signing a contract, evaluate the company's services. Consider the following steps before ending the three-day waiting period.

Step 1: Payment terms

The company contract must outline its payment terms for the services it will provide to you. An outline of payment terms must include a reference to total cost. Review the contract for its payment terms.

Step 2: Service Description

The company contract must provide a detailed description of its services, specifically the services that it will perform for you. Review the service description.

Step 3: Length of Services

The company contract must outline the length of services for your account. How long will it take to complete the solutions for your case? A detailed description regarding the length of services must be clearly expressed within the contract. Review the clause that references the length of services.

Step 4: Company Information

The company contract must reference the name of the company and the business address. Locate this information and review it for accuracy.

These steps will help you become familiar with contract terminology used within the context of credit repair solutions. Before signing up with a credit counselor, know what the company does, know what the company will require you to do, and know what the costs will be, especially to your budget.

BUSINESS PLANNER

Small business entrepreneurs currently in the process of repairing their credit will find the *Calculating Debt and Repayment Worksheet* beneficial. In addition, small business owners who have signed a personal guarantee for some credit and loan applications understand today the importance of ensuring that a business debt is repaid and paid on time. Signing a personal guarantee allows a lender to place a defaulted debt onto a personal credit report.

For new small business owners who are not aware of this fact, it is important that you have an understanding of the basic language of a standard personal guarantee agreement. You may download a copy off the internet to give you an idea of what to expect when a lender offers the document as a condition for receiving the loan. Here are some tips to remember.

Tip #1: Guarantee payment of obligation.

With a personal guarantee, you agree to bind yourself to pay to the lender/creditor the sum that becomes due whenever your company fails to pay.

Tip #2: Irrevocability.

Personal guarantees are typically irrevocable and continuing.

Tip #3: Waiver.

With a personal guarantee, you waive your right to submit a notice of default for nonpayment. Under these conditions, you consent to any modification of the credit agreement, which is at the discretion of the creditor/lender.

Tip #4: Coverage

Not all personal guarantees are one page. For more specialized industries, a personal guarantee can reference multiple requirements. Within this context, the personal guarantee would cover the principal of the loan, but also the interests, penalty interests, compound interests, and damages and related costs. Costs might include litigation expense, arbitration expense, attorney fees, and related contract costs.

These are tips that are beneficial for business owners who are in the process of developing a debt repayment plan that might include applying for a corporate line of credit, small business line of credit, and other related business and/or commercial loans. Once you sign a personal guarantee, and you default, the lender/creditor will send the information to your personal credit report.

The most important goals for a small business owner are to reduce debt and increase cash flow. Forget the financing. If you cannot present a record of sustainable cash flow, then your loan application will not be approved. Therefore, to hedge against credit issues, it becomes vitally important for the small business owner to begin a savings campaign. This type of campaign will help you not only repay your debt, but also help you save money at the same time.

This campaign is ideal for small business owners that receive a consistent income each month. Creating a savings campaign using variable income is difficult, because you need to know what you bring in in order to develop strategic goals. This savings plan below will help you to establish goals for your company.

SMALL BUSINESS DEBT REPAYMENT & SAVINGS PLANNING WORKSHEET

Establishing Goals

The first part of the process is to establish goals for debt repayment. On a basic level, calculate your disposable income.

Goal #1: Determine your total revenue. List the categories and the amounts.

_____
_____
_____
_____
_____

Goal #2: Determine your necessary business expenses.

Necessary business expenses include salaries, telephone and internet, water and electricity, property rates and taxes, insurance, advertising costs, fuel, stationery and marketing materials, bank charges, and tax expenses.

_____
_____
_____
_____
_____

Goal #3: Calculate disposable income.

After you subtract necessary business expenses from gross revenue, you must consider the disposable income you have to put towards saving for the business. Your goal should be to save the equivalent of what it will cost to fulfill a project, contract, or job. For example, if you charge $1,500 to complete one project, and you have a contract signed, then you will need to have at least three times this amount in a business reserve. From disposable income, what percentage can you put towards creating a financial reserve for the business?

_____
_____
_____
_____

Creating a Business Savings Plan

Now that you have calculated your business's disposable income, you must create a savings plan that will ensure you can meet the requirements of your projects. You need an emergency fund for your business as well as a savings fund to meet business expenses. Establish goals to save for an emergency fund and for the following types of business expenses.

	Month 1	Month 2	Month 3	Total
Emergency Fund				
Salaries Fund				
Overhead Expenses Fund				
Property Rates/Taxes Fund				
Insurance Fund				
Advertising and Marketing Fund				
Banking Fund				
Related Business Expenses Fund				
Project Fund				

To meet a project, you must have at least three times that amount plus the cost of salaries, overhead expenses, property rates, insurance, advertising and marketing, and banking costs. In the same way that a prospective apartment application requires that you have at least three times the rent in the bank, you must consider the same principle for your business.

Going forward, what issues are currently preventing you from creating a strategic savings plan?

_____

_____

Chapter Key Points

Credit repair is the process of fixing bad credit. This process includes ordering a credit report, disputing inaccuracies, establishing a sound budget, and repaying obligations. Credit repair does not necessarily restore financial health.

Small business owners must be doubly concerned about credit repair. Most lending institutions are now requiring that small business owners sign a personal guarantee. If a business owner defaults on a loan, then the lending institution can report the default to not only the business credit report, but also to the owner's personal credit report.

There are different types of credit repair options. Companies and organizations offer credit repair solutions, assuming that consumers are too afraid to confront the problem. Organizations believe that consumers lack the ability to evaluate their credit reports and design a solution.

Repairing your own credit is simple as ordering a credit report, studying it for mistakes and errors, and then disputing the inaccurate information.

Credit reporting agencies provide opportunities for consumers to dispute information free of charge. In order to dispute information on your report, you must request a recent report.

Chapter Key Terms

Credit counseling company: a company that offers to help you fix your credit and create a budget.

Credit repair company: a company that offers to fix your credit for a fee.

Disputing: the process of submitting a request for a credit reporting agency to investigate an error and/or an inaccuracy on the report.

Equifax: a credit reporting agency.

Experian: a credit reporting agency.

TransUnion: a credit reporting agency.

Group Work Prompt

Design a model business savings plan for Company X. Include the following categories:
- Emergency funding
- Salaries funding
- Overhead expenses funding
- Property rates and taxes funding
- Insurance funding
- Advertising and marketing funding
- Related business expenses funding

Design a plan that also considers a debt repayment plan. Company X receives $35,000 per month in revenues, but expenses range from $15,000 to $20,000. Expenses include salaries.

Research the field and develop a model that would encompass at least two industries. Start the project in class and finish it at home.

Homework Exercise

Sometimes small business entrepreneurs receive variable income. It is difficult to plan with variable income, but you must. If you and/or your company receive variable income, develop a strategy for how you would consider converting variable income into fixed income. Use the questions below as a guide. You may start this project in-class and finish it up at home.

1. What is your variable income? What is the source? What is the amount you receive?

_____
_____

2. Review your bank statement or project receipts. How often did one customer require your company's services?

_____
_____

3. How likely is it that you could put this customer on contract for monthly services? In other words, design a monthly plan that will ensure you receive a fixed amount each month.

_____
_____

4. What percentage of this income could you put towards saving for overhead expenses and emergencies?

_____
_____

Assessment

1. What is credit repair?

2. What are examples of credit repair types?

3. What is the Fair Credit Reporting Act?

4. What is disputing?

5. What are the three major credit reporting agencies?

Helpful Websites

Federal Trade Commission: Credit Repair: How to Help Yourself
http://www.ftc.gov/bcp/edu/pubs/consumer/credit/cre13.shtm

Federal Trade Commission: How to Dispute Credit Report Errors
http://www.ftc.gov/bcp/edu/pubs/consumer/credit/cre21.shtm

TransUnion Credit Report Disputes
http://www.transunion.com/personal-credit/credit-disputes/credit-disputes.page

CHAPTER 13

Cash Flow Planning

Learning Objectives

- Define "cash flow"
- Establish spending goal
- Categorize and register transactions
- Reconcile checking account
- Record transactions on business cash flow statement

WHAT IS CASH FLOW?

Cash flow is a common term that refers to the movement of money in and out of a business or financial product. Business analysts, accountants, and small business entrepreneurs measure cash flow as a method for determining the value of a company, a project's rate of return, problems with the liquidity of a business, the quality of income, and risks surrounding a financial product.

TYPES OF CASH FLOW

With this in mind, there are different types of cash flow. One type is **operational cash flow**. Under this type, cash is received and/or expended as a result of internal business activity. The second type is **investment cash flow**. Under this type, cash is received from the sale of long-life assets; cash may also be spent on capital expenditures, which include investments, acquisitions, and other long-life assets. The last type of cash flow is **financing cash flows**. Under this category, businesses receive cash from the issuance of debt and equity; or cash may be received from dividends, debt repayments, and share repurchases. Under these categories, businesses manage the inflow and the outflow of cash as a way of measuring the company's solvency, and/or insolvency.

PERSONAL CASH FLOW

Don't be alarmed by these terms. The same terms can be applied within a personal context. Cash flow is a generic term and as you can see it is often defined differently within multiple contexts. Although **personal cash flow** is not an official term, it is one that is specific to personal finance budgeting. Understanding the importance of this term within a personal budgeting context will allow you to design a plan for your money. On a simple level, budgeting is just planning the direction of your money. If you don't have a plan, someone else will plan your money. If businesses must ensure that they manage the flow of cash, then you should also consider this principle. There are common signs that you are losing control over your money and the following examples represent problems you must consider when developing a plan.

- Checking account overdrafts
- Bounced checks
- Over-the-limit credit card fees
- Unbalanced, unreconciled checking account
- Unpaid debts
- Loaned money to multiple parties

These are some of the common problems that many people face when they don't have control over their money. It is important to develop a plan that includes how you will both receive and expend money. Although cash flow, as a term, may be used often within multiple business contexts, it is important to consider this principle within a personal context because you live primarily outside of your home. You conduct business with the outside world. The outside world also affects what you do in your home and with your finances. If 75% of your money is still spent on fast food, and not home cooking, then you are not giving your money sound purpose. You are giving it some purpose, but the fast food will go in one area and out the other and you will have no money to show for it. Keep this in mind as you work through some of the exercises in this chapter.

Concept Checker	*What is cash flow?*

The most important thing you can do with your money is to give it a goal. You have to pay housing costs. This is a goal. You have to pay transportation costs. This is a goal. You have to pay for other types of costs such as insurance (life, health, and auto); you also have to consider funding for retirement and college. These are all goals that fall under your life plan. In other words, you must have a vision for your life. Having a vision and setting goals includes first learning how to balance your checkbook.

Balancing the Checkbook

With every checking account comes a checkbook and checkbook register forms. It is important to keep your checking account register current by subtracting checks, debit card purchases, and withdrawals. You also keep the register current by adding deposits.

One of your goals for managing cash flow should be to balance your checking account within the first 72 hours of receiving your banking statement. You may access your banking statement online or receive it by mail. Review your statement for any inaccuracies and then begin the process of reconciling your transactions. You will need the following items in order to balance your account. These items are standard for every checking account.

- Account register
- Last bank statement
- Reconciliation sheet

The reconciliation sheet is typically located at the back of an account statement. You will also see this statement at the end of your checkbook. Before moving into the exercises within this chapter, let's review a case study that provides insight into this topic.

> **Case Study:**
> **Jane Loses Balance**
>
> Jane has been very good with her money. She has saved since high school. However, when she entered college, she struggled to manage her money because she didn't have the comfort of accountability from mom and dad. It was her first time being away from home. She was now responsible for herself, her studies, and her money.
>
> The pressure to learn so much information (education) and maintain a habit of personal budgeting began to take a toll on Jane. She started spending money for comfort and not for purpose. Instead of fixing herself breakfast in the morning or getting breakfast at a local restaurant, she waited until midday, which encouraged her hunger even more. Because she was hungry, she didn't purchase well. She purchased fast food, candy, soda, and other related items that added no value to her day. By the time she got home from school, she didn't cook. She started eating out. Burgers, pizza, and anything else became the norm. Jane began to lose balance emotionally, psychologically, and financially. Only when she started to lose money and couldn't determine the reason did she realize the importance of balancing her checkbook.
>
> In high school, Jane had a checking account, but she didn't bring in the kind of income that required so much attention to managing her finances. She worked at the local burger place, earned pay, put some into a college account by request from her parents, and spent the rest going out with her friends. Jane's only responsibility was to put some of the money she earned toward the college account her parents established. In other words, Jane didn't even establish the account, so she never knew the value of establishing it as a goal.
>
> In addition, since Jane's checking account was linked to her parents' accounts, if she overdrew by a few dollars, the money would be replaced from her parents'

account. Jane never became fully involved with understanding the value of money, what it does, and what it is supposed to do.

In college was where Jane learned that if she didn't start giving attention to her finances, which included receiving scholarships and loans, she would be broke by graduation. To begin her journey, Jane began reconciling her checkbook every month and by semester since this was when she received a large inflow of cash. Below is an example of Jane's process and what she realized.

Jane Balances her Checkbook

Checking Account Register						
Check #	Date	Fee	Transaction	Payment	Deposit	Balance 564.46
2001	8/31/96	X	Campus Store	57.40		507.06
2002	9/2/96		Car Ins.	101.00		406.06
	9/5/96		Scholarship		700.00	1106.06
2003	9/5/96		Cell Phone	50.00		1056.06
2004	9/5/96		Campus Store	66.00		990.06
	9/30/96	X	Bank Service Fee	2.50		987.56*

*The last figure in the account register should match the one that results from reconciling the checkbook.

Before moving into the rest of the exercise, here is an explanation of the above transactions and activities. When balancing your checking account activities, consider the steps below. You will need the following:

- a printout of your bank statement
- the checking account register
- the reconciliation sheet

You will need these three items to perform the following steps.

Step 1: Categorize the transactions. This is the research part of the exercise.

Determine which transactions represent checks, debit card purchases, withdrawals, and deposits. Transactions also include bank service charges such as monthly maintenance fees and paid interest. To better list the information on the reconciliation sheet, you may want to write the type of transaction within the white space on the printout.

Step 2: Register and list the transactions.
List the transactions within your checking account register. You may choose to list the transactions by date or by category. If you choose the latter, this will give you a view of the type of money you spend on certain items. This may inform you of how to budget for the next month. In addition, list transactions on your reconciliation sheet that are not listed on the bank statement. These transactions still include checks, withdrawals, and other types of deductions. Lastly, transactions include deposits. In this case study, Jane receives a scholarship for $700. This is considered a deposit or credit to Jane's account and must be considered when reconciling the transactions.

Step 3: Subtract from the ending balance.
Your checking account will always give you an ending balance, even if the account is overdrawn and the balance is in the negative. Once you have located the ending balance, subtract from this balance the total number of account withdrawals (i.e., checks, debit card purchases, etc.). Add to this total the number for deposits. These are deposits that are not on your statement. Let's view the transaction in process. The ending balance for Jane's account on 9/30/96 was $504.56.

Non-Statement Withdrawals
Enter the withdrawals that you have put in your register that were not on your statement.

Car Insurance	2002	9/2/96	101.00
Cell Phone	2003	9/5/96	50.00
Campus Store	2004	9/5/96	66.00
			TOTAL: $217

Subtract the ending balance from the non-statement withdrawals balance.

Step 4: Add all deposits.
Now that you have performed the subtractions, it is time to add any deposits. In Jane's case, she received a deposit in the form of a scholarship. Add all deposits to the non-statement withdrawals balance.

| Scholarship | n/a | 9/5/96 | 700.00 |

Here's a recap of the transactions:

Balance from Jane's bank statement: $504.56
Balance of non-statement withdrawals: (-) $217.00
Balance of scholarship deposits received: (+) $700.00
TOTAL (Register Balance)   (=) **$987.56**

The above register balance was the same figure that Jane found at the end of her checkbook where she listed all of her transactions, which included the one deposit.

Jane learned a valuable lesson in reconciling her checkbook. She learned the importance of seeing for the first time where her money went and what type of money came in. Spending too much at the campus store and buying non-essential items was her greatest expense. Instead of spending money on chips, cookies, and burgers, Jane started buying sandwich meat and bread and began taking her lunch for those times she got hungry throughout the day. Choosing this method helped to save her budget and prevent future health problems related to fast-food eating.

Jane's first try at reconciling her checkbook was successful. In order to maintain this habit, she will have to do this every month. In addition, to manage the money she receives from scholarship and from earnings, Jane will need to perform these calculations by semester also.

BUSINESS PLANNER

Creating a goal for how cash will flow throughout your personal and business finances will require you to sit down and consider multiple factors. For every month, you will need to reconcile your financial accounts. The principle behind balancing the personal checkbook is equally applicable to the business cash flow statement. You must understand the importance of how cash flows throughout your company's operations. You must also understand how cash is used for investing and for financing. In this section, you will learn about a financial statement that is central for businesses.

WHO USES THE CASH FLOW STATEMENT?

The **cash flow statement**, or statement of cash flows, is a financial statement that provides insight into how changes in the company's balance sheet and income statement affect cash and cash equivalents. Accounting personnel use cash flow statements to determine if the company will be able to cover payroll as well as immediate expenses. Lenders and creditors require the cash flow statement to determine if a company has the ability to repay. Investors evaluate the cash flow statement to determine if a company is financially sound. Shareholders of a company also review the cash flow statement to measure the quality of their investment.

Purpose and Structure

The purpose of the cash flow statement is to provide insight into the company's liquidity and solvency status, provide information for evaluation of asset and liability changes, and measure the probability of cash flows.

The cash flow statement is divided into three segments:
- Cash flow from operating activities
- Cash flow from investing activities
- Cash flow from financing activities

Money coming into the business is considered **cash inflow**; money going out of the business is considered **cash outflow**.

| Concept Checker | *What is a cash flow statement?* |

Operating Activities

Operating activities include receipts from the sales of company goods and products and services; receipts from the sale of loans and debt instruments; interest received on loans; payments to suppliers for goods and services; payments to employees; and the purchase of merchandise. Businesses arrive at cash flows when certain items are added back to the net income figure. These line items include depreciation, deferred tax, amortization, and gains or losses from the sale of a non-current asset.

Investing Activities

Investing activities include the purchase or sale of an asset. An asset for the purpose of business is determined to be land, building, equipment, and securities. Investing activities also include loans made to suppliers and loans received from customers; payments incurred during the process of a merger or acquisition; and the receipt of dividends.

Financing Activities

Financing activities represent the inflow of cash from investors. Within this context, investors include banks and shareholders. Under financing, the outflow of cash is made to investors in the form of dividends. This is based upon the ability of the company to generate income. Financing activities include proceeds from short-term and long-term debt; dividends; payments incurred for the repurchase of company shares; and the company's repayment of debt principle.

The following table provides a sample cash flow statement to give you an idea how a company calculates and display their solvency to interested parties.

Sample Cash Flow Statement

Cash Flows from Operating Activities		
Cash receipts from customers	7,500	
Cash paid to suppliers and employees	(2,000)	
Cash generated from operations **(sum)**	**5,500**	
Interest paid	(1,000)	
Income taxes paid	(2,000)	
Net cash flows from operating activities		2,500
Cash Flows from Investing Activities		
Proceeds from sale of equipment	10,500	
Dividends received	(2,500)	
Net cash flows from investing activities		8,000
Cash Flows from Financing Activities		
Dividends paid	(5,500)	
Net cash flows from financing activities		(5,500)
Net increase in cash and cash equivalents		5,000
Cash and cash equivalents, beginning of year		1,000
Cash and cash equivalents, end of year		6,000

To best understand the process of determining cash inflows and cash outflows, you will need to review your company's transactions and prepare the information to be entered on the statement. Once you have researched and evaluated all of the figures, then you will be able to enter the totals on the cash flow statement worksheet. For now, let's enter information and notes on the **Cash Flow Statement Research Worksheet** that follows.

Cash Flow Statement Research Worksheet

In this section, you will perform the following exercises to help you plan for this part of your business. You will need your *income statement* and *balance sheet* in order to create the cash flow statement. You can find sample worksheets of these forms in the appendices section of this book.

1. List all cash receipts the company received from customers. What is the total?
_____
_____

2. How much cash was paid to suppliers? How much cash was paid to employees? Total both.
_____
_____

                Sum of cash generated from operations: _____
                                      Change in total: _____

3. What interest did the company pay?
_____
_____

4. How much did the company pay in income taxes?
_____
_____

                Net cash flow from operating activities: _____
                                      Change in total: _____

5. What equipment did the company sell? What were the proceeds from the sale?
_____
_____

6. What dividends did the company receive? What were the proceeds from the process?
_____
_____

                Net cash flow from investing activities: _____
                                      Change in total: _____

7. What dividends did the company pay out? Do the payout of dividends fall under multiple categories.
_____
_____

                Net cash flow from financing activities: _____
                                      Change in total: _____

Special Notes: What other factors need to be considered before finalizing the statement.
_____
_____

Now that you have researched the figures and have had time to think about what they mean and how they should be represented within a statement of cash flows, it is time to enter the data. Use the following sample form to enter the data. The form will help you to view the figures more comprehensively.

CASH FLOW STATEMENT WORKSHEET

Cash Flows from Operating Activities
Cash receipts from customers   _____
Cash paid to suppliers and employees   _____
Cash generated from operations (sum)   _____
Interest paid   _____
Income taxes paid   _____
Net cash flows from operating activities   _____

Cash Flows from Investing Activities
Proceeds from sale of equipment   _____
Dividends received   _____
Net cash flows from investing activities   _____

Cash Flows from Financing Activities
Dividends paid   _____
Net cash flows from financing activities   _____
Net increase in cash and cash equivalents   _____
Cash and cash equivalents, beginning of year   _____
Cash and cash equivalents, end of year   _____

Chapter Key Points

Cash flow is a common term that refers to the movement of money in and out of a business or financial product.

Personal cash flow is not an official term; it is one that is specific to personal finance budgeting.

The most important thing you can do with your money is to give it a goal.

One of your goals for managing cash flow should be to balance your checking account within the first 72 hours of receiving your banking statement.

The **cash flow statement**, or statement of cash flows, is a financial statement that provides insight into how changes in the company's balance sheet and income statement affect cash and cash equivalents.

Chapter Key Terms

Cash flow: term that refers to the movement of money in and out of a business or financial product.

Cash flow statement: term refers to a financial statement that provides insight into how changes in the company's balance sheet and income statement affect cash and cash equivalents.

Cash inflow: term that refers to money coming into a business.

Cash outflow: term that refers to money going out of a business.

Investment cash flow: term that refers to how cash is received from the sale of long-life assets; cash may also be spent on capital expenditures, which include investments, acquisitions, and other long-life assets.

Personal cash flow: term specific to personal finance budgeting.

Statement of cash flows: See *Cash Flow Statement*.

Group Work Prompt

Jane will soon be graduating from college. She will need to maintain the same budgeting habits that she has adopted in college. To do this, Jane will have to know her expenses and what budgets she will consider. Jane doesn't have a job now, but a budget can still be created based upon receiving minimum wage or two times more than that.

In considering that Jane may get a job where she is earning at least $2,500 per month, develop budgetary policy for Jane's future home expense categories. Common home expense categories typically represent the following: Housing, Utilities, Food, Transportation, Clothing, Medical, Personal, and Debt. There are further sub-categories under each major worksheet line item.

Establish and discuss the budgets for these categories. Next, using these budgets, create both a *Monthly Cash Flow Plan* and an *Allocated Spending Plan* for Jane. Use the worksheets at the end of this chapter. Start this project in class and finish it at home as a group.

Budgetary Expense Policy

Housing (Rent): _____

Utilities

In order to create the Utilities budget policy, you will need to conduct some market research. For now you are just submitting considerations to Jane. You don't know if she can yet afford one or more of the utilities.

Market Research Estimates
Time Warner: _____
AT&T: _____
Gas/Electric: _____
Water: _____

Budgets for Jane
Electric: _____   Gas: _____   Trash: _____
Water: _____   Phone: _____   Cable: _____

Food

Jane will need to budget for groceries and for eating out. If she doesn't budget for this, then she will be blindsided. Develop reasonable budgets based upon her take-home monthly pay.

Groceries: _____   Restaurants: _____

Transportation

Transportation has multiple sub-categories. Jane wants to get a car, but she also lives by a bus stop in Dallas, Texas. The transit system also offers multiple train lines. You will need to research the market to determine the best option(s) for Jane. Should she purchase a car or ride the bus? For how many months or years should she do this? Since you do not know what kind of car Jane wants, suggest to Jane what she should consider based upon her monthly pay.

Bus Fare: _____   Train Fare: _____
Gas Cost: _____   Car Repair: _____
License: _____   Taxes: _____

Mark Research Estimates
Car Payment: _____
Car Insurance: _____

Suggestions:
_____
_____

Clothing

_____

_____

Medical

Future medical costs will include a health insurance premium, a deductible, doctor bills, and medications. Since you do not know if Jane's company offers medical insurance and if Jane will have to make co-pays, develop a budgetary policy based upon your market research. Choose Aetna or BlueCross BlueShield as the basis for your estimates. Make a suggestion to Jane.

_____

_____

Personal

Personal costs include toiletries, hair care, and life insurance. Develop budgetary policy for the bare minimum in this area. However, you will need to research life insurance estimates. Jane lives in Dallas, Texas. Therefore, research two or three life insurance companies and provide suggestions to Jane on which type of life insurance would be of greater benefit.

Toiletries: _____   Hair Care: _____
Market Research Estimates
Life Insurance #1: _____
Life Insurance #2: _____
Life Insurance #3: _____
Suggestions:

_____

_____

Debt

Jane will undoubtedly graduate with some student loan debt. Jane can elect to sign up for the Income Contingent Plan through Direct Loans. Figure for Jane a minimum of $200 per month.

_____

_____

Now that you have developed budgetary policy for Jane, enter the numbers on the following worksheet. Don't worry about the Actual Spent and Total columns yet. This sheet gives you an idea of what to expect and how to plan your budget.

Monthly Cash Flow Plan Budget Worksheet

Category	Budget	Actual Spent	Total
Housing (rent)			
Utilities			
Electric			
Water			
Gas			
Phone			
Trash			
Cable			
Food			
Groceries			
Restaurant			
Transportation			
Car Payment			
Car Insurance			
Gas			
Repairs			
License/Taxes			
Clothing			
Medical			
Personal			
Toiletries			
Hair Care			
Life Insurance			
Debt			
Student Loan			

Jane currently doesn't have credit card debt.

Now that you have established policy and budgets for Jane, you must go one step further and develop a projected allocated spending plan so Jane will be prepared to spend money in the first month. In addition, you have not created a savings plan for Jane. Therefore, you will need to come up with a plan for how Jane can save an emergency fund of $1,000 over the course of three to six months. Consider this before completing the following **Projected Allocated Spending Plan Sheet**.

Note: Jane receives $2,500 per month and is paid bi-weekly. As you enter the budgeted amount for the expense categories based upon the figures from the previous worksheet, next to the budgeted amount, enter the balance. In other words, subtract from income and from the preceding balances. The first line item, Charitable, is done for you.

PROJECTED ALLOCATED SPENDING PLAN SHEET

Pay Period (week/month)	___/___	___/___	___/___	___/___
Income	$1,250	$1,250	$1,250	$1,250
Charitable	$20 / $1,230	___/___	___/___	___/___
Saving	___/___	___/___	___/___	___/___
Emergency Fund	___/___	___/___	___/___	___/___
Retirement Fund	___/___	___/___	___/___	___/___
Housing	___/___	___/___	___/___	___/___
Utilities				
Electric	___/___	___/___	___/___	___/___
Water	___/___	___/___	___/___	___/___
Phone	___/___	___/___	___/___	___/___
Trash	___/___	___/___	___/___	___/___
Cable	___/___	___/___	___/___	___/___
Food				
Groceries	___/___	___/___	___/___	___/___
Restaurant	___/___	___/___	___/___	___/___
Transportation				
Car Payment	___/___	___/___	___/___	___/___
Car Insurance	___/___	___/___	___/___	___/___
Gas	___/___	___/___	___/___	___/___
Repairs	___/___	___/___	___/___	___/___
License/Taxes	___/___	___/___	___/___	___/___
Bus Fare	___/___	___/___	___/___	___/___

Clothing	___/___	___/___	___/___	___/___
Medical	___/___	___/___	___/___	___/___
Personal	___/___	___/___	___/___	___/___
Toiletries	___/___	___/___	___/___	___/___
Hair Care	___/___	___/___	___/___	___/___
Life Insurance	___/___	___/___	___/___	___/___
Debt	___/___	___/___	___/___	___/___
Student Loan	___/___	___/___	___/___	___/___

HOMEWORK EXERCISE

Before moving on into the next section of this chapter, reconcile your own checkbook by following the steps provided. If you need help, refer to the case study exercises. Remember that you will need **1)** a printout of your bank statement; **2)** the checking account register; and **3)** the reconciliation sheet.

Step 1: Categorize the transactions. This is the research part of the exercise.

Category	How many?	Totals
Checks		
Debit card purchases		
Withdrawals		
Deposits		
Bank service charges		
Paid interest		

Special considerations:
_____
_____

Step 2: Register and list the transactions by date. Use additional paper if necessary.

Checking Account Register						
Check #	Date	Fee	Transaction	Payment	Deposit	Statement Balance

Special considerations:
_____
_____

Step 3: Using a reconciliation sheet, subtract from the ending balance.

What is your account's ending balance? _____

What is the total number of <u>statement account withdrawals</u>? See Step 1.
_____

What is the total number of <u>non-statement account withdrawals</u>?
_____

Subtract **total withdrawals** from the ending balance.
_____

What is the ending balance?
_____

Step 4: Add all deposits to the ending balance.

Add to this total the number of deposits that are not on your statement.
_____

Add to this total the number of deposits that are on your statement.
_____

What is your **reconciliation sheet balance**?
_____

Your reconciliation sheet balance here should reflect the same balance within your register. Your register balance is not the beginning balance, but the total after you have added and subtracted withdrawals and deposits. See Step 2.

Assessment

1. What is a cash flow statement?
   _____
   _____

2. What are the documents you need for balancing your checkbook?
   a. a printout of your bank statement
   b. the checking account register
   c. the reconciliation sheet
   d. all of the above

3. What are the three segments of a cash flow statement?
   _____
   _____

4. True or False: Operating Activities is the first segment of a cash flow statement.

5. What two sheets are suggested for managing monthly cash flow?
   _____
   _____

Helpful Websites

Cash Flow and Budgets
Personal Money Management Center, The University of Utah
http://www.asuupmmc.utah.edu/students/cashflow.html

How to Avoid Budgeting Problems with a Positive Cash Flow Statement
http://www.moneycrashers.com/positive-cash-flow-statement-analysis-personal-budgeting-problems/

Better Cash Flow and Budget Tracking
http://www.mint.com/blog/updates/better-cash-flow-and-budget-tracking/

Creating a Cash Flow Budget
http://www.soundmoneymatters.com/creating-a-budget/

Free Personal Budget Software
http://toolsformoney.com/personal_budget_software.htm

Free Budget Planning Software
https://www.budgetpulse.com/

Cash Flow Planner, YouTube Video
http://www.youtube.com/watch?v=ev_vxX7P6nc
http://stoplivingwithdebt.com

Budgeting and Cash Flow Business Case Studies
http://businesscasestudies.co.uk/business-theory/finance/budgeting-and-cash-flow.html#axzz2ED8zpz66

Chapter Forms

On the next pages are all of the forms discussed within this chapter. You may photocopy, scan, and print them out. Some forms you will need to complete the group work and the homework.

BALANCE SHEET PLANNING WORKSHEET

Company Name: _____

Ending Quarter/year: _____

ASSETS

CURRENT
Cash _____
Accounts receivable _____
Deposits and prepaid expenses _____
Inventory _____

PROPERTY, PLANT, EQUIPMENT _____
INVESTMENTS _____

LIABILITIES

CURRENT
Bank Overdraft _____
Bank Loan _____
Accounts payables/accrued liabilities _____
Long-term debt—current portion _____
Income tax payable _____

LONG-TERM DEBT _____

SHAREHOLDER'S EQUITY

Stated Capital _____
Retained Earnings _____

Note: The figures under **ASSETS** should match the totals of **LIABILITIES** and **SHAREHOLDER'S EQUITY**. In other words, they should balance. Consult a standard textbook on the subject for help.

STATEMENT OF INCOME PLANNING WORKSHEET

Company Name: _____

Ending Quarter/year: _____

REVENUE _____

COST OF SALES
Opening Inventory _____
Delivery _____
Purchases _____
Closing Inventory _____

GROSS PROFIT _____

OPERATING EXPENSES _____

INCOME FROM OPERATIONS _____

OTHER INCOME (EXPENSES)
Loss on disposal of property, equipment, plant _____
Gain on sale of investment _____
Miscellaneous _____

NET INCOME BEFORE TAX _____
INCOME TAX EXPENSE _____
NET INCOME _____

Note: Most companies combine the income statement with the statement of retained earnings. If you choose this method, the line items after NET INCOME would be **(DEFICIT) – Beginning of Year**, if your company has a deficit; **DIVIDENDS**; and **RETAINED EARNINGS (DEFICIT) – End of year**. Enter the line items in the above order.

CHAPTER 14

Investing

Learning Objectives

- Define investing
- List the types of investment products.
- Outline the features of bond products.
- Define the term "stock."
- Define the three types of mutual funds.
- Create an investment plan.
- Interview a fee-only advisor.

WHAT IS INVESTING?

Investing, or investment, is an economic principle generally related to saving. Savings is money you typically set aside to accomplish one or more short-term goals. Money deposited into a savings account is generally safe and earns a meager amount of interest. You basically get back what you put in and some change. However, the concept has a different meaning in finance. As a finance concept, investing is the process of putting money into a financial product, expecting gains over a long period of time.

Investing within this context means you strategically put money aside to meet one or more long-term goals. For example, you put money aside for future income and/or profit. In other words, you wouldn't put just $1,000 away; you would at least save six times your monthly income for twelve months up to three years, placing the money into interest-bearing accounts and also onto stock market to achieve greater gains. The potential earnings here are typically more than what you would make by just leaving your money in a savings account.

Investing involves risk. For example, investments in equities, property, and interest securities are subject to inflation risks. In essence, the fact is the higher the potential for a reward, the higher also the risk. Therefore, it is important to do some research before investing in a financial product, financial institution, and/or brokerage firm. It takes time and careful consideration to invest. Be aware of investment scams and money-making schemes that promise quick returns that will eventually prove to be worthless and costly to your finances. Review disclosure documents and consult an attorney before signing any investment contract.

Small business entrepreneurs interested in developing an investment program must adopt simple strategies to ensure long-term success. It is important for the small business investor to keep fees low, spread out investments, and research mutual funds and exchange traded funds (ETFs). This means that it is important to create an investment portfolio that requires little maintenance and reflects sound investing.

Types of Investing

There are different types of investing, or investment vehicle. An **investment vehicle** is any product used by investors for the purpose of earning a positive return. An investment vehicle can be low-risk; examples of low-risk vehicles include certificates of deposits and/or bonds. An investment vehicle can also incur greater risk. Examples of high-risk investment vehicles include individual stocks, options, and futures. There are other types of investment vehicles, namely annuities, collectibles, mutual funds, and exchange-traded funds.

Bonds

Bonds are grouped under the category called fixed-income securities. A **fixed-income security** is a type of investment vehicle that provides a return that is in the form of fixed periodic payments. It provides the eventual return of the maturity. It is unlike the **variable-income security**, where payments often change due to short-term interest rates. Payments derived from a fixed-income security are known in advance.

| Concept Checker | *What is investing?* |

With bonds, the process is simple. You purchase a bond and you receive interest from the issuer, which is typically a company or government. When you purchase the bond, you are essentially lending money to the entity; they, in turn, agree to give you interest on the money and pay back the money at a predetermined date.

Bonds are relatively safe. For example, when purchasing bonds from a stable government, the investment is risk-free and guaranteed. However, because there is little risk involved, they don't provide much potential regarding return. The rate on a bond is lower than most securities.

Features

The features of a bond are standard. The **principal** represents the face amount; how much interest the issuer pays in determined by the face amount. The face amount is synonymous with the terms "nominal" and "principal." Bond issuers are required to repay the nominal amount by a certain date, which is referenced as the **maturity date**; but after this date, they are no longer obligated.

The maturity date is defined as the final payment date of a loan and/or type of financial instrument. In finance, the principal and remaining interest must be paid on this date.

The length of time leading to the maturity date is referred to in one of three ways: term, tenor, or bond maturity. With this in mind, the term of this type of debt security is commonly set at 30 years, but may be 50 years or more. For example, with U.S. Treasury securities, debt securities typically fall under the following three categories:

- Short-term: these are bills where the maturity ranges from one to five years
- Medium-term: these are notes where the maturity ranges from six to twelve years
- Long-term: these are bonds where the maturity is greater than twelve years.

Coupon is an additional feature of bonds. The **coupon** is defined as the interest rate paid by the issuer to the bond holder. The interest rate is typically fixed over the term of the bond. Rates can also vary by money market indexes such as LIBOR.

The **yield** on a bond is defined as the rate of return that a bondholder receives from investing into the bond. It is typically referred to one of two ways: current yield or yield to maturity or redemption yield. The **current yield** is calculated by dividing the annual interest payment by the current market price of the bond. The current market price is referred to as the **clean price**. The **yield to maturity**, or redemption yield, also measures the return of the bond. It considers the current market price and the amount and timing of coupon payments remaining; it also considers the repayment due on maturity.

Concept Checker	*What are the features of a bond?*

The **credit quality** is a feature of a bond. Bonds are issued based upon the probability that bond holders will receive amounts promised by the due dates. A range of factors is considered. A **high-yield bond** is typically rated below investment grade by a credit rating agency. A **credit rating agency** (CRA) is a company that assigns a credit rating for an issuer of certain types of debt obligations. A CRA also assigns a credit rating for the debt instrument. High-yield bonds are more risky, but return a higher yield. High-yield bonds are called **junk bonds**.

Lastly, **market price** is an additional feature of a bond. The market price for tradeable bonds is influenced by a variety of factors which include currency, timing of interest payments, amount of capital repayment due, credit quality of the bond, and available redemption yield.

Types

There are different types of bonds. A discussion of the most common types is necessary.

- **Fixed-rate bond**: this is a bond whose coupon remains constant throughout the term of the bond.

- **Floating rate notes** (FRNs): this type of bond has a variable coupon and is often linked to a reference rate of interest. The LIBOR and the Euribor are considered reference rates of interest. A **reference rate** determines the pay-off outlined within a financial contract; the pay-off is determined outside the control of all parties to the contract. Examples of reference rates are consumer price index and unemployment rate. The following rates are typically used to determine short-term interest rates for floating rate notes and other types of bonds.

    - **Euribor:** Euro Interbank Offered Rate
    - **LIBOR:** London Interbank Offered Rate
    - **SIBOR:** Singapore Interbank Offered Rate
    - **TIBOR:** Tokyo Interbank Offered Rate
    - **WIBOR:** Warsaw Interbank Offered Rate
    - **MIBOR:** Mumbai Interbank Offered Rate
    - **PRIBOR:** Prague Interbank Offered Rate
    - **BUBOR:** Budapest Interbank Offered Rate

    The rate represents an average interest rate estimated by the above leading banks that is charged to borrowers from other banks.

- **Asset-backed securities:** for this type of bond, the interest and principal payments are guaranteed by the underlying cash flows from other assets. Examples of asset-backed securities are mortgage-backed securities (MBSs), collateralized mortgage obligations (CMOs), and collateralized debt obligations (CDOs). A **mortgage-backed security** has a claim on the cash flows that result from mortgage loans; the process is called securitization. A **collateralized mortgage obligation** is a debt security issued for a special purpose. The institution that creates and operates the debt security for the entity does not owe the debt. Instead, the entity is the legal owner. For example, the entity that owns a set of mortgages submits them to an investment institution that **pools** them together. They become CMOs. Investors in CMOs buy the bonds that the entity issues and they in turn receive payments from the income that generates from the mortgages, or collateralized mortgages. A **collateralized debt obligation** is a structured asset-backed security (ABS) that includes multiple tranches; a **tranche** is one of many related securities a part of the same transaction. A CDO is issued by a special purpose entity and is collateralized by multiple debt obligations which include both bonds and loans.

- **Treasury bond:** a treasury bond is also called a government bond, which is issued by a federal government. A bond under this category is not exposed to default risk. It is typically referred to as the safest bond. If offers a lower interest rate and it is backed by the "full faith and credit" of the issuer, the federal government.

- **Municipal bond:** a municipal bond is issued by a state, city, local government, agency, and a U.S. territory. The interest income that bond holders receive is exempt from federal income tax and from state income tax. However, municipal bonds issued for a specific purpose may not receive tax exemption.

The last features of bond include the issue of bonds in foreign securities, the valuation of bonds as determined by a variety of factors, and the trading of bonds by central banks, pension funds, insurance companies, hedge funds, banks, and sovereign wealth funds (SWFs). A **sovereign wealth fund** is a state-owned investment fund that is composed of multiple financial assets, which include stocks, bonds, precious metals, property, and relate financial instruments.

Stocks

A **stock** is a type of security instrument that reflects ownership in a corporation. It represents your claim on part of the corporation's assets and/or earnings. It is commonly referred to as "shares" or "equity." A **shareholder** is defined as a holder of stock.

When purchasing stocks, you are purchasing an equity share in a company. You become a part owner of the business, a shareholder, based upon the number of shares you purchased. For example, a company issues stock; on their books the company has 1,000 shares outstanding. An individual who purchases and/or owns 100 shares would have a claim of 10% of the company's assets. However, if a common shareholder and a preferred shareholder owns the same amount of shares, a preferred shareholder would have a greater claim to the company's assets should the company go bankrupt.

In addition, with stock in a company, you are entitled to vote at a shareholder's meeting and you are allowed to receive a portion of the profits that the company allocates to the owners. A share of the profits you receive is called **dividends**.

There are two types of stock: common and preferred. With a **common stock** purchase, you are entitled to vote at a shareholder's meeting and receive dividends. However, when your purchase is for **preferred stock**, you typically are not entitled to voting rights, but you do have a higher claim on the corporation's assets and/or earnings. Your claim is higher than those who have purchased common stock. For example, if you are an owner of preferred stock, then you would receive a dividend before a common shareholder. You would also receive priority in the event that the company pursues bankruptcy.

It is important to note that unlike bonds, stocks are volatile. They fluctuate on a daily basis and they offer no real guarantees of a return. Some stocks don't pay dividends. If a stock doesn't pay a dividend, then the only way you could see a gain is if the stock increases in its value. There is no guarantee that this will happen.

Although stocks are a risky product, they are typically the foundation of an investment portfolio and they tend to outperform many other investment vehicles.

Mutual Funds

Another investment vehicle is the mutual fund. A **mutual fund** represents a collection of both stocks and bonds. With a mutual fund, your money is pooled together with a number of investors. As a group, you pay a professional manager to select securities that will benefit you. Mutual funds are typically operated by a money manager who invests the fund's capital with the goal of producing capital gains and income.

A mutual fund can be made up of large stocks, small stocks, government bonds, company bonds, stocks and bonds, stocks, and foreign country stocks. Mutual funds are low maintenance and do not require the time and consideration that riskier investment vehicles need. A shareholder of a mutual fund receives a share, or unit, proportionate to his or her capital investment. The shares can be redeemed at the fund's current net asset value (NAV). **Net asset value** is defined as the value of an entity's assets less the value of its liabilities. The calculation of net asset value falls under one or more accounting methods: securities accounting, investment accounting, and/or portfolio accounting.

There are three types of U.S. mutual funds: open-end, unit investment trust, and closed-end. The Investment Company Act of 1940 established three types of entities called **registered investment companies**, or RICs. The RICs are essentially open-end funds, unit investment trusts (UITs), and closed-end funds. An open-end mutual fund is the most common type. An exchange-traded fund (ETF) is an example of an open-end fund and/or unit investment trust that is traded on the exchange.

Open-End Funds

There are rules specific to the trading of open-end funds. Open-end funds are the common type of mutual fund. The shares of open-end mutual funds are bought back by their investors by the end of every business day; they are bought back at the net asset value for the day. The shares of open-end mutual funds are sold to the public every business day; they are also priced at the net asset value computed for the day. Professional investment managers oversee the portfolio of open-end mutual funds; they are responsible for buying and selling securities. Investment into an open-end mutual fund is based upon the number of share purchases, share redemptions, and market valuation fluctuations. There is no legal limit imposed on buying and selling open-end mutual fund shares.

Closed-end funds

Closed-end funds are another type of mutual fund. They are declining in popularity. The shares of closed-end mutual funds are sold only to the public. This is during the time they are created as a result of an **initial public offering** (IPO), which is a public offering where a private company sells shares of its stock to the general public to raise expansion capital, monetize the investments of private investors, and become a publicly-traded company. Shares of company stock are sold on the **securities exchange**, which provides an environment for stock brokers and traders to trade bonds, stocks, and related securities. An initial public offering is synonymous with the term **stock market launch** and serves as the means by which a private company transforms into a public company.

Concept Checker	*What are the three types of mutual funds?*

With this context in mind, after closed-end funds are created through an IPO, the shares are then listed on a stock exchange for trading purposes. Once the open-end mutual fund is listed on the exchange, investors will not be able to sell their shares back to the fund. Only an open-end mutual fund permits resales. Investors sell their shares to other investors in the market; the price the investors receive is typically different from the net asset value. The price received may be higher, called "premium," or lower, which is called "discount." These prices are in direct proportion to net asset value. Similarly to open-end mutual funds, a professional investment manager oversees the portfolio, buying and selling when appropriate.

Unit Investment Trusts

A **unit investment trusts** (UITs) are shares sold to the public one time; and this only when they are created. Investors redeem UITs with the fund or sell them on the market. Unlike closed-end funds and open-end funds, UITs do not have a professional investment manager buying and selling securities. The portfolio of securities begins and ends at creation and UITs have a limited life span. To date, they have declined in popularity.

Exchange-Traded Funds

Exchange-traded funds, or ETFs, are structured as open-end investment company. An ETF may also be structured as a unit investment trust, partnership, investment trust, grantor trust, and/or bond. A bond within this context is called an **exchange-traded note** (ETN), which is a type of debt security issued by an underwriting bank. An ETN has a maturity date and is backed by the credit of the issuer. Exchange-traded notes provide returns that are predicated on the performance of a market benchmark. They are not equities or index funds.

Exchange-traded funds are similar to closed-end funds because they are traded throughout the day on a stock exchange; an ETF is traded at a price that is determined by the market. Similar to open-end funds, investors of exchange-traded funds receive a price that is typically close to net asset value and are redeemed in large blocks of shares held by institutional investors. Exchange-traded notes are also considered as index funds and are continuing to gain in popularity.

BUSINESS PLANNER

A small business entrepreneur interested in developing an investment program must begin to research the field of investing to ensure success. There are many financial products and a wide-range of rules that could easily deter the novice investor from navigating this world. In addition, the seasoned investor must also be aware of new trends that require familiarity with brokerage policy.

Mack found out the hard way. An investment in one mutual fund did not provide in totality the type of return he needed to grow his business. Mack can't convert his private company into a public company because he has proven that he can create sustainable cash flow. Therefore, he decided to research stocks and bonds. He researched the concept of diversification and began a path to creating and growing sound returns.

**Case Study:
Mack Researches Index Funds**

Mack Jones is a small business entrepreneur. He is also an avid investor, who prefers to work with brokerage houses and let them provide the management and maintenance he needs. Mack's business is in real estate development. He owns multiple properties which include apartment buildings, houses, and small commercial buildings.

Mack discovered the value of index funds and began to look into establishing accounts with Charles Schwab and other companies. Before this, Mack wanted to refresh his memory concerning investment principles and researched a couple of websites on the topic. Mack's search took him to an article housed on the Charles Schwab website.

Here is a summary of the article that Mack read.

1. Create a Plan

It is important to create an actionable investment plan. A sound investment plan considers the following:

- **States your goals:** How much money do you need and when?
- **Considers current savings:** How much have you saved? How much should you invest?
- **Evaluates current assets:** What is the total value of all current assets? What are the categories?
- **Considers decreases:** How do a decrease in debt securities and other investment products affect the investment portfolio?

- **Estimates returns:** What are the potential returns? What are the current economic conditions?

Creating a sound investment plan will provide insight into diversification and asset allocation objectives.

2. Diversify

It is important to understand the risks involved when it comes to investing in stocks, bonds, index funds, and related financial products. There are multiple ways to manage risks. The following list includes some highlights. However, the list is not all-inclusive. Consult your investment provider for help.

- **Across asset classes:** Diversify asset classes that offer long-term asset allocation. These are asset classes that combine multiple types of instruments such as the following:
    - Domestic stocks
    - International stocks
    - Bonds
    - Cash investments
    - Commodities
    - Real Estate Investment Trusts (REITS)
- **Within asset classes:** Diversify asset classes that offer to reduce risks associated with concentration in one market sector. Concentration risks also include those associated with concentrating asset classes within one company and/or country.
- **Equity styles:** Diversify equity styles that allow you to hold both value and growth stocks. This will help you to reduce risks associated with multiple strategies.
- **Bonds:** Diversify bonds. Hold both short-term and long-term maturities. Other options include government and corporate bonds, municipal bonds, and Treasure Inflation Protected Securities, or TIPS. Applying this method will help you to create balance within your fixed income portfolio.

3. Allocate Assets

Creating balance within an investment portfolio is important for balancing risk. From time to time, you will need to adjust the percentage of each asset within the portfolio to ensure that you manage risks. Before you can learn how to allocate assets, you must understand the many classifications. The following represents a list of assets for which small business owners must develop a strategy.

- Cash and cash equivalents
- Fixed-interest securities (i.e., bonds)
- Stocks
- Commodities

- Commercial or residential real estate (RITs)
- Collectibles
- Insurance products
- Derivatives
- Venture capital

Research the many classifications before adjusting the allocation percentage within the investment portfolio.

4. Conduct Periodic Checkups

Consider the volatility of some stocks when allocating assets under an investment plan. In addition, consider those assets that have too much concentration. Periodically evaluate when your bonds are maturing and the change in credit quality of a bond. It is also important to check for changes in a stock's rating (i.e., an A-rated stock falls to a D within any given year).

5. Renew Benchmarks

Set benchmarks for short-term and long-term success. In addition, renew those benchmarks when making changes to assets and when you have multiple asset classes within one investment portfolio. For example, the same benchmark for a bond may not be appropriate for a stock. Compare the performance of stocks, bonds, and cash investments. Compare the results against the portfolio's benchmark index. Then compare those results against a blended benchmark. Measure the value of deposit and withdrawal activities during the year using an internal rate of return calculation guide. Continue to measure the performance of an individual investment against its index.

There are more investing principles that Mack learned as a result of conducting research on the topic. These are the ones that applied to him and the objectives for his business.

Before purchasing any investment product and/or composing an investment portfolio, know the difference between a retail broker and an independent, fee-only advisor. The **retail broker's** first duty is not to you, the client. It is to the firm. A retail broker is compensated based upon the number of trades he or she generates; compensated for selling investment products; and limited to selling only the investment products that are approved by the firm.

On the other hand, an **independent fee-only advisor** is legally required to act as a fiduciary to the client. Advisors don't receive commissions; instead, they receive a fee that represents a percentage of the amount of money he or she manages for you. The advisor uses a third-party custodian such as Charles Schwab or Fidelity for safe-keeping of your assets. Therefore, when considering a fee-only advisor, use the **Independent, Fee-Only Advisor Questionnaire & Worksheet** at the end of this chapter to help guide the process of choosing the appropriate advisor for you and your investment objectives.

Financial Wellness | 303

Chapter Key Points

Investing, or investment, is an economic principle generally related to saving. Savings is money you typically set aside to accomplish one or more short-term goals.

Investing involves risk. For example, investments in equities, property, and interest securities are subject to inflation risks.

An **investment vehicle** is any product used by investors for the purpose of earning a positive return.

Bonds are grouped under the category called fixed-income securities.

The **yield** on a bond is defined as the rate of return that a bondholder receives from investing into the bond. It is typically referred to one of two ways: current yield or yield to maturity or redemption yield.

A **stock** is a type of security instrument that reflects ownership in a corporation. It represents your claim on part of the corporation's assets and/or earnings. It is commonly referred to as "shares" or "equity." A **shareholder** is defined as a holder of stock.

Another investment vehicle is the mutual fund. A **mutual fund** represents a collection of both stocks and bonds.

There are three types of U.S. mutual funds: open-end, unit investment trust, and closed-end. The Investment Company Act of 1940 established three types of entities called **registered investment companies**, or RICs.

A **unit investment trusts** (UITs) are shares sold to the public one time; and this only when they are created. Investors redeem UITs with the fund or sell them on the market.

Exchange-traded funds, or ETFs, are structured as open-end investment company. An ETF may also be structured as a unit investment trust, partnership, investment trust, grantor trust, and/or bond. A bond within this context is called an **exchange-traded note** (ETN), which is a type of debt security issued by an underwriting bank.

The **retail broker's** first duty is not to you, the client. It is to the firm.

On the other hand, an **independent fee-only advisor** is legally required to act as a fiduciary to the client.

Chapter Key Terms

ABS: acronym stands for asset-backed security.

Asset-backed securities: term refers to type of bond where the interest and principal payments are guaranteed by the underlying cash flows from other assets.

Bond: term refers to a type of instrument of indebtedness between the bond issuer and the bondholder. It is a debt security.

BUBOR: acronym stands for Budapest Interbank Offered Rate.

CDO: acronym stands for collateralized debt obligation.

Clean price: term refers to the current market price of a bond.

Closed-end funds: term refers to a type of mutual fund.

CMO: acronym stands for collateralized mortgage obligation.

Collateralized debt obligation: term refers to a structured asset-backed security (ABS) that includes multiple tranches.

Collateralized mortgage obligation: term refers to a debt security issued for a special purpose.

Common stock: term refers to a shareholder's right to vote at a shareholder's meeting and receive dividends.

Coupon: term refers to the interest rate paid by the issuer to the bond holder.

CRA: acronym stands for credit rating agency.

Credit quality: term refers to a feature of a bond.

Credit rating agency: term refers to a company that assigns a credit rating for an issuer of certain types of debt obligations.

Current yield: term refers to a calculation by dividing the annual interest payment by the current market price of the bond.

Dividend: term refers to a share of the profits a shareholder receives.

ETF: acronym stands for exchange-traded fund.

ETN: acronym stands for exchange-traded note.

EURIBOR: acronym stands for Euro Interbank Offered Rate.

Exchange-traded fund: term refers to the structure of an open-end investment company.

Exchange-traded note: term refers to a type of debt security issued by an underwriting bank.

Fixed-income security: term refers to a type of investment vehicle that provides a return that is in the form of fixed periodic payments.

Fixed-rate bond: term refers to a bond whose coupon remains constant throughout the term of the bond.

Floating rate notes: term refers to a type of bond that has a variable coupon and is often linked to a reference rate of interest.

High-yield bond: term refers to a type of bond that is typically rated below investment grade by a credit rating agency.

Independent fee-only advisor: term refers to a type of advisor legally required to act as a fiduciary to the client. Advisors don't receive commissions; instead, they receive a fee that represents a percentage of the amount of money he or she manages for the client.

Initial public offering: term refers to a public offering where a private company sells shares of its stock to the general public to raise expansion capital, monetize the investments of private investors, and become a publicly-traded company.

Investing: term refers to an economic principle generally related to saving.

Investment vehicle: term refers to any product used by investors for the purpose of earning a positive return.

IPO: acronym stands for initial public offering.

Junk bonds: term refers to high-yield bonds. See *High-Yield Bonds*.

LIBOR: acronym stands for London Interbank Offered Rate.

Market price: term refers to an additional feature of a bond; market price is influenced by currency, timing of interest payments, amount of capital repayment due, credit quality of the bond, and available redemption yield.

Maturity date: term refers to a date a bond issuer is required to repay a nominal amount to a bondholder.

MBS: acronym stands for mortgage-backed security.

MIBOR: acronym stands for Mumbai Interbank Offered Rate.

Mortgage-backed security: term refers to a claim on the cash flows that result from mortgage loans; the process is called securitization.

Municipal bond: term refers to a bond issued by a state, city, local government, agency, and/or a U.S. territory.

Mutual fund: term refers to a collection of both stocks and bonds.

NAV: acronym stands for net asset value.

Net asset value: term refers to the value of an entity's assets less the value of its liabilities.

Open-end funds: term refers to a common type of mutual fund.

Pool: term refers to the activity of an entity that owns a set of mortgages and submits them to an investment institution that pools them together.

Preferred stock: term refers to a type of shareholder who is not entitled to voting rights, but has a higher claim on the corporation's assets and/or earnings.

PRIBOR: acronym stands for Prague Interbank Offered Rate.

Principal: term refers to the face amount of a bond.

Redemption yield: see *Yield to Maturity*.

Reference rate: term refers to a type of rate that determines the pay-off outlined within a financial contract; the pay-off is determined outside the control of all parties to the contract.

Registered investment companies: term refers to three types of entities established by the Investment Company Act of 1940.

Retail broker: term refers to a type of advisor whose compensation is based upon the number of trades he or she generates and selling of investment products; retail broker is limited to selling only the investment products that are approved by the firm.

RICs: acronym stands for registered investment companies.

SEC: acronym stands for the U.S. Securities and Exchange Commission.

Securities exchange: term refers to an environment for stock brokers and traders to trade bonds, stocks, and related securities.

Shareholder: term refers to a holder of stock.

SIBOR: acronym stands for Singapore Interbank Offered Rate.

Sovereign wealth fund: term refers to a state-owned investment fund that is composed of multiple financial assets, which include stocks, bonds, precious metals, property, and relate financial instruments.

Stock: term refers to a type of security instrument that reflects ownership in a corporation.

Stock market launch: term refers to the means by which a private company transforms into a public company.

TIBOR: acronym stands for Tokyo Interbank Offered Rate.

Tranche: term refers to one of many related securities a part of the same transaction.

Treasury bond: term refers to a government bond.

UIT: acronym stands for unit investment trust.

Unit investment trust: term refers to shares sold to the public one time; and this only when they are created.

Variable-income security: term refers to when payments often change due to short-term interest rates.

WIBOR: acronym stands for Warsaw Interbank Offered Rate.

Yield: term refers to the rate of return that a bondholder receives from investing into the bond.

Yield to maturity: term refers to the redemption yield, or measurement of return of a bond.

Group Work Prompt

As a group, create an investment plan. Refer to the tips outlined in the chapter case study. Begin this project in class and finish it as a group out-of-class. Use the following questions to complete the exercise.

Part One: Creating the Plan

1. What are your goals?

2. What are your current savings?

3. What is the value of your current assets?

4. What are your potential returns? Provide an estimate.

Part Two: Developing Diversification Objectives

1. What are your diversification objectives?

2. What asset classes are you considering?

3. What are your long-term considerations? What are your short-term considerations?

4. Which asset classes will reduce risk?

5. Does your portfolio hold both value and growth stocks? If not, what are your plans for diversifying by equity style?

6. Does your portfolio hold bond securities? What are the maturities?

7. How are assets allocated?

Part Three: Establishing Periodic Checkup Objectives

1. What are your periodic checkup objectives?

2. How often and when will you evaluate your current portfolio to ensure risks are minimized?

Part Four: Reevaluating Benchmarks

1. What are benchmarks objectives?
2. How often will you reevaluate these objectives?

HOMEWORK EXERCISE

For homework, evaluate your current financial condition. List current debt obligations and savings totals. Based upon the information, create an individual investment plan where you consider stocks, mutual funds, and bonds. Refer to the ideas expressed in this chapter. In addition, visit sites such as Charles Schwab, Fidelity, and Merrill Lynch for insight into how to create the plan.

HELPFUL WEBSITES

Federal Trade Commission: Consumer Information, Investment Risks
http://www.consumer.ftc.gov/articles/0238-investment-risks

The New York Times
Small Business: Investing Advice for the Small-Business Owner, Jeff Brown (June 16, 2009)
http://www.nytimes.com/2009/06/16/business/smallbusiness/16investing.html?pagewanted=all&_r=0

Investopedia: Investing 101: Types of Investments
http://www.investopedia.com/university/beginner/beginner5.asp#axzz2FFnGT5Um

Charles Schwab: Investing Principles
http://www.schwab.com/public/schwab/resource_center/investing_basics/investing_principles

BOOKS FOR CONSIDERATION

The Investment Answer, Learn to Manage Your Money & Protect Your Financial Future (2010), Daniel C. Goldie, CFA and Gordon S. Murray.

CHAPTER FORMS

On the next pages are all of the forms discussed within this chapter. You may photocopy, scan, and print them out. Some forms you will need to complete the group work and the homework.

Assessment

1. What is investing?

2. What are the major types of investing? What are the most common investment vehicles?

3. **True or False**. The maturity date is a feature of a bond.

4. Which of the following represents a type of bond?
    a. Fixed-rate bond
    b. Floating rate note
    c. Asset-backed security
    d. All of the above

5. Define "stock." Relate the definition to the term "shareholder." What two types of stock can a shareholder purchase?

6. What are mutual funds?

7. Define RIC, UIT, IPO, ETF, and ETN.

8. Based upon the ideas expressed in Chapter: Investing, suggest an investment plan to Mack, the subject of the chapter's case study.

INDEPENDENT, FEE-ONLY QUESTIONNAIRE & WORKSHEET

Date: _____

Advisor/Contact: _____
Fee: _____

Custodian: _____
Contact: _____

Questions

1. What is the advisor's investment philosophy?
_____
_____
_____

2. What are the advisor's professional qualifications?
_____
_____
_____

Financial Designations*:
CFP_____ CFA_____ CPA_____

3. What is the advisor's educational background?
_____
_____
_____

4. What is the advisor's level(s) of experience with financial services and accounting?
_____
_____
_____

5. What is the current business structure of the advisor's business?

Sole Proprietorship_____ Partnership_____ Unincorporated Business_____
Other: _____

6. What services does the advisor offer? Is a brochure available for evaluation?
_____
_____
_____

7. What are the advisor's current clients? How long have they been with the advisor?
_____
_____
_____

Special Notes & Considerations
_____
_____
_____
_____
_____

*Certified Financial Planner (CFP); Chartered Financial Analysis (CFA); Certified Public Accountant (CPA)

Creating an Investment Plan
Questionnaire & Worksheet

Part One: Creating the Plan

1. What are your goals?
2. What are your current savings?
3. What is the value of your current assets?
4. What are your potential returns? Provide an estimate.

Part Two: Developing Diversification Objectives

1. What are your diversification objectives?
2. What asset classes are you considering?
3. What are your long-term considerations? What are your short-term considerations?
4. Which asset classes will reduce risk?
5. Does your portfolio hold both value and growth stocks? If not, what are your plans for diversifying by equity style?
6. Does your portfolio hold bond securities? What are the maturities?
7. How are assets allocated?

Part Three: Establishing Periodic Checkup Objectives

1. What are your periodic checkup objectives?
2. How often and when will you evaluate your current portfolio to ensure risks are minimized?

Part Four: Reevaluating Benchmarks

1. What are benchmarks objectives?
2. How often will you reevaluate these objectives?

Special Notes and Considerations

_____
_____
_____
_____
_____

CHAPTER 15

Retirement Options

Learning Objectives

- Define retirement.
- List the types of retirement options.
- Define annuities.
- Recite a scenario.
- Complete worksheet.
- Define mutual funds.
- Define bond funds.
- List the different types of IRAs.

WHAT IS RETIREMENT?

Retirement is the time at which a person stops working completely. Many people choose to retire at different junctures in their lives. Some people retire for private benefits. Others retire for public pension benefits. Some people are forced to retire due to health reasons making it impossible for them to continue working. There are common factors that contribute to early and/or late retirement decisions. These factors include Social Security, where people are retiring at normal retirement ages (i.e., ages 62 and 65); greater wealth, where wealthier individuals enter early retirement and "purchase leisure"; financial crisis, where individuals are foregoing retirement because they don't have the long-term financial cushion to meet future demands; and health status, where some individuals are forced to retire because of health reasons.

As many people continue to get older, as prices increase, as people are discovering that they don't have sufficient savings, retirement is beginning to look like a goal that would take many more years to reach. To be successful at retiring, you must become a strategic investor. In other words, you must learn the language of investing, researching various financial products and plans that will help you later in life.

You must create a retirement budget that will help you to consider what will be necessary for you at a later age. The money you earn now will not be the same money you earn and/or receive in retirement. Unless you enter the world of entrepreneurship, age will play a factor in the types of post-employment jobs you seek and the retirement plans you choose. That's why it is important to think beyond just your pension. Your pension perhaps may be the foundation of your retirement plan, but it shouldn't be the only option you consider.

This chapter explores various retirement options to give you a comprehensive view of what to expect in terms of planning and preparing for taxes.

Small business entrepreneurs must also consider retirement options, especially if you are a self-employed individual. It is important that you plan to purchase products that will help to hedge against emergencies. This chapter provides insight into both private and public retirement options.

Types of Retirement Options

There are multiple types of retirement options specific to individuals working for a public entity as well as for individuals working within the private industry. For each type of plan, whether it is through a public or private entity, you must choose where you want your money allocated. Reread Chapter: Investing for insight into what each category of asset classes means within the context of finance and investing.

Public Choice: The 403(b) Plan

Employees of a public school typically have access to a retirement savings plan called a 403(b) plan. A 403(b) plan is tax-deferred and it is available to members of the clergy, non-profit entities, and employees of public schools. Taxes are not paid on the amount you contribute for the year in which you contribute the amount. This allows you to lower your tax burden in the present year. With a 403(b) plan you can also defer the income tax assessed on contributions. However, when you make withdrawals from the 403(b) plan account, after you retire, then you can expect to pay income taxes. However, the earnings through the account grow tax-free until withdrawal.

Investment Options

There are multiple investment options for a 403(b) plan. The choice of options is predicated on how the employer structures the plan. Once you understand the plan's structure, you can then choose the investments that will meet your financial objectives. A 403(b) plan offers both annuities and mutual funds.

Concept Checker	*What is retirement?*

Annuities

In general, annuities typically offer tax-deferred growth. They often include a death benefit where the beneficiary is paid a specific amount after the death of the policyholder. Tax is deferred particularly on earnings growth. However, when withdrawals are made against the account, this is considered gains, which is considered taxable income. Gains are taxed as ordinary income rates, not capital gains rates.

Expect to pay surrender charges to the insurance company when withdrawing money from an annuity. In addition, there are tax penalties for withdrawing money from the annuity too early. To begin the discussion, there are three types of annuities: fixed, indexed, and variable.

Fixed Annuity

A **fixed annuity** is a type of contract that an insured (i.e., policyholder) has with an insurance company. The purpose of an annuity is to guarantee that the insured earns a minimum rate of interest during the time that the annuity account is growing. The insurer guarantees that the insured will receive fixed periodic payments. The insured may receive periodic payments for a specific period (i.e., 20 years). Periodic payments may also be received for an indefinite period which may represent your lifetime or the lifetime of both you and your spouse.

Indexed Annuity

Indexed annuities are called officially **equity-indexed annuity**, which may be referred to as **fixed index annuities** or **simple indexed annuities**. They are special types of contracts between an insurance company and the insured. For example, an insured may make a lump sum payment or choose to make a series of payments during the **accumulation period**, which represents a period of time when the **annuitant**, the person entitled to receive benefits from the annuity, makes contributions (to the annuity) for the purpose of building up the value of the annuity account. The annuitant receives guaranteed payments for a specific period of time during the **annuitization phase**. Typically, the annuitant receives these payments during the rest of his or her life.

Concept Checker	What are the types of annuities?

With an equity-indexed annuity, the payments the annuitant makes are credited by the insurance company. The credits are based upon changes within an equity index such as the S&P 500. The insurance company guarantees that the annuitant will receive a minimum return based upon a minimum interest rate typically set between one-percent and three-percent. However, minimum return rates vary and the annuitant is only guaranteed this rate until the end of the surrender term. After the annuitant's accumulation period, the insurance company makes periodic payments based upon the value of the insurance contract. Payments are typically made in a lump sum.

Indexed annuity contracts are typically suitable for asset portfolios where the owner wants to avoid incurring risk during his or her retirement period. The objective of purchasing this type of product is realize gains that are greater than those typically received from a certificate of deposit, money market account, and/or bond. With an indexed annuity, the principal is protected.

Variable Annuity

With a **variable annuity**, the insured makes a lump sum payment or a series of payments to an insurance company. Payments are made into a tax-deferred account. After the accumulation period, the insurance provider, or insurer, agrees to make periodic payments to the insured immediately or at some future date. The insured can then choose to invest the purchase payments in a number of investment options, which typically include mutual funds. The value of a variable annuity account often varies and is dependent upon the performance of the investment options. In addition, you typically receive no additional tax advantage from a variable annuity.

For variable annuity accounts, there are two standard phases: the accumulation phase as discussed above and the payout phase. The **payout phase** is defined as the period of time when the insurer makes payments to the annuitant. During the accumulation period the annuitant can allocate purchase payments to a number of investment options. For example, forty percent of the purchase payment could be allocated to a bond fund, forty percent to a stock fund, and the remainder to an international stock fund. The monies allocated to each mutual fund investment option will increase or decrease depending upon the fund's performance.

With a variable annuity account, an annuitant can allocate part of his or her purchase payment also to a fixed account. A fixed account typically pays a fixed rate of interest. However, the insurance company can reset the rate periodically. It is here where Barbara learned the importance of paying more into her annuity account.

Case Study:
Barbara Increases her Purchase Payment

Barbara Simms invests in annuity accounts. She retired last year after 30 years as a public school teacher. Barbara has been investing in a 403(b) account for the majority of her service to Davis Public School. Prior to retirement, Barbara invested primarily in mutual funds. Now she is interested in purchasing an annuity. She researched the topic, discovering some valuable information. Barbara realized that in increasing her purchase payment, she could also increase the value of her annuity account.

For example, with a first-year purchase payment of $10,000, Barbara allocates 50% to a bond fund and 50% to a stock fund. Barbara keeps the account for a year. After the year, the stock fund earns a return of 10% and the bond fund earns a 5% return. At the end of the first year, Barbara's annuity account has a total value of $10,750, subject to fees and charges.

Barbara realized that just by increasing her purchase payment by $500 or $1,000 in the second year she could easily grow a greater return that would increase the value of her annuity account.

During the accumulation phase, the annuitant can transfer money between investment options without paying tax on investment income and gains.

However, the insurance company can charge fees for transfers. If the annuitant withdraws money during the accumulation phase, surrender charges apply; a federal 10% tax penalty will also apply for withdrawals prior to age 59½.

A variable annuity has a **death benefit**, which is defined as the amount on a life insurance policy that will be payable to a beneficiary when the annuitant dies. For example, if the insured dies before the insurance company (insurer) begins to make payments, then the beneficiary on the policy will receive guaranteed payments, an amount specific to the purchase payment. The beneficiary will receive this amount at the time of the insured's death. To be sure, the beneficiary will still receive a benefit even if the account value is less than the guaranteed amount.

Scenario #1
For example, Barbara's annuity account by year three is valued at $50,000. This is the total of her purchase payments. Barbara withdraws $5,000 from the account at the end of year three. Because of the withdrawal and some losses, Barbara's annuity account is valued at $40,000. If Barbara dies at any time, then her beneficiary would receive $45,000. This represents $50,000 less the total amount of withdrawals. Although Barbara's account is currently valued at $40,000, she only withdrew $5,000. The beneficiary would receive the balance of Barbara's investment into the annuity account, not necessarily the current value of the account due to losses related to interest rate increases/decreases and/or account charges.

With this in mind, there are different types of variable annuity charges assessed to an annuity account. Charges to the account reduce its value and the return on the investment. For example, each annuity account has a **surrender period** where the surrender charge to the account declines gradually over a period of years. A **surrender charge** is a fee that the insurance policyholder must pay upon cancelling the policy. The fee covers the costs related to keeping the insurance policy on the insurer's books. Withdrawals of money from an annuity account after the initial purchase payment and within a certain period, which is typically six to eight years, will be assessed a surrender charge. The surrender charge is the equivalent of a sales charge. The charge to the account pays the commission of the financial professional who sells the variable annuity to the insured.

Concept Checker	What is death benefit for a variable annuity?

The surrender charge is typically a percentage of the amount withdrawn. The surrender charge is typically assessed differently each year. There might be a 7% charge assessed during for a first-year withdrawal after the purchase payment. In subsequent years, the charge may go down to 6% for the second year and 5% for the third year. In the eighth year, the surrender charge may no longer apply. What if Barbara wanted to withdraw money from her annuity account? What would be her surrender charges and what amounts would be assessed what charge?

Scenario #2
When Barbara purchased her variable annuity account, making an initial purchase payment of $10,000, she signed a contract that provided a schedule of surrender charges. For account withdrawals, a 7% charge will be assessed in the first year and the charge would decline each year thereafter. There is also a provision that allows Barbara to withdraw 10% of the contract's value each year free of surrender charges. Barbara decides to withdraw $5,000, or one-half of her contract's value. A charge of 7% would not be assessed on the $5,000. Instead, Barbara would receive the first $1,000 free of surrender charges. This is 10% of the contract value. The 7% charge would apply to the $4,000 withdrawn.

There are additional charges to a variable annuity account. This type of account is subject to a **mortality and expense risk charge** of 1.25% per year. This charge covers the insurance company's costs related to insurance risks under the annuity contract. Earned profit compensates the insurer for costs related to selling the variable annuity. Costs include compensating financial professionals. There are also **administrative fees** that the insurer deducts to for record-keeping purposes. The insurer may deduct account maintenance fees within the range of 0.15% assessed per year. Insurers may deduct **underlying fund expenses**; these are charges imposed by mutual funds within the variable annuity. Lastly, the insured can expect to be charged special fees. If an insurance policy provides long-term care insurance or guaranteed minimum income benefit, then there will be charges for initial sales loads and transferring fees.

When considering any annuity product, research and ask questions before you invest. Financial professionals have a duty to advise you and answer any questions you may have. Variable annuity contracts typically offer a "free look" period benefit, where a prospective annuitant can "try out" the variable annuity for a prescribed period usually ten or more days. During the period, the annuitant can terminate the contract without assessed charges to the initial purchase payment.

Before purchasing a variable annuity, consider the questions in the following **Variable Annuity Planning Questionnaire and Worksheet.**

Variable Annuity Planning Questionnaire & Worksheet

Date: _____

Company/Contact:
_____
_____

Preliminary Questions

1. Is the purpose of the variable annuity to save for retirement?

    Yes_____No_____

2. Is the purpose of the variable annuity for another long-term goal?

    Yes_____No_____

What is the long-term goal?
_____
_____

3. Is the investment in the variable annuity through a retirement plan?

    Yes_____No_____

Is the investment in the variable annuity through an IRA?
Yes_____No_____

Note that investment through an IRA means that you will not receive additional tax-deferral benefits from the variable annuity.

4. Do you understand the risk that the account value may decrease as a result of underlying mutual fund investment performing poorly?

    Yes_____No_____

What are the risks?
_____
_____
_____
_____

Worksheet

Research a prospective variable annuity contract. Answer the following questions.

5. What are the features of the variable annuity?
_____
_____
_____
_____

6. What are the fees and expenses that the variable annuity charges?
_____
_____
_____
_____

7. What is the policy on the variable annuity for surrender charges related to withdrawing money?
_____
_____
_____
_____

8. What is the policy on bonus credits? Do they outweigh any other higher fees?
_____
_____
_____
_____

9. What are the features of the variable annuity? Is long-term care insurance a feature?
_____
_____
_____
_____

10. What are the tax consequences of purchasing a variable annuity?
_____
_____

Special Notes & Considerations
_____
_____
_____
_____
_____

When researching this topic, it is important that you get a good understanding of the contract policy before making the final purchase. Visit and read online publications on the subject of investing wisely.

Mutual Funds

A **mutual fund** is a type of collective investment vehicle that pools together money from multiple investors for the purpose of purchasing securities. A **collective investment vehicle** is defined as a method of investing where investors benefit from the inherent advantages of working as a group. Advantages include hiring a professional investment manager, sharing costs, and diversifying to reduce risks. In addition to mutual funds, a collective investment vehicle is often referred to as investment funds and managed funds (or simply funds).

Mutual funds are offered in a multitude of varieties. Some of the most common include index funds, stock funds, bond funds, and money market funds. Each type of fund has a different investment objective and strategy. Mutual funds are subject to risks, volatility, and assessed fees and expenses.

Index Fund

An **index fund** is a type of mutual fund. The portfolio of an index fund is structured to match and/or track the components of the particular market index such as Standard & Poor's Index (S&P 500). Index funds also track other indexes such as the Russell 2000 for smaller companies; the DJ Wilshire 5000 for the total stock market; the MSCI EAFE for foreign stocks offered in Europe, Australia, and the Far East; and the Lehman Aggregate Bond Index for the total bond market.

An index fund has broader market exposure with lower operating expenses and low portfolio turnover. Indexing, in general is a passive form of fund management. Indexing is successful in outperforming most managed mutual funds.

Tracking, within the context of indexing, is defined as the process of holding all securities in the index in the same proportions as the index. Additional methods include sampling the market and holding "representative" securities. Indexes typically rely on a computer model that requires little or no human input, hence the term **passive management**, or passive investing. Passive management is defined as a financial strategy used by an investor or fund manager. The fund manager's investing decisions are based upon a pre-determined strategy that doesn't require the need for forecasting. **Forecasting**, within this context, is related to market timing or stock picking.

Stock Funds

A **stock fund** is defined as a fund that invests in stocks, which are called equity securities. In this regard, a stock fund is synonymous with equity fund. Stock funds are different from bond funds and money funds. A **bond fund**, or debt fund, invests in bonds and related debt securities. A money fund, or **money market fund**, is an open-end mutual fund that invests in short-term debt securities, which include U.S. Treasury bills and commercial paper.

The assets of a stock fund are held in stock with some amount of cash. A stock fund may be a mutual fund or an exchange-traded fund. The objective of a stock fund is to create long-term growth through capital gains. Dividends have been an important source of return for stock funds.

Stock funds are distinguishable between multiple properties. Stock funds have a specific style related to value and/or growth. They are typically invested solely into the securities of a country or into the securities of multiple countries. There are additional components to stock funds which include stock picking. There are different types of stock funds. An index fund invests in securities to match a specific index.

Concept Checker	*What is passive management?*

A **growth fund** invests in the stocks of companies that are experiencing rapid growth. Growth companies reinvest profits for research and development instead of paying dividends. A **value fund** invests in value stocks. Companies that offer value stocks are typically established businesses that pay dividends. A **sector fund** invests in a particular area of industry. Sector funds typically invest 25% of their assets in a specialty. Sector funds offer high appreciation potential; with these funds also come higher risks. Examples of sector fund investments include gold funds, technology funds, and utility funds. An **income fund**, or equity income fund, invests in the stocks of companies that have a long history of paying dividends. Example types of companies include utility stocks, blue-chip stocks, and preferred stocks.

A **balanced fund** invests in bonds for income and stocks for appreciation. The goal of a balanced fund is to provide regular income payment to a fund holder. **Asset allocation funds** split investments between multiple options, which include growth stocks, money market funds, and income stocks/bonds. Fund advisers generally switch the percentage of holdings between multiple asset categories. This is in accordance with performance.

For example, an asset allocation fund may invest 60% into stocks, 20% into bonds, and 20% into the money market. However, if a stock market is expected to perform well, then the fund adviser may switch the percentages where 80% may be allocated to stocks and 20% invested into bonds and cash investments. Lastly, a **hedge fund** often trades stocks to reduce the risk of investments.

Bond Funds

A **bond fund** invests in bonds and related debt securities. A bond fund typically pays dividends. The payment of dividends includes interest payments that are assessed as a result of the fund's underlying securities. A bond fund also realizes capital appreciation. Bond funds pay higher dividends than certificate of deposits and money market accounts and they pay out more frequently than individual bonds.

There are different types of bonds: government, mortgage, corporate, and municipal. **Government bonds** are considered the safest form of investment. The government can always print more money. However, the yield on a government bond tends to be low. A **mortgage bond** is issued and/or guaranteed by government agencies, which include the Federal National Mortgage Association (Fannie Mae), the Federal Home Loan Mortgage Corporation (Freddie Mac), and the Government National Mortgage Association (Ginnie Mae). A **corporate bond** is issued by a corporation. Corporate bonds are guaranteed by the issuing company, which is also the borrower. The risks for corporate bonds are predicated on the company's ability to pay the loan at maturity. Bonds that specialize in high-yield securities are considered junk bonds. Junk bonds are corporate bonds that carry a higher risk; the risk is based upon the (potential) inability of the issuer to repay the bond. Corporate bond funds that specialize in junk bonds pay higher dividends. Lastly, municipal bonds are issued by state and local governments. They are subject to tax preferences and are exempt from federal taxes. Some municipal bonds are exempt from state and local taxes.

Concept Checker	What are the different types of stock funds?

In general, bond funds may be classified by yield (high-income), term (short, medium, long), and specialty (zero-coupon, international, multi-sector, convertible). The advantages of investing in a bond fund versus individual bonds include dedicated management by fund managers; diversification; automatic income reinvestment; and liquidity, meaning a bond holder can sell its shares at any time. Common disadvantages include fees charged to bond funds versus individual bonds; variable dividends meaning bonds are not fixed and are subject to fluctuate; and variable net asset value. This means that the bond fund can change over time.

Money Funds

A money fund, or **money market fund**, and also known as money market mutual fund, is a type of open-ended mutual fund. The fund invests in short-term debt securities, which include Treasury bills and commercial paper. Money market funds are usually safe for investment purposes and provide a higher yield. Money market funds are regulated by the U.S. Securities and Exchange Commission (SEC) and subject to the provisions of the Investment Company Act of 1940. They are providers of liquidity to financial intermediaries. The objective of money market funds is to limit exposure to losses as a result of credit, market, and liquidity risks.

There are two major types of money market funds. An **institutional money fund** requires a high minimum investment, but offers a low expense share class. Institutional money funds are typically marketed to corporations, fiduciaries, and governments. Fund managers structure institutional money funds so money is swept to a company from its main operating account. Large national chains are examples of companies that have many accounts with multiple banks. Institutions withdraw a majority of funds that are on deposit and transfer funds to a concentrated money market fund. The JPMorgan Prime Money Market Fund is the largest institutional money fund. There are additional companies and banks that offer an institutional money fund. Examples of such companies are Western Asset, Bank of America, Dreyfus, and BlackRock.

A **retail money fund** is a product offered primarily to individuals. Retail money funds represent approximately 33% of all money market fund assets. There are different types of retail money funds, which include government-only funds, non-government funds, and tax-free funds. Yields under a retail money fund tend to be higher than a regular savings account. Investors typically achieve higher yields under the non-government class where the principal holdings represent high-quality commercial paper. The largest retail fund providers are Fidelity, Vanguard, and Schwab.

Private Considerations: The 401(k) Plan

The **401(k) plan** is a type of retirement savings account in the United States. The name of the plan derives from a subsection (401(k) of the Internal Revenue Code (Title 26 of the United States Code). The 401(k) plan is a "defined contribution plan." Annual contributions cannot exceed approximately $17,000. Contributions to the plan are tax-deferred. They are deducted from the employee's paycheck before taxes. When the plan participant makes a withdrawal from the account, then taxes are assessed on the withdrawal. Some employers match an employee's contribution.

Contributions & Tax Considerations

Plan Structure

There are tax consequences associated with a 401(k) plan. Each company structures its plan differently. Some companies structure their 401(k) plan to allow employees to make contributions on a pre-tax basis; other companies allow contributions to be made on a post-tax basis. Before contributing to the plan, review the company's literature to determine which type of structure it offers.

Tax-Deferred Earnings

Earnings generated from a company 401(k) plan are tax-deferred. Earnings are defined as interest, dividends, and/or capital gains. A unique feature of a 401(k) plan is the resulting compounding interest where taxes on the interest are delayed, provided the interest is held over a long period of time. As of the writing of this book, since 2006, employees have been able to designate contributions as a Roth 401(k) deduction. Contributions under this category are similar to the provisions that outline requirements for selecting a Roth IRA. The contributions are after taxes; earnings are tax-deferred and tax-free upon a qualified distribution. To ensure that employees receive these options, the company sponsor must amend the plan.

Pre-Tax Contributions

Regarding pre-tax contributions, employees do not have to pay federal income tax on the current income he or she defers to a 401(k) account. For example, Sam earned $50,000 in 2011. He deferred or submitted a total of $3,000 to his 401(k) account. Based upon this scenario, Sam's income was only $47,000 on his tax return. As long as Sam stays within a certain tax bracket and there are no adjustments, then he would recognize a savings in taxes. However, Sam would have to pay taxes on the money he withdraws from his plan. In this respect, tax-favored capital gains are converted into ordinary income.

Ordinary income is defined as income that is other than **capital gain**, which is profit that results from the disposing of a capital asset. Examples of ordinary income include wages, salaries, tips, commissions, bonuses, interest, dividends, net income, rents, royalties, and gambling winnings. **Capital assets** are stocks, bonds, and/or real estate. A **capital gain tax** is assessed when the amount received from the disposition exceeds the price of purchase. Capital gains may also refer to investment income in relation to property and financial assets as well as intangible assets such as goodwill. **Goodwill** is defined as those intangible assets that provide a "prudent value." The reputation of a company with its clients is considered an example of "goodwill."

Concept Checker	What is a 401(k) plan?

After-Tax Contributions

The contributions of employees who have made after-tax funding to a non-Roth 401(k) account are coupled together with the pre-tax funds. When the distributions are made, only the taxable portion is calculated as the ratio of non-Roth contributions to the total amount of the 401(k) basis. The remainder of the distribution is tax-free and it is not included in the gross income earned for the year.

For designated Roth accounts, the accumulated after-tax contributions and earnings are considered "qualified distributions," which are made tax-free and penalty free. There are two requirements that must be met for a distribution to be eligible as a qualified distribution. The first requirement is that the distribution must occur a minimum of five years after the Roth IRA owner establishes the first Roth IRA. For the second requirement, one of four requirements must occur:

- **Age:** The Roth IRA holder must reach the age of 59.5 at the time of distribution.
- **First Home:** Distributed assets that do not exceed $10,000 must be used towards the purchasing or rebuilding of a first home for the Roth IRA holder. This requirement applies also to a qualified family member.
- **Disability:** The distribution must occur after the Roth IRA owner becomes disabled.
- **Death:** Assets distributed to the beneficiary must occur after the Roth IRA owner's death.

Under these conditions, a Roth contribution is irrevocable. It cannot be converted into a pre-tax contribution base. A Roth contribution must be made to a separate account. Good record-keeping practices are important. Records should indicate that the amount of contribution is distinguishable from the corresponding earnings that receive Roth treatment.

The Roth IRA is different in some respects from the Roth 401(k). With the latter, there is no income limit capping eligibility. An employee and/or individual who is otherwise ineligible or disqualified from contributing to a Roth IRA may contribute funds to their Roth 401(k). However, individuals and/or employees who are qualified to make contributions into both Roth 401(k) and Roth IRA may contribute the maximum statutory amounts for both plans. This qualification includes funding up under the **catch-up contribution** provision, which is a type of retirement savings contribution for people over the age of 50. The provision allows people to make additional contributions to their 401(k) plan and related individual retirement accounts. The provision was created by the Economic Growth and Tax Relief Reconciliation Act of 2001 (EGTRRA).

Withdrawals

Companies tend to impose restrictions on Roth IRA plan withdrawals before the age of 59½, especially while the employee is currently in service. Fund withdrawals permitted before this age will be subject to an excise tax; the tax is equal to ten percent of the amount distributed. This is on top of ordinary income tax that also the employee has to pay. Employees may make withdrawals on the basis of hardship expenses. Exceptions apply. Consult your plan's sponsor for more information. In addition, read the Internal Revenue Code, section 213 to determine allowable withdrawals and required deductions during a given tax year.

Concept Checker	What are the after-tax contributions for a 401(k) plan?

Hardship

Companies reserve the right to disallow a withdrawal necessary for a hardship cause. An employee wishing to withdraw funds from a 401(k) plan would most likely have to resign from the company. To maintain a tax advantage for income deferrals, money must be kept in the plan until an employee reaches 59½ years of age. Money withdrawn prior to this age will occur the 10% penalty as discussed in the preceding paragraph. However, there are exceptions to the 10% penalty. The following represents a list of exceptions that employees should be aware.

- Employee's death
- Employee's total and permanent disability
- Separation from service in/after the year employee reaches age 55
- Substantially equal periodic payments selection
- Qualified domestic relations order
- Deductible medical expenses

Each 401(k) plan has exceptions and requirements that employees must meet before requesting consideration.

Loans

Employees with a 401(k) plan are allowed to take out loans, but the loans must be repaid with after-tax funds. Loans are disbursed with a predetermined interest rate and the interest proceeds are added to the 401(k) balance.

Loans are not taxable income and they are not subject to the 10% penalty fee assessed for early withdrawals. The repayment provisions of 401(k) loans are subject to section 72(p) of the Internal Revenue Code. The section requires the repayment of a loan not to exceed five years, provided that the employee has not purchased a primary residence. A reasonable rate of interest is charged with equal payments required at least every calendar quarter through the life of the loan.

Employer-sponsored 401(k) plans tend to be more restrictive. In general, when an employee fails to repay the loan during the required term, the outstanding loan balance will be considered in default. Defaulted loans accrue interest on the current loan balance, become a taxable distribution in the year of default, and are accessed tax penalties and withdrawal fees.

As you continue to develop retirement planning objectives, consider all of the tax implications by researching such issues on the IRS website.

Other Considerations: IRA, SEP IRA, and SIMPLE IRA

IRA

An **Individual Retirement Arrangement** is a type of retirement plan. It is typically provided by financial institutions and it provides tax advantages for retirement savings. This type of retirement plan is best described in IRS Publication 590, Individual Retirement Arrangements (IRAs). An IRA plan falls under multiple categories. An IRA represents a type of custodial account available for the benefit of taxpayers and their beneficiaries. An IRA is also considered an individual retirement annuity; taxpayers purchase an annuity contract from a life insurance company. With this in mind, there are different types of IRA plans. The sections that follow represent the standard list on the topic.

Traditional IRA

A **Traditional IRA** offers unique benefits. Contributions are tax-deductible; transactions and earnings have no tax impact; and withdrawals are taxed as income. A traditional IRA may fall under multiple categories, which include: deductible IRA and/or non-deductible IRA. The Traditional IRA was introduced by a statute titled the Tax Reform Act of 1986.

The IRA is typically held at a custodian institution (i.e., bank or brokerage) and invested in anything that the institution allows. For example, a bank may allow an individual to use the IRA to invest in certificates of deposit (CDs). On the other hand, a brokerage firm may allow an individual to invest in stocks and mutual funds.

The Traditional IRA requires sufficient income for making contributions. It has more restrictions in withdrawals in contrast to the Roth IRA. Transactions, which include capital gains, dividends, and interest, incur no tax liability. The income limits are defined by category. For example, in 2011, the income limit for "Married Filing Jointly or Qualified Widow" was between $90,000 and $110,000. Contact the plan sponsor for more information about eligibility. You may also find information about tax implications on the IRS website.

Roth IRA

With a **Roth IRA**, an employee makes contributions with after-tax assets. Transactions that fall under a Roth IRA have no impact and fund withdrawals are typically tax-free. The Roth IRA was introduced by the Taxpayer Relief Act of 1997 and was named after Senator William V. Roth, Jr.

Concept Checker	*What are the different types of IRAs?*

A Roth IRA can contain investments in securities (stocks and bonds) through mutual funds. A Roth IRA can also be an individual retirement annuity purchased from a life insurance company. A Roth IRA offers a flexible tax structure. For example, tax breaks for a Roth IRA plan are granted for money withdrawn from the plan during retirement. Income limits are based upon three major categories: Single filers (up to $110,000), Joint filers (up to $173,000), and Married filing separately (based upon two major factors and type of contribution). The current contribution limits are $5,000 (tax year 2012) and $6,000 (for over 50 years of age).

Direct contributions to a Roth IRA may be withdrawn tax-free at any time. Taxpayers who rollover or convert their Roth IRA plans before the age of 59½ may withdraw funds with tax and penalty after the fifth year and/or seasoning period. This provision is different from the Traditional IRA plan where withdrawals are often taxed as ordinary income and penalty fees apply for early withdrawals.

Review IRS Publication 590 for more guidance on this product.

SEP IRA

The **Simplified Employee Pension Individual Retirement Arrangement**, or SEP IRA, is a type of individual retirement account in the United States. A SEP IRA is typically used by business owners providing retirement benefits. This plan is ideal for small business owners and self-employed persons. If the self-employed individual has employees, then all persons of the company must receive the same benefits under the plan. A SEP IRA account is treated as an IRA for tax purposes, which funds can be invested similarly to an IRA.

To be eligible for a SEP IRA account, employees must be at least 21 years of age; have worked for the employer a minimum of three years; and currently recently at least $500 in compensation.

A SEP IRA fund is taxed as ordinary income for qualified withdrawals after the age of 59½; in addition, contributions to this type of plan are tax-deductible, which allows the employee to lower their income tax liability for the current year.

Contributions are typically made into a Traditional IRA established in the employee's name rather than the name of the employer.

For more information about SEPs, read the IRS Publication 560 Retirement Plans for Small Business.

SIMPLE IRA

A **Savings Incentive Match Plan for Employees**, or SIMPLE, requires that an employer matches the contributions of its employees. Although similar to a 401(k) plan, the SIMPLE IRA has a lower contribution limit.

There are rules specific to a SIMPLE IRA plan. For example, eligible employers are considered those with no more than 100 total employees. An employee is not required to make a regular contribution. This type of plan requires a minimum contribution from the employer. The minimum contribution is subject to one of two conditions. The employer can match the employee's contribute dollar-for-dollar or can contribute up to three-percent of the employee's compensation. The employer may choose to contribute a flat fee of two-percent of the employee's compensation. In addition, the contribution limit for employees is approximately $11,500 and the plan includes a catch-up provision for participants over the age of 50.

Concept Checker	*What is the difference between a SEP IRA and a SIMPLE IRA?*

The SIMPLE IRA plan is typically funded with either an IRA or a 401(k) account. The SIMPLE IRA plan cannot be rolled over to a Traditional IRA before the two-year waiting period. There are also early withdrawals penalties assessed by the Internal Revenue Service. Keep in mind that a SEP IRA and a Traditional IRA cannot be rolled over into a SIMPLE IRA.

Self-Directed IRA

A **Self-Directed IRA** allows the account holder to investment on behalf of the retirement plan. Regarding a Self-Directed IRA account, there are IRS stipulations. The IRS requires that a custodian and/or trustee hold the IRA assets on behalf of the IRA owner. The trustee maintains the assets, records transactions, files the required IRS reports, issues client statements, educates the IRA owner on the rules and regulations, and performs administrative tasks. The IRA owner can invest in stocks, bonds, and mutual funds; other permissible investments under the law are allowed.

The IRS prohibits certain types of assets such as life insurance, collectibles, stamps, gems, coins, and tangible personal property. There are additional prohibited transactions that fall under the Self-Directed IRA. Here is a list of the following that are specific to an IRA.

- You can't borrow money from it.
- You can't sell property to it.
- You can't receive unreasonable compensation for managing it.
- You can't use it as a security for a loan.
- You can buy personal property with IRA funds.

Permitted investments include real estate, stocks, mortgages, franchises, partnerships, private equity, and tax liens. For the purposes of an IRA, real estate is typically defined as residential and commercial properties, farmland, raw land, new construction, property renovation, and passive rental income. An individual who purchases real estate using a self-directed IRA can have a mortgage placed against the property, which would allow the amount of cash needed to be lowered. There are restrictions under this category. The IRA or the account owner of the IRA cannot have a personal liability on the mortgage.

The categories of a business investment include partnerships, joint ventures, and private stock. The platform for the investment may involve funding to start a business or for-profit venture. Alternative investments include hedge funds, foreign stock, commodities, commercial paper, royalty rights, equipment and leases, United States T-bills, and American depository receipts.

These are the standard plans available to employees, small business, and self-employed individuals.

When developing retirement planning objectives, consider the following Retirement Planning Research Worksheet and Questionnaire.

Retirement Planning Research Worksheet and Questionnaire

Date:
Plan: 403(b)____ 401(k)_____ Roth IRA____ Traditional IRA___ SEP___ SIMPLE IRA___
Custodian: _____

Plan Investments:
Mutual Fund_____ Stock_____ Bond_____ CD_____ Other_____
Tax-deductible contribution:
                                      Yes_____No_____   _____
Withdrawals taxed as ordinary income:
                                      Yes_____No_____   _____
Withdrawals tax-free: Yes_____No_____   _____
Early withdrawal penalty: Yes_____No_____   _____
Contribution limits: Yes_____No_____   _____
Employer match: Yes_____No_____   _____
Rollovers/Conversions/Transfers:
                                      Yes_____No_____   _____
Prohibited transactions: Yes_____No_____   _____
Income limits: Yes_____No_____   _____
Distribution penalty: Yes_____No_____   _____
Waivers: Yes_____No_____   _____
Loans: Yes_____No_____   _____

Notes & Special Considerations
_____
_____

1. What are my retirement planning goals?

Goal #1: _____

Goal #2: _____

Goal #3: _____

2. What is my current budget for retirement planning investment?
_____

3. Based on my current budget, how much money can I allocate per month to creating a retirement plan?
_____

Business Planner

Start-up small business owners and self-employed individuals who have decided to hire that one employee must consider the importance of retirement planning. The following sections will help to provide insight into what you will need to consider as you grow your business.

Establish Goals

Before challenges surface, you should always prepare them. You will undoubtedly encounter some of the most common. Therefore, it is important to establish goals for retirement whether you choose a plan for yourself or for yourself and one or more employees. Create goals that will ensure you don't hinder cash flow, but that you are able to safeguard your future and the future of others.

Create an Inventory

Create an inventory of your retirement needs. Do you need an IRA plan? Which one? Do you also need a life insurance plan? Which one? These are some of the questions you must consider when developing and maintaining retirement planning objectives. Your age should always play a factor in your planning goals.

Make a Contribution

If you are self-employed and working for an employer, then contribute to the retirement savings plan with the company. Your taxes will be lower and the company may match your contribution. Compound interest and tax deferrals are two particular benefits of most company-sponsored plans. Develop a budget based upon your net income and your necessity expenses. If you are expending any type of miscellaneous expense and/or blow money, then consider allocating those funds to a retirement account.

Develop Investment Objectives

You should now know the differences between stocks, mutual funds, and bonds. You should know their value and what value they could bring to an IRA, 401(k), and/or 403(b) account. Since you know and understand these concepts, then advance to the next level by researching what types of risks are inherent in choosing certain investment products. What is inflation risk? How would it affect your investment options? How might you diversify your current portfolio to reduce risk? These are the questions you must consider when developing investment objectives.

Keep the Principal and Interest

This key point is central to maintaining your retirement planning objectives. Don't withdraw your retirement savings too early. Early withdrawals are always subject to tax implications and penalties. You lose tax benefits when you withdraw too early. Consider rolling over your contributions into an IRA account or a new employer's plan.

These are all suggestions for helping you create and manage your retirement planning objectives. These suggestions are also useful for helping you to grow your contributions. Continue to research this topic. Becoming knowledgeable in this area will continue to help you on the road to financial success.

Chapter Key Points

Retirement is the time at which a person stops working completely. Many people choose to retire at different junctures in their lives.

Employees of a public school typically have access to a retirement savings plan called a 403(b) plan. A 403(b) plan is tax-deferred and it is available to members of the clergy, non-profit entities, and employees of public schools. Taxes are not paid on the amount you contribute for the year in which you contribute the amount.

In general, annuities typically offer tax-deferred growth. They often include a death benefit where the beneficiary is paid a specific amount after the death of the policyholder. Tax is deferred particularly on earnings growth.

With a variable annuity, the insured makes a lump sum payment or a series of payments to an insurance company. Payments are made into a tax-deferred account. After the accumulation period, the insurance provider, or insurer, agrees to make periodic payments to the insured immediately or at some future date.

A **mutual fund** is a type of collective investment vehicle that pools together money from multiple investors for the purpose of purchasing securities. A **collective investment vehicle** is defined as a method of investing where investors benefit from the inherent advantages of working as a group.

A **stock fund** is defined as a fund that invests in stocks, which are called equity securities. In this regard, a stock fund is synonymous with equity fund. Stock funds are different from bond funds and money funds.

The **401(k) plan** is a type of retirement savings account in the United States. The name of the plan derives from a subsection (401(k) of the Internal Revenue Code (Title 26 of the United States Code). The 401(k) plan is a "defined contribution plan."

Companies tend to impose restrictions on Roth IRA plan withdrawals before the age of 59½, especially while the employee is currently in service. Fund withdrawals permitted before this age will be subject to an excise tax; the tax is equal to ten percent of the amount distributed.

An **Individual Retirement Account** is a type of retirement plan. It is typically provided by financial institutions and it provides tax advantages for retirement savings.

Chapter Key Terms

Accumulation period: term refers to a period of time when the annuitant, the person entitled to receive benefits from the annuity, makes contributions (to the annuity) for the purpose of building up the value of the annuity account.

Administrative fee: term refers to what the insurer deducts to for record-keeping purposes.

Annuitant: term refers to the person entitled to receive benefits from an annuity. Annuitization phase: term refers to when the annuitant receives guaranteed payments for a specific period of time.

Asset allocation funds: term refers to a type of fund that splits investments between multiple options, which include growth stocks, money market funds, and income stocks/bonds.

Balanced fund: term refers to a type of fund that invests in bonds for income and stocks for appreciation.

Bond fund: term refers to a type of fund that invests in bonds and related debt securities.

Capital asset: term refers to stocks, bonds, and/or real estate.

Capital gain: term refers to profit that result from the disposing of a capital asset.

Capital gain tax: term refers to a type of tax assessed when the amount received from the disposition exceeds the price of purchase.

Catch-up contribution: term refers to a provision within a Roth IRA that allows people over the age of 50 to make additional contributions to their 401(k) plan and related individual retirement accounts.

Collective investment vehicle: term refers to a method of investing where investors benefit from the inherent advantages of working as a group.

Corporate bond: term refers to a type of bond that is issued by a corporation.

Death benefit: term refers to as the amount on a life insurance policy that will be payable to a beneficiary when the annuitant dies.

Debt fund: see *Bond Fund*.

Equity-income fund: see *Income Fund*.

Equity-indexed annuity: see *Indexed Annuity*.

Fixed annuity: term refers to a type of contract that an insured (i.e., policyholder) has with an insurance company. The insurer guarantees that the insured will receive fixed periodic payments.

Fixed index annuity: see *Indexed Annuity*.

Forecasting: term refers to market timing or stock picking.

Goodwill: term refers to intangible assets that provide a "prudent value."

Government bond: term refers to a type of bond that represents the safest form of investment.

Growth fund: term refers to a type of fund that invests in the stocks of companies that are experiencing rapid growth.

Hedge fund: term refers to a type of fund that often trades stocks to reduce the risk of investments.

Income fund: term that refers to a type of fund that invests in the stocks of companies that have a long history of paying dividends.

Indexed annuity: term refers to a special type of contracts between an insurance company and the insured.

Index fund: term refers to a type of mutual fund.

Individual Retirement Account: term refers to a type of retirement plan.

Institutional money fund: term refers to a type of fund that requires a high minimum investment, but offers a low expense share class.

IRA: acronym stands for Individual Retirement Account.

Money market fund: term refers to an open-end mutual fund that invests in short-term debt securities, which include U.S. Treasury bills and commercial paper.

Mortality and expense risk charge: term refers to a percentage used in calculating a rate per year (1.25%).

Mortgage bond: term refers to a type of bond that is issued and/or guaranteed by government agencies, which include the Federal National Mortgage Association (Fannie Mae), the Federal Home Loan Mortgage Corporation (Freddie Mac), and the Government National Mortgage Association (Ginnie Mae).

Mutual fund: term refers to a type of collective investment vehicle that pools together money from multiple investors for the purpose of purchasing securities.

Ordinary income: term refers to income that is other than capital gain. See *Capital Gain*.

Passive investing: see *Passive Management*.

Passive management: term refers to indexes that typically rely on a computer model that requires little or no human input.

Payout phase: term refers to the period of time when the insurer makes payments to the annuitant.

Retail money fund: term refers to a type of product offered primarily to individuals.

Retirement: term refers to the time at which a person stops working completely.

Roth IRA: term refers to a type of retirement savings plan where an employee makes contributions with after-tax assets.

Savings Incentive Match Plan for Employees: term refers to a plan that requires an employer to match the contributions of its employees.

Sector fund: term refers to a type of fund that invests in a particular area of industry.

Self-Directed IRA: term refers to a type of retirement savings plan that allows the account holder to investment on behalf of the retirement plan.

SEP IRA: acronym stands for Simplified Employee Pension Individual Retirement Arrangement.

Simple Indexed Annuity: see *Indexed Annuity*.

SIMPLE IRA: acronym stands for Savings Incentive Match Plan for Employees.

Simplified Employee Pension Individual Retirement Arrangement: term refers to a type of individual retirement account in the United States used by small business owners and self-employed persons.

Stock fund: term refers to a fund that invests in stocks, which are called equity securities.

Surrender charge: term refers to a fee that the insurance policyholder must pay upon cancelling the policy.

Surrender period: term refers to a time when the charge to the annuity account declines gradually over a period of years.

Traditional IRA: term refers to a type of IRA account where contributions are tax-deductible; transactions and earnings have no tax impact; and withdrawals are taxed as income.

Underlying fund expenses: term refers to charges imposed by mutual funds within the variable annuity.

Value fund: term refers to a type of fund that invests in value stocks.

Variable annuity: term refers to when the insured makes a lump sum payment or a series of payments to an insurance company.

GROUP WORK PROMPT

As a group, visit the IRS website. Review the information for SEP IRA and SIMPLE IRA. Take notes on the information based upon your own retirement planning objectives. After this process, create an essay outline of how you would begin to synthesize the information into a cohesive document. Begin the project in class and finish it up at home. Dedicate a section to each group member. The paper would range between 10 and 12 pages. As a group, create both the introduction and conclusion paragraphs.

HOMEWORK EXERCISE

As an individual, research the major categories that fall under IRA. Create an essay comparing and contrasting the categories. Your paper should not exceed 10 double-spaced pages.

HELPFUL WEBSITES

U.S. Securities and Exchange Commission: Evaluating Your Retirement Options
http://www.sec.gov/investor/pubs/teacheroptions.htm

United States Department of Labor: Top 10 Ways to Prepare for Retirement
http://www.dol.gov/ebsa/publications/10_ways_to_prepare.html

HELPFUL RESOURCES

IRS Pub 560 Retirement Plans for Small Business
IRS Pub 590 Individual Retirement Arrangements
IRS Form 5305 SEP Agreement

Assessment

1. What is the 403(b) plan? Describe its features, investment options, giving special attention to "variable annuity."

2. What are the different types of mutual funds that fall under the category of retirement savings planning? List and describe at least three.

3. What is the 401(k) plan? What are the tax benefits? What is the policy for pre-tax and after-tax contributions? Explain.

4. What is IRA, SEP IRA, and SIMPLE IRA? Provide brief definitions.

IRA

SEP IRA

SIMPLE IRA

CHAPTER 16

Estate Planning

Learning Objectives

- Define estate planning.
- List the types of estate planning options.
- Define living will.
- Summarize the chapter case study.

WHAT IS ESTATE PLANNING?

Estate planning is a type of process where an individual anticipates and arranges for the disposal of an **estate**, which is defined as the net worth of a person at any point in time. Estate planning eliminates uncertainties involved in probate administration and maximizes the value of an estate by reducing its taxes and related expenses. A guardian is often designated for children and other beneficiaries of an estate.

Estate planning involves multiple factors. It includes the creation of wills, trusts, beneficiary designations, powers of appointment, and rights to property ownership. It also involves the assignment of gifts and powers of attorney. The multiple processes of estate planning is subject to litigation and media coverage and attorneys that provide services within this field often advise their clients to create a **living will**, which is a legal document within which an individual outlines his or her wishes regarding the continuation of medical treatments. An individual also provides guidelines for how to be buried or cremated.

It is important to consider and develop estate planning objectives, particularly for tax purposes. Individuals can set up a charitable remainder trust or a qualified personal residence trust where the trust owns the personal residence and it is left to the beneficiaries (i.e., children) without the incurring of estate tax. In addition, since the proceeds of a life insurance policy are not taxed as income, individuals can use a life insurance trust to pay for estate taxes. Estate planning is important for the sole purpose of mediating potential conflicts.

Business owners that want to enter the field of estate planning must consider various certifications to ensure they have comprehensive knowledge of the legal, financing, and accounting services required to provide solutions for individuals, business owners, and high net-worth individuals. With this in mind, most estate planners have a background in law, accounting, and/or finance.

Developing a sound estate plan will require an individual to research products that are beneficial, offer tax advantages, and help to meet financial goals.

TYPES OF ESTATE PLANNING

There are different types of estate planning that individuals should know as they plan the next years of their lives. The following sections provide insight into how to develop a sound estate plan.

Will

A **will** is a written declaration, or testament, by a person, the testator, who names one or more persons to manage the estate and provide for the transfer of property. The **testator** is defined as the person who has written and executed a last will and testament that takes effect at the testator's death. A will typically provides guidelines for how to dispose of personal property, but may also be used as a tool for creating a **trust**, which is defined as a relationship whereby real, personal, tangible, or intangible property is held by one party that will serve to benefit another.

Types of Wills

There are different types of wills. They include the following:

- **Noncupative:** These are wills that are oral or dictated. They are typically limited to sailors or military personnel.

- **Holographic:** These are wills that are written by the hand of the testator.

- **Self-proved:** These are wills that include affidavits of subscribing witnesses. The purpose of this type of will is to avoid probate.

- **Notarial:** This is a will in public form. It is prepared by a civil-law notary.

- **Mystic:** These are wills that are sealed until death.

- **Serviceman's Will:** This is a will of a person in who is an active-duty military servicemen.

- **Reciprocal/Mirror/Mutual/Husband and Wife Wills:** These are wills made by two or more parties (typically between spouses) that mirror provisions that are in favor of the other.

- **Unsolemn Will:** This is a will in which the executor is named.

- **Will in Solemn Form:** This is a will that is signed by both the testator and the witnesses.

With some wills there are constraints on the disposition of property. For example, with a holographic will, the testator outlines his or her wishes by hand. A distinctive feature of a holographic will is that it doesn't have to be witnessed, which may make it difficult for a prospective beneficiary to prove that the testator left property in the will. These constraints also plague the noncupative will where a beneficiary might find it difficult to prove even the existence of a will, let alone the wishes that the testator desired to leave property. With this in mind, there are restrictions that govern the creation of wills.

Restrictions and Requirements

In general, there is no legal requirement that a testator be required to create a will. The general consensus is that if someone has a will, it helps to provide guidelines for how the person wants the assets of the estate treated in terms of disposition and assignment of responsibility. Although there is no legal requirement for someone to create a will, there are, however, restrictions on who can create one and on the format and structure of a will.

Age of Majority

For example, the person creating the will must be over the **age of majority**, which is defined as the threshold of adulthood. It is typically conceptualized in law as a legal and/or statutory principle. The age is the point at which a minor is no longer considered to be a child and is able to assume control over their own person, their actions, and their decisions. This age terminates the legal control and legal responsibility of the parent and/or guardian. Most countries set the age of majority at 18 years (of age).

Sound Mind

In addition, the person creating the will must be of **sound mind**. This means that the person must have the mental capacity to draft his or her own will without the necessary services of a lawyer. In other words, the person should possess the mental capacity to compose one or more sentences. In addition, sound mind refers to sanity. In terms of law and general knowledge, a person is sane if he or she is rational.

With this in mind, the testator must be able mentally to identify himself or herself as the maker of the will and attest to the fact that he or she is making the will. In legal terms, this is called publication. The maker of the will usually references these common words: "last will and testament."

If there are any previous wills, the new will the maker creates must include a revocation clause that essentially revokes any and all previous wills and related **codicil**, which is a separate document that amends a previously executed will; a codicil doesn't replace a will. Instead, it amends it and typically conforms to the same legal standards that are specific to the creation of a will.

Without a reference to the revocation of a previous will, then by default, any subsequent document will revoke one or more previous wills. In addition, the maker of the will must demonstrate the mental capacity, or sound mind, when it comes to the issue of disposing of personal property. There are further implications for understanding the creation and revocation of previous wills. For more information about this issue in the law, refer to your state's guidelines on estate planning and probate law.

Signature and Witnesses

The testator must sign the will. In addition, he or she must date the will to prevent any future conflict with the law. The will must be signed and dated in front of witnesses that do not have an interest in the will. In other words, the witnesses cannot be beneficiaries. Some local jurisdictions provide insight into what determines a valid will. In fact, there are some states such as Pennsylvania that do not require two witnesses. On the other hand, Louisiana requires two witnesses and the document must be notarized by a licensed notary public. In terms of holographic wills, where the testator handwrites his or her own will, witnesses are not required.

When it comes to a beneficiary receiving property under the will, there are some restrictions. A beneficiary who will be the recipient of the testator's personal property and who is also a witness may find the process difficult. Some jurisdictions may disallow the status of a beneficiary-witness, thus preventing the individual from receiving under the will. On the other hand, the same jurisdiction may invalidate the beneficiary as a witness. A testator's signature is placed at the end of the will. Any text following the signature is typically ignored. However, if the material is significant, then the whole will may be invalidated. References to the beneficiaries must be clearly stated in-text. Refer to your state's guidelines for more insight.

Living Will

A **living will** is a type of legal document that outlines a person's wishes regarding medical treatments. A living will is referred to synonymously as an **advance directive**, a **health care directive**, or a **physician's directive**. The living will represents a set of written instructions where the person specifies what type of actions he or she wants for their health in the event that he or she is not able to make any decisions.

In the living will, the person appoints someone, who by law is called an agent, to make medical treatment decisions. In this regard, the living will is considered an advance directive, where the agent is left instructions for what to do. There are additional requirements and documents that support a living will.

Power of Attorney

Another form supports the living will and provides authorization duties for the agent. This form, called **power of attorney**, or **health care proxy**, is a type of written authorization for an appointed person to represent and/act on someone's behalf. The appointed person would have power of attorney to make decisions regarding personal, business, and legal matters.

Within this context, the person authorizing another is called the **principal** and may be referred to synonymously as the grantor and/or donor. The person authorized to act is called the **agent**, or attorney. Some common law jurisdictions refer to the agent as an **attorney-in-fact**, which means that the person acts as a fiduciary to the principal. A **fiduciary** is defined as a legal and ethical relationship of trust between two parties. The fiduciary must be ethical in his or her dealings with the principal. If the fiduciary is receiving payment from the principal, then he or she would typically agree to terms within a contract, which is separate from the power of attorney itself. The contract is kept private between the attorney-in-fact and the principal. Only the power of attorney is shown to interested parties, if requested.

Structure and Requirements

The person who creates a power of attorney is called a **grantor**. With this in mind, the person must have the mental capacity to make the power valid. If a grantor, or donor, loses mental capacity to grant duties to the agent, and this happens after the power of attorney has been created, then the agent would lose the power to make decisions and the power of attorney would no longer be effective.

However, before a grantor becomes incapacitated, he or she may provide instructions and sign a power of attorney granting rights to the agent to make decisions after he or she becomes incapacitated. This type of power is referred to as **durable power of attorney**, a type of document where the grantor specifies that the power of attorney is effective even if the grantor becomes incapacitated.

In other cases, if a grantor does not have the capacity to execute a power of attorney, then the only options for the other party would be to request that the court impose a **conservatorship** or a **guardianship**. These are types of orders that are put into place for severely mental individuals who cannot carry out basic daily and life functions without the assistance of another.

It is important for an individual to create a living will, granting another person the right and/or power to make decisions on his or her behalf. Without a living and a power of attorney, an individual's wishes regarding medical treatments would be challenged and the court would have to decide what is in the best interest of the party in question. Terri Schiavo is one such person who did not have a living will on record. Terri Schiavo's collapse in her St. Petersburg, Florida home; subsequent brain damage leading to a two and half months coma; and permanent diagnosis (vegetative state) sparked a national controversy regarding the medical wishes and the decision of Michael Schiavo to terminate his wife's life support. Following is a summary of the events of the case.

Case Study:
The Terri Schiavo Case

The Terri Schiavo case was a legal struggle that lasted from 1998 to 2005. At issue was the determination of the court to prolong Terri Schiavo's life support while in a **persistent vegetative state**, which is defined as a disorder of consciousness. Patients with PVS are severely brain damaged; they are essentially in a state of partial **arousal**, which means that a patient is physiologically and psychologically awake and can react to stimuli but has no sense of true awareness. Arousal includes the activation of a certain part of the brain stem, the autonomic nervous system, and the endocrine system which leads to increased heart rate and blood pressure, sensory alertness, and readiness to respond, but the patient isn't aware that he or she is actively contributing to the operation of these systems. A diagnosis of vegetative state, or VS, is given by a doctor (to a patient) after four weeks. However, a diagnosis of PVS is typically given after the patient has been in a persistent vegetative state for at least one year.

In the case of Terri Schiavo, Michael Schiavo petitioned the Sixth Circuit Court of Florida (Pinellas County) in 1998 to remove his wife's feeding tube pursuant to a Florida statute (Florida Statutes Section 765.401[3]). Because Terri Schiavo did not have a living will, a trial was held on her behalf to determine her "end-of-life wishes." Michael Schiavo requested to be Terri's legal guardian on June 19, 1990, which the latter's parents did not dispute. However, when Michael Schiavo petitioned to remove Terri Schiavo's feeding tube in May of 1998, this request caused her parents to intervene and request a court-appointed guardian.

Richard Pearse enters the case as a second **guardian ad litem** (GAL), which is a type of person who is typically appointed in under-age children cases and who serves as the voice of the child. Pearse concluded on December 29, 1998 that Terri Schiavo was, in fact, in a persistent vegetative state, based upon the diagnoses of her doctors, and as defined by the Florida statute. Pearse also concluded that because Terri's husband and parents believed they had a vested interest in her estate, there existed a conflict of interest.

The case resulted in Michael Schiavo winning a malpractice suit, receiving an award, and Terri's parents demanding that Michael share some of the malpractice money with them. The seven-year case generated many years of controversy and activism. Schiavo's ashes where finally buried in Florida.

The case could have been avoided had Terri created a living will.

The importance of providing instructions for how you want your loved ones to make medical decisions should be of great priority. An individual of sound mind now should consider the future with regard to not only the "right to die wish," but also when it comes to organ donation. Therefore, it becomes vitally important for everyone to create a will, a living will, and assign power of attorney rights.

With this in mind, in some jurisdictions, a power of attorney may be oral. If it is witnessed, it will hold up in court as if it is in writing. However, there are some laws that require the power of attorney to be in writing. For example, hospitals, banks, nursing homes, and the IRS require the power of attorney to be in writing.

There are additional structures and requirements for laws that govern the power of attorney. The **equal dignity rule** is a legal principle that requires authorization for one person, who is typically the agent and who performs a certain act on behalf of the grantor, to conduct one or more acts with the same formality required for all the acts. For example, the grantor may authorize the agent to sell the grantor's property. The equal dignity rule requires a contract for the sale of the property to be in writing. The contract is required under the Statute of Frauds. When it comes to property, the signing of a sales contract and a deed must be in writing. Because of the law, the authorization for the agent to sign the sales contract and the deed must be in writing. The power of attorney that requires the execution of a deed must be given by deed.

Trusts

A **trust** is a common law principle that outlines a relationship between parties and property. One party holds property for the benefit of another party. The trust is created by a **settlor**, a person who transfers some or all of his or her property to a **trustee**, who holds the property in trust for the benefit of the beneficiaries. The trustee may be a natural person or a company. The trustee may also be a public body. There may be more than one trustee. Within the context of self-declared trusts, one person functions as both settlor and trustee. They are essentially the same person.

The trustee of a trust has legal title to the trust property. However, the beneficiaries of the trust have equitable title to the property. With this in mind, the trustee functions as a fiduciary to the beneficiaries, who are technically and legal the beneficial owners of the trust property. Within this context, the beneficiary may be a single person or multiple people. The settlor may also be a beneficiary.

The trustee governs the trust under the terms for which it was created. The terms are written down in a typical trust instrument called a deed. The terms of the trust specify the property and how it is to be transferred into the trust. The terms also specify the beneficiaries, spell out the duties and powers of the trustee, and reference local law. The duties of a trustee typically include *powers of investment*, which refers to the investment of some properties into securities and the assurance of a balanced portfolio; *powers to vary the interests of the beneficiaries*; and *powers of appointment*, which means that the trustee appoints or gives an asset of the trust to the proper beneficiary. A trust is also governed by local law and the trustee must administer the trust according to its terms.

Creation and Purpose

A trust can be created by a written trust agreement, initiated by the settlor; an oral declaration; the will of a decedent, which is called a testamentary trust; a **testamentary trust** is typically the product of a will that takes effect upon the death of the testator; and a court order.

The purposes of a trust are multiple. Some settlors create a trust for privacy concerns. Because a will is public, the terms of a trust are not subject to the same scrutiny. The purpose of a trust may include spendthrift protection, which includes protecting the beneficiaries from mishandling any items of the trust. A common purpose of a trust is to fulfill an estate planning objective. Additional purposes of a trust include asset protections, the setup of a pension plan where the employer is the settlor, and corporate structuring. When contemplating the provisions of a trust document, consider evaluating a standard sample trust document. This will provide you with insight into the necessary clauses.

Types

There are different types of trusts. For example, a **constructive trust** is a type of trust imposed by the law as an equitable remedy. With this type of trust, a wrongdoer has illegally acquired property under the trust and cannot be allowed to keep it. With a **dynasty trust**, or generation-skipping trust, assets are passed down to the grandchildren of the grantor and not directly to the grantor's children. With this method, the grantor avoids estate taxes. An **express trust** is defined as the settlor simply expressing the intention to create a trust. The United States Statute of Frauds requires that an express trust be put into writing. An **inter vivos trust** (living trust) is defined as a settlor who creates a trust at the time he or she is still living. A **revocable trust** can be amended, altered, or revoked by the settlor. In contrast, an **irrevocable trust** cannot be amended or revised; the terms of the trust must be fully executed and completed. An **offshore trust** is a type of instrument where the trust is resident in a jurisdiction other than the resident of the settlor. Lastly, a **unit trust** is defined as the right of the beneficiaries, or unitholders, to possess a certain share (called units) of the trust and request that the trustee pay money out of the trust in direct proportion to the units they hold.

Tax Considerations

There are tax consequences regarding trusts. For example, if an individual forms an irrevocable trust during his or her lifetime, then he or she can expect to pay a gift tax of approximately 45 percent. The gift tax is considered a progressive tax. However, an irrevocable trust does not incur gift taxes. With this type of trust, the ownership of property within the trust is never transferred and the main beneficiary is typically the grantor. In other words, according to federal law, it is impossible for a grantor to gift something to himself or herself.

When a trust is created for the benefit of a charity and the grantor or a stated beneficiary, then two types of tax benefits apply. For one, the **Charitable Lead**

Trust (CLT) reduces the taxable income of the beneficiaries. The settlor donates a portion of the income earned through the trust to one or more charities. After a specific period of time has passed, the remainder of the income is transferred to the beneficiaries.

With a **Charitable Remainder Trust**, the donor (or grantor) donates property or money to a charity, uses the property while living, and receives income from it. The beneficiaries of the trust receive income, but the charity receives the principal after a period has passed. With this type of trust, the grantor avoids standard capital gains tax on the donated assets. The grantor also gets an income tax deduction on the remainder interest earned by the trust; the grantor receives the deduction at fair market value.

Lastly, the IRS allows for a marital deduction in relation to trust law. A spouse that transfers property to another spouse will not incur taxes, because U.S. tax laws allow an unlimited marital deduction. The marital deduction falls under both marital trusts and property in trusts vehicles.

Property Ownership

There are three major types of property ownership that typically fall under trust law. They are as follows:

- Joint tenancy with rights of survivorship
- Tenancy in common
- Tenancy by the entirety

With **joint tenancy**, also referred to as concurrent estate or co-tenancy, property is owned by one or more parties at a single time. When more than one person owns the same property, then property law considers each person to function as co-owners, co-tenants, and/or joint tenants. Multiple jurisdictions refer to joint tenancy as **joint tenancy with right of survivorship**, which means that upon the death of one of the owners (or tenants), ownership of the property passes to the surviving tenants who are also called successors. Local bodies treat joint tenancy as the same as **tenancy in common**, which is defined by law as one or more owners owning a distinct share of the same property. In essence, with tenancy in common, all co-owners own equal shares.

United States property law determines the rights of the parties that are joint tenants of a property. Each party has a right to sell his or her interest in the property to others. Each party also has the right to will the property to their devisees. Lastly, each owner of the property has the right to sever their interest in the property. Because local laws can vary, it is important to consult an attorney for more help with this legal principle.

A tenancy in common owner owns a percentage of the undivided property. The property is typically not divided into units or apartments. The deed shows the ownership percentage. Each owner has rights to the property, which may include dwelling rights. If a co-owner wants to dwell on the property, then each owner would sign a written contract called a Tenancy in Common Agreement. Tenancy in common is typically used for co-owners that are not married and have contributed amounts to the purchase of the property. What is unique about this type of ownership is that tenants in common do have right of survivorship. This means that if one of the tenant in common dies, the interest in the property of that tenant will become a part of his or her estate and pass by inheritance to the tenant's heirs. This is usually outlined in a will.

Tenancy by the entirety is a type of concurrent estate where real property is held by a husband and wife. Each party owns the whole of the property, which is undivided. Right of survivorship is typically coupled with tenancy by the entirety to ensure that one party receives the decedent's share. Tenancy by the entirety offers unique credit protection features. An individual spouse's creditor cannot attach to and sell the interest of a debtor spouse. However, the creditor of the couple may, in fact, attach and sell the interest in the property owned. For this reason, a tenancy by the entirety can only be created by married people. Either party cannot sell his or her interest in the party without the consent of the other. Upon the death of either party, the surviving spouse receives the deceased spouse's interest, not the heirs. This is where right of survivorship is central. Keep in mind that a tenancy by the entirety cannot automatically change to a joint tenancy or a tenancy in common by one or more parties conveying a property. The couple would have to divorce, annul the marriage, or amend the title to the property to make the tenancy by the entirety of none effect.

Reverse Mortgage Tips

Reverse mortgage has become the new buzzword for retirement planning. Senior citizens, recently retired, and the elderly are choosing this option as an opportunity to receive cash money drawn against their homes. But just like any idea, there are drawbacks. Homeowners must consider all of the alternatives before choosing to enter a reverse mortgage agreement with a financial institution.

A **reverse mortgage** is a type of loan that is available to homeowners who are of retirement age. The loan enables the homeowner to have access to a portion of their home's equity. Because a reverse mortgage is a loan, the homeowner can draw the mortgage principal in a lump sum. The homeowner will in turn receive monthly payments over a specific period of time, typically over their lifetime. The homeowner receives the mortgage principal as a revolving line of credit.

In legal terms, the reverse mortgage is a type of **equity release**, or lifetime mortgage, which means that the homeowner retains the use of their house. The house represents capital value. While retaining use of the house, the homeowner also receives a lump sum which is considered a steady stream of income. The amount the homeowner receives is based upon the value of the home.

There is a drawback. The income-provider, which is typically the bank, requires the homeowner to repay the loaned amount at a later date, usually when the homeowner dies. In essence, equity release is useful for elderly persons who are not able to leave a large estate for their heirs when they die. For this reason, there are different types of equity release arrangements. They are as follows:

- **Lifetime mortgage:** This is a mortgage loan that is secured against the borrower's home. Compounded interest is assessed and added to the capital; this happens throughout the term of the loan. The loan is repaid by the sale of the property when the borrower dies or moves out. While living in the home the borrower retains legal title to the home and also is responsible for the costs of ownership.

- **Interest only:** This is a mortgage. The capital is repaid when the borrower dies. The borrower is responsible for making interest payments while still living in the property.

- **Home reversion:** With this option, the borrower agrees to sell all or part of their home to a third party. The third party is typically a reversion company or an individual. Part or all of the borrower's home now belongs to someone else. The borrower receives either regular income or a cash lump sum or both. The borrower can continue to live in the home.

- **Shared appreciation mortgage:** The borrower receives a loan from the lender. The loan is a capital sum. In return for the loan, the lender receives a share of the increase in the property's value. The borrower reserves the right to live in the property until his or her death. Lenders typically receive a smaller share of the owner's property.

- **Home income plan:** This is a type of lifetime mortgage. The capital is used to provide income. With this plan, an annuity is purchased and provided by the lender.

There are advantages to an equity release, or lifetime mortgage. This type of mortgage provides tax-free cash or a steady income (annuity). It reduces the amount of inheritance tax assessed against your estate. The borrower is protected against housing market downturns by receiving a "no negative equity guarantee" (NNEG). Borrowers can refinance their mortgages as a result of low interest rates.

On the other hand, there are disadvantages to a lifetime mortgage. Receiving a lifetime mortgage will decrease the amount your family can inherit when you die. In addition, this type of mortgage prevents you from donating shares of your assets to charity.

Therefore, understanding the difference between a reverse mortgage and a conventional mortgage is important. With a conventional mortgage, the homeowner makes an amortized payment to the lender. With each payment, the equity in the home increases by the amount of the principal. When the borrower pays the mortgage in full, he or she is released from the mortgage.

In the case of a reverse mortgage, the homeowner receives the equivalent of a line of credit that is revolving. The borrower doesn't have to make payments of principal or interest. The interest accrues and is added to the mortgage balance. Title to the property remains with the homeowners and the property can be disposed of as the homeowners wish. However, the property is also encumbered by the unpaid loan under the mortgage.

A reverse mortgage may be refinanced provided enough equity is present in the home. In addition, a reverse mortgage line is recorded at a higher dollar amount than the amount disbursed at loan closing. It is important for borrowers to consult a reverse mortgage specialist for help.

Eligibility

Borrowers in the United States must be 62 years old to qualify for a reverse mortgage. In addition, borrowers must occupy the property and it must be considered their principal residence. In addition to the age requirement, the current mortgage on the home must be low enough to offset the reverse mortgage proceeds.

Borrowers are not subject to minimum income or credit requirements because payments are not required on the mortgage. Borrowers may use the proceeds from the loan at their own discretion; loan proceeds are not subject to income tax payment. Credit qualification is not part of the process. However, if a borrower is undergoing bankruptcy, he or she would have to obtain court approval prior to loan closing.

A reverse mortgage typically follows FHA guidelines. With this in mind, standard family dwellings, FHA-approved condominiums and PUDs, and manufactured housing qualify under the FHA guidelines.

Eligible applicants must complete an approved counseling course before starting the loan process with an FHA/HUD reverse mortgage. Counseling is available at low or no cost to the borrower. The counseling process safeguards the borrower and ensures that he or she completely understands the reverse mortgage process. The reverse mortgage counselor will explain legal ramifications and financial obligations. The borrower receives a certificate of completion, which makes him or her eligible to enter the loan process.

Loan Size

There are maximum lending limits for reverse mortgages, but they vary by county. In total, a reverse mortgage loan cannot exceed $625,500. A reverse mortgage for a home over the maximum limit is called a **jumbo reverse mortgage**. Jumbo reverse mortgages are considered **proprietary reverse mortgages**. These are mortgages that are structured and supported by private companies. Owners of higher-valued homes are typically offered larger loan amounts, but the loans are uninsured by the FHA. The fees for these loans are also higher.

The amount the borrower will receive is determined by age, the lesser value of the home or the lending limit of the county, and the interest rate the borrower selects. The primary factors for determining the amount of the loan include the following: appraised value, interest rate, age of the borrower, payment type (line of credit, lump sum, or monthly payment). These factors are summed up and/or support the Total Annual Lending Cost (TALC), which is the single rate that includes all of the loan costs.

Costs

There are standard costs associated with a reverse mortgage. The costs of private sector loans tend to be higher and they tend to exceed certain types of mortgages. The exact costs of a reverse mortgage loan are based upon the program of the lending institution.

Scenario

To give you an idea of what it will cost for an FHA-insured Home Equity Conversion Mortgage (HECM), these are the costs a prospective borrower can expect to pay:

- **Mortgage Insurance Premium** (MIP): This is typically 2% of the appraised value.

- **Origination Fee:** This is dependent upon the home's appraised value. For homes that are appraised under $125,000, the borrower can expect to pay an origination fee of $2,500. However, for homes appraised over $125,000, the borrower will have to pay 2% of the first $200,000. The borrower would have to pay an additional 1% of the value that is over $200,000. The value is capped at $6,000.

- **Title Insurance:** Title insurance varies by state and county.

- **Title, Attorney, County Recording Fees:** Costs under this category vary by state and county.

- **Real Estate Appraisal:** To receive a real estate appraisal, the borrower will be responsible for paying between $300 and $500.

- **Survey:** The costs for a survey range from $300 to $500. In some counties, it is required.

There are additional costs. For example, borrowers can expect to pay a monthly service charge which is added to the balance of the loan. An annual Mortgage Insurance Premium is assessed and is equal to 1.25% of the mortgage balance. The MIP is paid at settlement.

Interest Rate

The interest rate for a reverse mortgage is determined by program, but it is typically below any other available interest rate within the standard mortgage marketplace. A reverse mortgage loan is secured by the home itself and backed by HUD.

Some institutions offer adjustable interest rates. Rates are adjusted on a monthly, semi-annual, or annual rate. In addition, lenders now offer the FHA HECM reverse mortgages, which provide fixed rates. The downside to a fixed rate reverse mortgage is that the cash proceeds are limited and the borrower must take out the entire amount at loan closing. States and local jurisdictions offer reverse mortgages, but these programs are typically restrictive. Consult your local bodies for more information.

Taxes and Insurance

A reverse mortgage borrower is responsible for costs related to taxes and insurance and both must be kept current throughout the term of the loan. The funds for taxes and insurance are not paid into escrow; they must be paid directly by the homeowner. A lapse in payment for each will result in a default on the reverse mortgage.

Monies received from a reverse mortgage are considered a loan advance. According to the IRS, a loan advance is not considered income. Therefore, the loan advance of a reverse mortgage is not taxable. For more information on the tax consequences of reverse mortgages, review the American Bar Association guide to reverse mortgages; it highlights the responsibilities of borrowers receiving Medicaid, Social Security Insurance, and public benefits.

Due Date

The reverse mortgage loan becomes due essentially when the borrower dies, sells the house, moves out of the house for more than 12 consecutive months, and/or fails to keep the taxes and insurance current. When the mortgage becomes due, the borrower and/or the heirs of the borrower's property have the option to refinance the home in order to keep it. They also have the option of selling it and/or cashing out remaining equity. They may also turn the home over to the lender.

When the mortgage due, lenders may grant a borrower an extension, giving them up to a year to make a decision about refinancing. However, once the property is turned over to the lender, the borrower and/or heirs no longer have a claim to the property or the equity. The lender has no recourse against the borrower, but only against the property. Thus, the reverse mortgage falls under the non-recourse limit, which characterizes a type of debt that is secured by collateral (i.e., real property), but the borrower is not personally liable.

Business Planner

Small business owners that want to enter the industry of estate planning are typically attorneys who have had some experience with bankruptcy law, property law, and estate planning. They are also financial advisors. Most estate planners also have received some designation that solidifies their experience in the industry. With this in mind, small business entrepreneurs should consider becoming a certified estate planner. Here are a few designations to consider.

Chartered Trust and Estate Planner (CTEP)
A Chartered Trust and Estate Planner is a type of designation offered by the certifying body American Academy of Financial Management. Professionals who earn the CTEP must first have at least three years of experience in estate planning or trust creation. Candidates for the designation must also possess an undergraduate and/or graduate degree in finance, tax, accounting, financial services, or law. Candidates may also possess a CPA license, an MBA, a MS, a PhD, or a JD from an accredited school. Candidates must have completed five approved courses and meet annual continuing education requirements. To receive the designation, candidates must complete the full certification training course.

Accredited Estate Planner (AEP)
The Accredited Estate Planner is awarded by the National Association of Estate Planners and Councils (NAEPC). Candidates for the AEP designation must possess the following:

- **License and Certification:** Licensed to practice law and/or practice as a Certified Public Accountant (CPA); or possess one or more of the following designations: Chartered Life Underwriter (CLU), Chartered Financial Consultant (ChFC), Certified Financial Planner (CFP), or Certified Trust & Financial Advisor (CTFA).

- **Activities:** Engaged in estate planning activities as one or more of the following: an attorney, an accountant, a life insurance professional, a financial planner, or as a trust officer.

- **Experience:** Completed a minimum of five years of experience in estate planning and estate planning activities.

- **Graduate Coursework:** Completed two graduate courses offered through The American College.

- **Continuing Education:** Completed at least 30 hours of continuing education coursework within the past 24 months; fifteen of the 30 hours must represent estate planning coursework.

For more information about the AEP designation, visit the NAEPC website.

Certified Trust and Financial Advisor (CTFA)

The Certified Trust and Financial Advisor designation is awarded by the American Bankers Association (ABA). The designation is awarded in conjunction with the Institute of Certified Bankers. Requirements for the CTFA designation include three years of experience in wealth management, completion of an approved wealth management training program, letter of recommendation, ethics statement, and completion of at least 45 credits of continuing education every one to three years.

Related Wealth Management Certifications

There are additional certifications that a small business owner may complete. These include: Chartered Wealth Manager, Chartered Asset Manager, Chartered Portfolio Manager, and Chartered Compliance Manager. Each designation requires breadth of knowledge including law, accounting, and finance as well as experience in the field. To be sure, review "The Importance of Estate and Contingency Planning" for more information about the field.

Chapter Key Points

Estate planning is a type of process where an individual anticipates and arranges for the disposal of an **estate**, which is defined as the net worth of a person at any point in time.

The multiple processes of estate planning is subject to litigation and media coverage and attorneys that provide services within this field often advise their clients to create a **living will**, which is a legal document within which an individual outlines his or her wishes regarding the continuation of medical treatments.

A **will** is a written declaration, or testament, by a person, the testator, who names one or more persons to manage the estate and provide for the transfer of property.

In general, there is no legal requirement that a testator be required to create a will. The general consensus is that if someone has a will, it helps to provide guidelines for how the person wants the assets of the estate treated in terms of disposition and assignment of responsibility.

In addition, the person creating the will must be of **sound mind**. This means that the person must have the mental capacity to draft his or her own will without the necessary services of a lawyer.

A **living will** is a type of legal document that outlines a person's wishes regarding medical treatments. A living will is referred to synonymously as an **advance directive**, a **health care directive**, or a **physician's directive**. The living will represents a set of written instructions where the person specifies what type of actions he or she wants for their health in the event that he or she is not able to make any decisions.

A **trust** is a common law principle that outlines a relationship between parties and property. One party holds property for the benefit of another party.

A **reverse mortgage** is a type of loan that is available to homeowners who are of retirement age.

Chapter Key Terms

Advance directive: estate planning term refers to a type of living will where a person outlines his or her wishes regarding the continuation of medical treatments.

Agent: estate planning term refers to the person authorized to act.

Age of majority: estate planning term refers to the threshold of adulthood.

Arousal: estate planning term refers to a patient who is physiologically and psychologically awake and can react to stimuli but has no sense of true awareness.

Attorney-in-fact: estate planning term refers to the person who acts as a fiduciary to the principal.

Charitable Lead Trust: estate planning term refers to a type of trust where the taxable income of the beneficiaries is reduced.

Charitable Remainder Trust: estate planning term refers to a process where the donor (or grantor) donates property or money to a charity, uses the property while living, and receives income from it.

CLT: acronym stands for Charitable Lead Trust.

Codicil: estate planning term refers to a separate document that amends a previously executed will; a codicil doesn't replace a will.

Concurrent estate: see *Joint Tenancy*.

Conservatorship: estate planning term refers to a type of guardianship; used in estate planning.

Constructive trust: estate planning term refers to a type of trust imposed by the law as an equitable remedy.

Co-tenancy: see *Joint Tenancy*.

Durable power of attorney: estate planning term refers to a type of document where the grantor specifies that the power of attorney is effective even if the grantor becomes incapacitated.

Dynasty trust: estate planning term refers to a type of generation-skipping trust where assets are passed down to the grandchildren of the grantor and not directly to the grantor's children.

Equal dignity rule: estate planning term refers to a legal principle that requires authorization for one person, who is typically the agent and who performs a certain act on behalf of the grantor, to conduct one or more acts with the same formality required for all the acts.

Equity release: term refers to a process where the homeowner retains the use of their house; falls under the concept of reverse mortgage.

Estate: term refers to the net worth of a person at any point in time.

Estate planning: term refers to is a type of process where an individual anticipates and arranges for the disposal of an estate, which is defined as the net worth of a person at any point in time.

Express trust: term refers to the settlor simply expressing the intention to create a trust.

Fiduciary: term refers to as a legal and ethical relationship of trust between two parties.

Grantor: term refers to the person who creates a power of attorney.

Health care directive: term refers to a type of living will where a person outlines his or her wishes regarding the continuation of medical treatments.

Health care proxy: see *Power of Attorney*.

Holographic will: term refers to wills that are written by the hand of the testator.

Home income plan: term refers to a type of lifetime mortgage.

Home reversion: reverse mortgage term refers to when the borrower agrees to sell all or part of their home to a third party.

Husband and wife will: term refers to wills made by two or more parties (typically between spouses) that mirror provisions that are in favor of the other.

Interest only: a reverse mortgage term refers to a process where the capital is repaid when the borrower dies.

Inter vivos trust: term refers to a settlor who creates a trust at the time he or she is still living.

Irrevocable trust: term refers to a type of document that cannot be amended or revised; the terms of the trust must be fully executed and completed.

Join tenancy: term refers to a legal principle regarding property owned by one or more parties at a single time.

Joint tenancy with right of survivorship: term refers to a process where upon the death of one of the owners (or tenants), ownership of the property passes to the surviving tenants who are also called successors.

Jumbo reverse mortgage: term refers to a type of mortgage structured and supported by private companies.

Lifetime mortgage: a reverse mortgage term refers to a mortgage loan that is secured against the borrower's home. See also *Equity Release*.

Living will: term refers to a legal document within which an individual outlines his or her wishes regarding the continuation of medical treatments.

Mirror will: term refers to wills made by two or more parties (typically between spouses) that mirror provisions that are in favor of the other.

Mutual will: term refers to wills made by two or more parties (typically between spouses) that mirror provisions that are in favor of the other.

Mystic will: term refers to wills that are sealed until death.

Notarial will: term refers to a will in public form.

Nuncupative will: term refers to wills that are oral or dictated.

Offshore trust: term refers to a type of instrument where the trust is resident in a jurisdiction other than the resident of the settlor.

Persistent vegetative state: term refers to a type of disorder of consciousness.

Physician's directive: term refers to a type of living will where a person outlines his or her wishes regarding the continuation of medical treatments.

Power of attorney: term refers to a type of written authorization for an appointed person to represent and/act on someone's behalf.

Principal: estate planning term refers to the person authorizing another.

Proprietary reverse mortgage: see *Jumbo Reverse Mortgage*.

Reciprocal will: term refers to wills made by two or more parties (typically between spouses) that mirror provisions that are in favor of the other.
Reverse mortgage: term refers to a type of loan that is available to homeowners who are of retirement age.

Revocable trust: term refers to a type of document that can be amended, altered, or revoked by the settlor.

Self-proved will: term refers to wills that include affidavits of subscribing witnesses.

Serviceman's will: term refers to a will of a person in who is an active-duty military servicemen.

Settlor: term refers to a person who transfers some or all of his or her property to a trustee.

Shared appreciation mortgage: term refers to when the receives a loan from the lender. The loan is a capital sum. In return for the loan, the lender receives a share of the increase in the property's value.

Sound mind: term refers to the mental capacity of a person to draft his or her own will without the necessary services of a lawyer.

Tenancy by the entirety: term refers to a type of concurrent estate where real property is held by a husband and wife. Each party owns the whole of the property, which is undivided.

Tenancy in common: term refers to a legal principle where one or more owners own a distinct share of the same property. In essence, with tenancy in common, all co-owners own equal shares.
Testamentary trust: term refers to the product of a will that takes effect upon the death of the testator; and a court order.

Testator: term refers to the person who has written and executed a last will and testament that takes effect at the testator's death.

Trust: term refers to a relationship whereby real, personal, tangible, or intangible property is held by one party that will serve to benefit another; it is also a common law principle that outlines a relationship between parties and property.

Trustee: term refers to a person who holds the property in trust for the benefit of the beneficiaries.

Unit trust: term refers to the right of the beneficiaries, or unitholders, to possess a certain share (called units) of the trust and request that the trustee pay money out of the trust in direct proportion to the units they hold.

Unsolemn will: term refers to a will in which the executor is named.

Will: term refers to a written declaration, or testament, by a person, the testator, who names one or more persons to manage the estate and provide for the transfer of property.

Will in solemn form: term refers to a will that is signed by both the testator and the witnesses.

GROUP WORK PROMPT

As a group, review the Sample Revocable Living Trust housed on the Newland & Associates, PLC website http://www.tax-business.com/RLT.htm. As a group, revise the content of the trust. Insert different names, types of properties, and distribution share. The objective of this project is to review and evaluate a trust document.

Study it, talk about it, and offer a critical view. Suggest changes you would make as an accountant, a lawyer, and/or a financial advisor. Begin this exercise in-class, and finish it at home. Develop an essay that reflects your evaluation. The final product doesn't need to be formal in structure; just present your observations in an outline format.

HOMEWORK EXERCISE

For homework, create a trust document. Review sample documents for insight. If you do not possess real property in terms of land, use any type of property you have as references within the document. You may reference computers, automobiles, and related. Reference any property that may be typically insurable. In addition, if you do not have kids, refer to your siblings or friends as beneficiaries of your trust. To complete this assignment, you do not have to reference real names. This exercise is practice-based.

HELPFUL WEBSITES

What is a Living Will?
http://www.alllaw.com/articles/wills_and_trusts/article7.asp

New Retirement: Jumbo Reverse Mortgage and Proprietary Reverse Mortgage Loans
http://www.newretirement.com/Services/Jumbo-Reverse-Mortgage.aspx

American Academy of Financial Management: Chartered Trust and Estate Planner (CTEP)
http://www.financialcertified.com/chartered_trust_estate_planner.html

The National Association of Estate Planners and Councils (NAEPC)
http://www.naepc.org/

Assessment

1. What are the types of estate planning? List them. Explain.

2. What is a health care directive? How is it typically used?

3. What are the different types of wills? Explain at least three.

4. What are the different types of equity release arrangements? Explain at least three.

5. Summarize the costs a prospective borrower can expect to pay for an FHA-insured Home Equity Conversion Mortgage. Refer to the chapter scenario.

ESTATE PLANNING CHECKLIST

When developing a sound estate plan, consider the following checklist. It provides insight overall into the documents required and steps you will need to take in order to make a sound transition.

	Done	Need to Do	Comments
Will/Living will			
Health care directive			
Financial power of attorney			
Assignment of custodian of children's property (protection)			
Beneficiary forms (bank accounts, insurance)			
Life insurance			
Reviewed estate tax laws			
Prepaid funeral arrangements			
Succession plan			
Named executor/attorney-in-fact			
Trust			
Certificates in stock, bonds, securities			
Bank accounts, mutual funds, safe deposit boxes			
Debts and unpaid taxes			
Letter of instruction			

CHAPTER 17

Business Coaching

Do you have business debt that needs to be paid off? Do you often wonder if you have enough money to invest in your business so it can grow? Do you find yourself mixing your business and personal finances? Do you ever lack savings for slow months? If you answer yes to any of these questions, you are a candidate for business coaching.

WHAT IS A SMALL BUSINESS?

The Small Business Association (SBA) has identified standards for what constitutes a small business, but the standards vary by industry and type of business. A common standard is a manufacturing business with 500 employees or less, or a nonmanufacturing business with less than $7.5 million in annual receipts. For more precise standards, see the SBA's 2014 report Summary of Size Standards by Industry Section: http://www.sba.gov/content/summary-size-standards-industry-sector

WHAT IS BUSINESS COACHING?

Business coaching teaches business owners and executives to create and maintain a sustainable business, and then holds them accountable for it.

Many people want to own their own business, but businesses face many challenges. A majority of businesses quickly fail. In the first year, twenty-five percent of small businesses fail. Of the remaining survivors, thirty-six percent fail in the second year. In year three, forty-four percent of the remaining businesses fail. Half of those fail in year four.

Why do so many businesses fail? Many fail due to a lack of leadership within management, poor money management, and lack of money management skill. According to *Entrepreneur Weekly*, lack of financial responsibility and awareness is one of the top twelve reasons small business fail. Business coaching aims to increase the success of businesses through education and planning. Improving money management skills and leadership will improve the overall health of a business.

Business Plan

Every business needs a **business plan**. The old adage is true: failing to plan is planning to fail. Many small businesses do not have a business plan, though. Business coaching helps business owners develop a written plan with goals and timeframes for reaching those goals. I recommend a one-page business plan for most businesses.

Marketing Plan

Every business needs a **marketing plan**. The marketing plan determines what actions a business will take to get in front and stay in front of their customers and potential customers. I recommend a one-page marketing plan.

Policies and Procedures Manual

Many small businesses never create a **policies and procedures manual** or **employee handbook** unless their board or a government agency requires one. But, these manuals guide the operations of a business. Anyone who reads the Policies and Procedures Manual should gain an understanding of how the business operates and where to find any documents related to its operations.

The policy and procedure manual allows the business to operate without the founder. Oftentimes, entrepreneurs create a business, but do not know how to get away from the business they have created. The policies and procedures manual gives direction as to what needs to get done, how to do it, and where to find the items needed to operate the organization. A thorough policy and procedures manual is necessary for everyone involved in the organization. For example, what would happen to your business if you are not at work making sure things happen and work gets done? A policy and procedures manual becomes your friend, because how to completely operate the business is spelled out in the manual.

Budget

Every business owner needs both a **business budget** and a **personal budget**. Many do not have either, and this can create real problems for them. A budget is more than just a spreadsheet with numbers on it. It directs one's finances, spending, and investing decisions. I recommend a business keeps a reserve of six months of retained assets (savings) for slow months. A business should also have a balance sheet, a financial snapshot of where the business stands financially at a given time. A business also needs an income statement to track monthly revenues and cash flow.

A business owner needs to have both a personal budget and a business budget to keep their finances separate. Commingling funds is a major threat that every business wants to avoid. Commingling funds means that business monies and personal monies are mixing together instead of being separated in different bank accounts and different money management systems. Commingling funds happens most often because a business may have cash flow problems. Bills, expenses, salaries, and accounts payable may be due, but revenue has not yet arrived to pay them. Perhaps monies have not come in from customer purchases yet. In response, many business owners pull from their personal funds to pay their business expenses, and *vice versa*.

This causes an accounting problem in determining which money belongs to the business. But it also creates serious problems for personal finances when a business owner takes money from their family to pay for the business. When that happens, the household may find itself without funds for the mortgage or rent, the utilities, and even food. Suddenly, business owners find themselves facing problems on every front: business, personal, taxes, and accounting. When people borrow from their personal life to pay for their business life, they put their family at risk. If they never recoup that money, the stress can culminate in foreclosure, bankruptcy, and divorce. Commingling funds can become a huge problem. Developing and sticking to both a business budget and a personal budget will help prevent these tragic events.

Business Reinvestment

Business investment means taking advantage of opportunities to grow and expand a business. **Reinvestment** utilizes a portion of the revenues from the business to purchase equipment and **expand the business**, or to buy out another company and expand one's market share. A business owner needs a process or a system where they can take advantage of these opportunities. In their budget, they need a line item to make purchases to expand and grow their business or extend its lifespan. We have discussed how many businesses fail. Business reinvestment gives business owners an edge on keeping their business healthy, solvent, and sustainable for the future.

Taxes

A small business should save a portion of their revenues for **taxes**. The IRS requires businesses to make **estimated quarterly tax payments** on their expected federal income and self-employment taxes. Late payments, failure to pay, or even failure to pay enough, can each result in penalties. But despite the threat of penalties, many small business owners do not set aside funds for quarterly taxes. The taxes then become delinquent. This becomes a drain on resources that makes it difficult to build retained assets for the business. It can also interfere with having funds for payroll and other monthly obligations.

BUSINESS QUESTIONNAIRE

1. Why are you in business? Are you passionate about your business?

2. What is going well in your business? What is not going well?

3. What do you enjoy about your business? What do you not enjoy?

4. What is your business mission statement? What are your business goals? Do these goals relate well with your personal goals?

5. Where do you see your business in the next year? 5 years? 10 years?

6. Do you currently use a working/Functioning Business Budget?

7. What are your main marketing efforts? (Internet, advertising, referrals, networking)

8. Who are your clients? (Other businesses, individuals, international)

Conclusion

It is my goal in this book to empower you with financial knowledge and help you to gain confidence as you complete some of the activities appropriate to your current financial situation. This book is interactive and practical. It helps to usher you on the road to financial success by encouraging you to spend time evaluating your current expenses, creating a working and functioning spending plan, creating and maintaining an emergency fund, getting rid of debt, systematically investing in your future and building and living a legacy.

At the beginning of the book, I introduced you to the financial coaching and financial planning industry. Knowledge of how the industry function is important because you need to know the different designations specific to the industry. Do you need an investment advisor a financial coach or a financial planner? Do you just need a CPA or a financial analyst? These are questions you need to address before pursuing the services of a professional. You are wasting your money and valuable time if you haven't established financial goals appropriate for your current situation.

The next few chapters are traditional concepts specific to life objectives. You must know what type of relationship you want to have with your bank. You must also know your career questionnaires and/or college considerations. These chapters encourage you to sit down and think about where you want to take you. Do you want to pursue college? Or do you want to become a small business owner? Or both? For either choice, do you have the necessary cash flow? If not, would you consider borrowing the money or are you committed to never borrow money? If you borrow the money, what are your plans for repaying the loan? These are questions you must ask yourself before assuming the risk(s). If companies develop risk management objectives, then you should too. In other words, you should run yourself like a business, because you are in the business of living.

The main body of the book offers both information and practical tips for negotiating additional aspects of business living. You need insurance: health, life, and auto. You need to know the system of mortgage lending in terms of purchasing your first home or investment home. You also need to know about credit and the pitfalls inherent in borrowing money. How you negotiate life as an adult is important. You can start the pattern of borrowing money and never fully repaying the debt(s) or you can start the pattern of choosing not to borrow money and to build real wealth over time.

It is not inevitable that you will have debt. However, it is inevitable that you will deal with money. I recommend, you decide now if you are going to participate in the cycle of borrowing money or if you are going to build the disciple to save and buy things in cash. You can't escape this idea. You will have to choose. It would be better to develop a budget that works and develop a cash flow management plan for how you want to distribute and allocate monies. In other words, develop a relationship with your money. Know how much money you are spending, saving and giving. If you don't have a spending plan, meaning you don't know where your money is going, you will end up broke. If you don't have a savings plan, meaning if you don't pay yourself, then you are leaving yourself and your family vulnerable and uncovered. If you don't have a plan for giving, then you are not truly living.

I hope you have had fun reading this book as well as completing some of the exercises. I wish you all the best as you begin, endure, and complete your journey towards personal financial success. God bless you.

Testimonies

College—the "other" American dream. It's what you're supposed to do to get a successful career. It's part of working hard and being a responsible citizen. And, if you don't have the cash, you just use student loans, right?

That's what we used to think. We both graduated college three years ago with mountains of student loan debt. We owed more on our student loans than we did on our mortgage. Money was tight, and our degrees had not made much difference in our income levels.

But, we started paying and tracking our student loans diligently. The first year, they didn't go down. In fact, they went up as some of the payments were less than interest-only. The second year, we tried harder and paid a little more, but the balance stayed the same. The third year, we paid as much extra towards our loans as we could, but in the end made only a small dent in the principal.

We calculated that, at our current rate of repayment, it would take at least 42 more years to pay them off. We were heartbroken. We felt like we had tried so hard yet failed, and we didn't know what else to do. To make matters worse, the minimum payments were doubling, and we couldn't afford that. How would we give our daughter a good life and help her fund college one day so she wouldn't end up in the same situation? How would we ever get to a point where we could save a significant amount towards retirement and take care of our aging relatives? We were stressed and depressed.

We discovered Dave Ramsey's website and selected an option to speak to a local financial coach to see if there was any way we could avoid bankruptcy and turn our situation around. That's when we met Taras Collum and everything changed for the better. Taras listened to our story. After understanding our goals, he shared that he could help us put together a plan to get out of debt, avoid bankruptcy, and have financial peace.

Taras helped us create a family budget, understand the hows and whys of paying for purchases in cash, and helped us manage our monthly cash flow plan. Suddenly, things started to change. In the first 45 days, we paid off $5,000 in principal on our student loans. Even after we had to make a $3,000 emergency home repair, which we paid in cash, we maintained $3,000 in savings.

We were thrilled, amazed, and shocked! It seemed like a miracle, and our paychecks seemed to stretch farther than they ever had before. Under Taras's guidance, we got better and better each month at developing and sticking to our cash flow plan. Now, just four months later, we've already paid over $15,000 towards our student loan principal debt, more than twice the amount we paid all of last year. Our student loan debt is finally lower than our mortgage debt and shrinking quickly.

Best of all, we have a financial peace and confidence we've never had before. Thanks to Taras, we've created and maintained a solid plan of action and are making strides towards becoming debt free. We no longer stress about how much to spend on food, clothes, emergencies, or occasional necessities because our budget accommodates all these items, plus a little spending cash.

Visiting Taras monthly is actually fun, because we report our successes, discuss and regroup with any challenges we face, and have a professional, successful coach to guide us along the way. By ourselves, we had tried our best to do the right things but didn't make much progress. We wanted and needed to take our financial game to the next level, and we never could have done it without Coach Taras. Thanks, Taras, for getting us started down a solid path of financial success, improving our financial skills, and helping us go from financial misery to financial wellness.

If you're serious about making a change in your finances and experiencing financial wellness, listen to Taras. His proven track record and wise advice will help get you where you want to be.

With gratitude,
Brian and Selene Nelson

When I met Taras at my church classes of Financial Peace University, I had already taken FPU two times before. But, I still had debt and hadn't put together the links between my own finances and what the FPU plan told me to do. I still didn't understand how to do a budget with an irregular income like mine. I was always coming up short when it came time to pay my bills, and had no clue where it was all going! I tried to save but was unable achieve financial peace.

After working with Taras, I now know where all my money is going. I paid off $2,500 of my debt and saved $4,000. I never thought I would come this far in such a short amount of time! In less than one year, I proved to myself that I can have financial peace and independence.

When my car had problems, I didn't have to worry. I had an envelope for that. What seemed like a huge burden in the past has now been lifted off my shoulders, because I followed the system Taras helped me perfect. I have also been able to get my debt down to only my house mortgage. And, by paying extra every month, I have decreased my mortgage from 20 years to only 17 years. I never imagined finishing off my mortgage sooner than expected.

Without Taras, I would still be struggling on my own. It was hard to find a true accountability partner among my family and friends, but having a financial coach was a huge help to staying accountable. Taras walked me through every step and listened to what I had to say! He helped me create monthly calendars. Following them to a T helps me balance my irregular budget. Taras was supportive every step of the way. He was knowledgeable, respectful, and friendly throughout the entire process.

Thank you, Taras!
Vicky Vos

Bankruptcy. Is this where our story ends? This is the question my husband and I were asking ourselves. We knew we put ourselves in a bad position and needed to get out, but was bankruptcy the answer? Would it fix the problem? We were working hard, making the minimum payments on our debts, and still getting nowhere. The first time we contacted Taras, he called back the same day. Who would have thought that one phone call could change our lives so drastically?

We started with Taras in August, 2014. Within two weeks, we had our $1000 emergency fund. We have been married for almost nine years and never had that. Then, Taras educated us on how we were going to pay off debt, and how fast, and that it wasn't going to be easy. Within a month, we paid off five credit cards. Within two months we paid off 10 credit cards totaling more than $2000 of debt. We also paid cash for several emergencies that totaled more than $2500: an unexpected dental bill, and replacing our car's tires, shocks, and water pump.

Before, we were up at night from the stress, and it seemed we were always fighting—mostly over money. When payday came, we paid our bills. But, by Monday our money was mostly gone. After meeting with Taras, we now feel like we have more money. It seems crazy, but it's true. We know exactly what to do and where every single penny goes.

The future looks bright. One of our friends said, "I know how you can save some money: Get rid of your financial coach." No, that's how we will lose money! Taras is always accessible. We can call and text whenever we want—and we do! Taras is always available, and he gives us peace of mind. We know we can count on him. It's amazing how one decision, one person, and our commitment can make such a difference in our life.

Sincerely,
Marco and Lisa Ramos

Taras,

I want to tell you how much I appreciate you and what you do. Since we met, I feel that you've helped me accomplish so much. I remember when I first looked you up on Dave Ramsey's website and checked out your YouTube videos. With a divorce pending, I knew I needed, since my husband handled all the finances. Not knowing what was in store for me in my new life was unnerving, but you've really helped me put the pieces of the puzzle in place.

Paying off credit, even though it was joint debt and I complained a lot, you helped me through planning and implementing a plan to pay off my credit card debt. Wow, what a difference it makes on my stress level to have less debt per month! I'm not 100% debt free yet, but I'm steadily making changes to push through my fears and uncertainty.

Your help with moral support and creative options have worked well for me. I'm glad you can see the forest through the trees of my situation. I often see through the trees of my clients' situations in real estate, but it's hard for me to see my own options when a lot of responsibility is now on my shoulders.

I feel we have a friendship that will last, and I know that I'll forever be a fan of you and your business.

Sincerely,
Carol Duffy

Before we met Taras, we were in debt. We filed bankruptcy. We fought all the time about finances and money. We were living way above our means and did not know how to get out of the hole we were in.

We have now been seeing Taras for more than six months. With his help, we have been able to pay off several loans and outstanding debt. We are still in the middle of the Chapter 13 bankruptcy we were already in when we joined Taras; but, with his assistance, we have been able to see how not end up here again. We have hit several barriers since starting with Taras, but he has been able to help us set goals and find a way out of debt.

We are now in a place where we can start saving three to six months of bills, and looking to a brighter future. We do not argue over money like we used to, and it has been a huge relief to know where all of our money is going. We don't feel like we are just working to pay bills now. We are able to live life and enjoy each other.

Taras has been great at helping us figure out what we were doing wrong with our finances. He helped us find peace in our marriage when it comes to money and finances. He is not only a financial coach, he is a counselor who cares about the people he works with. We know, with his continued assistance and coaching, we will be where we want to be when our Chapter 13 bankruptcy is over in 2017—and that is to never end up in debt again!

We have total faith in Taras and his ability to help us. We are thankful we found him and thank God for him.

Sincerely,
Dustin and Shanan Aven

I reached out to Taras because, as a creative person, I had come to terms with the fact that orchestrating the details of financial management was not one of my innate skills. I knew I needed to model myself after someone else who was already gifted and up to speed in this area, to have them coach me through the learning curve, so I could acquire the skills for myself. I also knew that I needed the repeated check-in from a coach to hold me on task until I mastered the habits myself.

Taras has been an amazing ally, not only because of his knowledge and insights, but also his rock-solid demeanor and focus to keep me on task. Thanks to working with Taras, confusion and disarray has given way to forging a clear path toward my dreams. I highly recommend him to anyone who needs a helping hand mastering this area of their life.

Sincerely,
Kirk Bianchi, Business Owner
Bianchi Design

Taras,

When I first came to you, I had two jobs but was living from paycheck to paycheck. I didn't know how to save my money, and I didn't have any discipline. I would get my bills paid, but then I would spend everything that I had left over. My savings account was very bare.

Now I am much better with my money. I write things out in a planner. I stay on top of paying things off and saving what I have left over. I have saved a generous amount of money, and I have paid off almost all of my small debts. I also started paying off some of the larger ones like my car and student loans. I have definitely been living a much less stressful life now that I am in a better place financially.

You helped me find financial peace by holding me accountable and forcing me to make tough financial decisions that I wasn't willing to make on my own.

Sincerely,
Rebekah Oliver

We called Taras at a point when we felt seriously overwhelmed by the weight of debts and the outlook of our financial lives. Our marriage was greatly affected by our finances and our communication was lacking.

When we came to Taras we found him easy to talk to. He helped us understand our situation. He did not sugarcoat anything. He was real—understanding, but truthful. We met with him about nine times. Our schedules did not permit us to meet during the day, but Taras made time to see us after hours.

We spoke at length about budgeting. Taras helped us create a budget that spanned over three months. He emphasized the difference between wants and needs. He stressed the need to have an emergency savings and helped us understand we can have a better financial future if we work at it.

We are far from our goals of financial freedom; but, we know that when we work together, we will make it work.

Thank you, Taras, for the great advice!
Eli and Judith Sidza

Over the last couple of years, our finances had been under a lot of pressure. My husband, James, was recently divorced and this had significant financial implications. I had moved countries, started a life in the US, taken time off work to have a baby, and blended a family. For some time I was unable to work in the US.

We were somehow managing from month to month when my husband lost his job overnight. It was a scary time, but, through the support and generosity of friends and family, we once again made it through. I ended up going back to work, and this helped us to manage. However, ongoing legal expenses, unsteady work (I work on a contract basis), and the stress of having to manage each month finally led me to want to do it differently. I could not take the uncertainty and stress any longer.

I wanted to take charge of this aspect of my life once and for all. I read a couple of Dave Ramsey books but was still not confident we could do it on our own. I was mostly unsure how to manage our irregular income. So, I found Taras online, got my husband on board, and organized to meet with him. We were sold at the first meeting!

Taras really helped us to break down what we needed to do into small easy steps. He especially helped us develop a monthly budget and understand how to manage irregular income. He insisted that we agree to pay all our debts.

We are now debt free! We have saved our baby emergency fund, and we are on our way to having a full emergency fund completed in the next few months. We now have health insurance and life insurance that we did not have before. We love the envelope system. We no longer have to worry at the register if we have enough money to pay. Preparing the monthly budget together is a good bonding experience, and the steps we have taken have led to a sense of peace and security with regards to money. We are looking forward to saving for a new car and beginning to plan for retirement and our kids' college.

We couldn't have done it without Taras' support, and we love going to meet with him every month!
Kate and James Wilson

My husband filed for bankruptcy in the summer of 2014. From the moment we filed, I felt this pressing in my heart that filing was the wrong decision. I searched out alternatives to bankruptcy and stumbled across financial planning.

Taras Collum was the name given to me by Dave Ramsey. I called and immediately felt a sense of peace. Over the next several months, we did not follow through with the bankruptcy. Instead, we set up a plan to get debt-free.

Today, we have a starter savings account and have paid off several small accounts. We fell off our budget for a time, but, with a little motivation, we are back on schedule and working harder than ever to pay off bills. I have learned that creating a budget and following it is a daily process, sometimes even a struggle, but with God's help we can achieve our goals!

Thank you,
Monique and Phillip Ulibarri

Taras doesn't present himself as a relationship counselor; but, since arguments about money are the top predictor of divorce, he should probably consider it!

When Bernadette and I began working with Taras, I felt we were on a financial treadmill to nowhere. She and I had the same broad goals and would discuss those together, but the plan to get from here to there wasn't aligned with our day-to-day actions. Plus, I travel for work quite a bit, and Bernadette is a stay at home mom. So, with our lives going this way and that, it seemed we were on different financial pages more often than not!

Once we met with Taras, all of that changed. We first reviewed our goals—the most pressing ones, as well as the more lofty or esoteric ones. Taras walked us through a framework to get our day-to-day actions aligned with our long-term goals. We consistently and constantly reaffirmed our commitment to those goals; and, more importantly, we agreed to the short-term actions aligned with our objectives.

The time we spend together each month helps us reaffirm the commitment we have to one another, our family, and our goals for our family. This agreement helps us maintain the discipline to continue our financial plan! The strength this process gives us as a couple truly cannot be measured with money. The discussion, agreement, and achievement we experience during our monthly meeting with Taras truly flavors all aspects of our life together!

Best regards,
John and Bernadette Moreno

About the Author

　　I grew up in impoverished neighborhoods in Mississippi. Food stamps and government assistance were the norm. Money always ran out before the end of the month. I remember eating out of garbage cans became normal. My grandmother used to bring home large trash bags of hamburgers that McDonald's would throw away at the end of the night and trash bags of day-old doughnuts that were thrown away.

　　I had an opportunity to move to San Diego, California from Greenville, Mississippi when I was 15. I didn't take advantage of the opportunity the first time around. I didn't want to leave my mother and siblings while they still were living in poverty. The second opportunity came and my mom quietly encouraged me to go. That decision changed my life.

　　In San Diego, I was faced with a fork in the road; I had to do some soul-searching. I could (1) continue with my unproductive life and questionable behavior, or I could (2) join the football team and better utilize my God-given talents. I chose to play football. I eventually graduated high school then went on to play college football.

　　Throughout this process, I kept remembering my mom's final words: "Make sure you get your college degree." So I did. I graduated from the University of San Diego earning my bachelors degree in business administration. Upon graduating USD, I relocated to Las Vegas to take advantage of the lucrative real estate and mortgage market. I worked in the real estate and mortgage industry for about four years.

Then came the "Great Recession." Remember, the sky was falling? I was no longer earning the income I once did when the market was booming. What's more, I had a baby on the way, my first born. I was scared. So, I did what my mother would have told me; that is, get a job and take care of my responsibilities. I found an opportunity and was hired as a banker. I didn't like banking so much.

So, after banking, and becoming debt free by working multiple jobs around the clock and paying off debt, I got involved in the home care industry working with the developmentally disabled and the elderly. To be more effective, I decided to start my own group home for troubled teens. I ate inferior goods such as cereal in the morning for breakfast, peanut butter and jelly along with beans and rice for lunch, and Ritz crackers and more beans and rice for dinner. This lasted for approximately 18 months. I sacrificed in order to save the money to start the group home endeavor.

So, here I am now helping people and their families learn how to use their money **God's way**. I love it because I get to help educate and teach people instead of selling products or services to customers that are not necessarily in the client's best interest.

I worked as a high school teacher and taught moral foundations and personal finance to high school seniors getting ready to graduate. I also taught personal finance to groups of young adults in my church. I currently coach individuals and couples on how to manage money, save money, pay off debt, and retire with dignity. I also speak on the topics of money and leadership.

When you work with me, you are working with someone who has the experience, skills, knowledge and insight gained from climbing out of poverty through education and discipline with tenacity and prayer. You are working with someone who genuinely cares about people, someone who has empathy and understands money problems—and how to overcome them.

Money is a tool. Learning to make your money behave will change your life and the lives of your children and of your children's children, changing your entire family tree. Success is not success without succession.

And finally, when you work with me, you work with someone who has actually started and run businesses—multiple businesses. I've been in the trenches daily. I understand how to make the necessary sacrifices, which are typically short term, in order to accomplish goals and dreams. I am available to speak to your group and coach you towards your goals and dreams, so you can one day retire with dignity!

Taras Collum, Sr.

For more information about personal finance coaching services, visit: TarasTheBull.com

Call Now! (888) 975-BULL

Glossary

529 Plan: a type of tax-advantaged investment vehicle that encourages saving for higher education expenses on behalf of a designated beneficiary.

ABS: Asset-backed security.

Accidental death: a type of limited life insurance where the insurance covers the insured should the policyholder die as a result of an accident.

Accumulation period: a period of time when the annuitant, the person entitled to receive benefits from the annuity, makes contributions (to the annuity) for the purpose of building up the value of the annuity account.

Adjustment cap: the limit of how much the rate can go up or down within a single adjustment period.

Adjustable-rate mortgage: a debt instrument that does not have a fixed rate of interest.

Administrative fee: what the insurer deducts to for record-keeping purposes.

Advance directive: estate planning, a type of living will where a person outlines his or her wishes regarding the continuation of medical treatments.

Agent: estate planning, the person authorized to act.

Age of majority: estate planning, the threshold of adulthood.

Alternative financing: non-bank financial products such as payday loans, rent-to-own agreements, sub-prime mortgage loans, car title loans, refund anticipation loans, and non-bank check cashing.

Amortization: the process of the principal of a mortgage loan decreasing over the life of the loan.

Ancillary costs: costs associated with property taxes and insurance.

Annual percentage rate: the rate the borrower pays to an institution (loan).

Annual percentage yield: mean a normalized representation of an interest rate that is based upon a compounding period per year.

Annual renewable term: a type of term insurance policy where it is only for one year.

Annuitant: the person entitled to receive benefits from an annuity.

Annuitization phase: when the annuitant receives guaranteed payments for a specific period of time.

Arousal: estate planning, a patient who is physiologically and psychologically awake and can react to stimuli but has no sense of true awareness.

Asset allocation funds: a type of fund that splits investments between multiple options, which include growth stocks, money market funds, and income stocks/bonds.

Asset-backed securities: type of bond where the interest and principal payments are guaranteed by the underlying cash flows from other assets.

ATM: Automated Teller Machine.

ATM card: a type of bank card issued by a financial institution that is used at an Automated Teller Machine (ATM) for the following transactions: deposits, withdrawals, and obtaining account information.

Attorney-in-fact: estate planning, the person who acts as a fiduciary to the principal.

Automatic deduction: a process by which you set up money to be taken out of the account and directed to meet an obligation.

Balanced fund: a type of fund that invests in bonds for income and stocks for appreciation.

Bank: a type of financial institution and a financial intermediary that provides for the acceptance of customer deposits of which it channels through lending activities.

Banking: as a process of depositing and withdrawing money from a bank.

Bankruptcy: the legal status representative of a person or organization that cannot repay the debt or debts he, she, or it owes to a creditor.

Bankruptcy Rules: the process, or procedural aspects, of bankruptcy and how they are governed and monitored by the Federal Rules of Bankruptcy Procedure.

Bank statement: term that refers to a document that displays banking activities.

Beneficiary: a person who receives benefits after the death of an insured policyholder.

Bilateral debt: a type of international debt.

BOE: business overhead expense.

Bond: a type of instrument of indebtedness between the bond issuer and the bondholder. It is a debt security.

Bond fund: a type of fund that invests in bonds and related debt securities.

BUBOR: Budapest Interbank Offered Rate.

Business banking: the process by which institutions provide services to mid-market businesses.

Business overhead expense disability insurance: type of disability insurance that reimburses a business when the owner suffers a disability.

Capital asset: stocks, bonds, and/or real estate.

Capital gain: profit that result from the disposing of a capital asset.

Capital gain tax: a type of tax assessed when the amount received from the disposition exceeds the price of purchase.

Car insurance: a type of insurance purchased for cars, trucks, motorcycles, and related road vehicles **Co-insurance:** is a fixed amount the insurer would have to pay over and above the co-payment.

Career counselor: a type of individual who specializes in career coaching.

Career questionnaire: a self-assessment tool used by career counselors and organizations to measure a respondent's primary and secondary interests, career choice, and aptitude for job placement.

Career questionnaire format: a structured document that serves as the basis for different types of questionnaires targeted to multiple student and non-student groups.

Cash flow: term that refers to the movement of money in and out of a business or financial product.

Cash flow statement: a financial statement that provides insight into how changes in the company's balance sheet and income statement affect cash and cash equivalents.

Cash inflow: term that refers to money coming into a business.

Cash outflow: term that refers to money going out of a business.

Catch-up contribution: a provision within a Roth IRA that allows people over the age of 50 to make additional contributions to their 401(k) plan and related individual retirement accounts.

CDO: collateralized debt obligation.

Certified financial planner: a professional certification mark conferred to financial planners by the Certified Financial Planner Board of Standards, Financial Planning Standards Council in Canada, and affiliated organizations in coordination with the Financial Planning Standards Board (FPSB).

CFP: Certified Financial Planner.

Chapter 7: term that refers to a type of bankruptcy for no asset cases.

Chapter 11: term that refers to a type of bankruptcy that is specific to commercial enterprises that want to undergo reorganization while continuing to operate the business and repaying creditors through a court-approved plan.

Chapter 13: term that refers to a type of bankruptcy that is designed for individuals with a regular source of income.

Charitable Lead Trust: estate planning a type of trust where the taxable income of the beneficiaries is reduced.

Charitable Remainder Trust: estate planning a process where the donor (or grantor) donates property or money to a charity, uses the property while living, and receives income from it.

Chartered Alternative Investment Analyst: a professional designation awarded through the CAIA Association.

Chartered Financial Analyst: a professional credential offered by the CFA Institute. Candidates who complete the program and related requirements will be awarded the CFA charter and will become officially a CFA charter holder.

Chartered Financial Consultant: a professional who assists individuals, small business owners, and professionals with information about financial planning.

Checking account: a standard product offered to each depositor.

Checking account register: term that refers to a bank document used to list current activities; used with a reconciliation sheet.

Clean price: the current market price of a bond.

Closed-end funds: a type of mutual fund.

CLT: Charitable Lead Trust.

CMO: collateralized mortgage obligation.

Codicil: estate planning a separate document that amends a previously executed will; a codicil doesn't replace a will.

Collateralized debt obligation: a structured asset-backed security (ABS) that includes multiple tranches.

Collateralized mortgage obligation: a debt security issued for a special purpose.

Collective investment vehicle: a method of investing where investors benefit from the inherent advantages of working as a group.

College planning: a process of preparing for academic work beyond the completion of secondary education.

Commercial auto insurance: a type of business for company vehicles used in the normal course of business.
Commercial bank: a general term used for normal banking.

Common stock: a shareholder's right to vote at a shareholder's meeting and receive dividends.

Community bank: a locally-operated financial institution that provides community empowerment.

Community development bank: a regulated institution that provides financial services and typically credit to underserved markets and populations.

Concurrent estate: see *Joint Tenancy*.

Conservatorship: estate planning a type of guardianship; used in estate planning.

Constructive trust: estate planning a type of trust imposed by the law as an equitable remedy.

Consumer debt: multiple categories such as secured, unsecured, revolving, and installment.

Co-payment: the amount the policyholder pays out of pocket before the health insurance company pays for a particular doctor's visit; a co-payment is typically paid each time and before the insured receives a particular service.

Corporate banking: a banking product tailored directly larger business entities.

Corporate bond: a type of bond that is issued by a corporation.

Co-tenancy: see *Joint Tenancy*.

Coupon: the interest rate paid by the issuer to the bond holder.

Coverdell Education Savings Account: a type of investment account that offers owners an opportunity to plan and save for college on behalf of their children.

Coverdell ESA: see *Coverdell Education Savings Account*.

CRA: credit rating agency.

Credit counseling company: a company that offers to help you fix your credit and create a budget.

Credit quality: a feature of a bond.

Credit rating agency: a company that assigns a credit rating for an issuer of certain types of debt obligations.

Credit repair company: a company that offers to fix your credit for a fee.

Credit union: is a not-for-profit cooperative that is owned by the depositors.

Current yield: a calculation by dividing the annual interest payment by the current market price of the bond.

Death benefit: as the amount on a life insurance policy that will be payable to a beneficiary when the annuitant dies.

Debt: an obligation involving two parties: a debtor and a creditor.

Debt fund: see *Bond Fund*.

Deductible: the amount the policyholder pays out-of-pocket; the individual must pay this expense before the health insurance will pay its share.

Deed in lieu of foreclosure: a type of document signed by the owner of a property, selling right to the property to the bank.

DI: disability insurance.

Direct bank: a type of institution without any physical bank branches. It wholly operates on a network of computers. See *Internet-only Bank*.

Direct Consolidation Loan: a federal loan that allows a borrower to combine one or more federal student loans into one new loan.

Direct Loan: a type of federal student loan that is made through the William D. Ford Federal Direct Loan Program.

Direct PLUS Loan: a type of federal student loan where the borrower is fully responsible for paying both the principal and the interest.

Disability income insurance: term synonymous with disability insurance. See **disability insurance**.

Disability insurance: type of insurance that insures the beneficiary's earned income against a particular type of risk.

Disputing: the process of submitting a request for a credit reporting agency to investigate an error and/or an inaccuracy on the report.

Distressed property: three types of properties that fall under short sale, bank purchase, and foreclosure auction.

Dividend: A share of the profits a shareholder receives.

Durable power of attorney: estate planning a type of document where the grantor specifies that the power of attorney is effective even if the grantor becomes incapacitated.

Dynasty trust: estate planning a type of generation-skipping trust where assets are passed down to the grandchildren of the grantor and not directly to the grantor's children.

Employer-supplied disability insurance: term synonymous with worker's compensation.

Encumbrance: The right of the lender on real property.

Endowment life insurance policies: the cumulative cash value and how it equals the death benefit of the insured at a certain age, which is called the endowment age.

Equal dignity rule: estate planning, a legal principle that requires authorization for one person, who is typically the agent and who performs a certain act on behalf of the grantor, to conduct one or more acts with the same formality required for all the acts.

Equifax: a credit reporting agency.

Equity-income fund: see *Income Fund*.

Equity-indexed annuity: see *Indexed Annuity*.

Equity release: a process where the homeowner retains the use of their house; falls under the concept of reverse mortgage.

ERISA: Employee Retirement Income Security Act of 1974.

ESA: see *Coverdell Education Savings Account*.

Estate: the net worth of a person at any point in time.

Estate planning: a type of process where an individual anticipates and arranges for the disposal of an estate, which is defined as the net worth of a person at any point in time.

ETF: exchange-traded fund.

ETN: exchange-traded note.

EURIBOR: Euro Interbank Offered Rate.

Exchange-traded fund: the structure of an open-end investment company.

Exchange-traded note: a type of debt security issued by an underwriting bank.

Exclusions: services that are not covered under an insurance policy.

Experian: a credit reporting agency.

Express trust: the settlor simply expressing the intention to create a trust.

Federal Deposit Insurance Corporation: United States government corporation that operates as an independent agency.

FDIC: Federal Deposit Insurance Corporation.

Federal Family Education Loan Program: a type of federal loan program where private lenders provide loans to students that are guaranteed by the government.

Federal Housing Administration: a federal agency whose goals are to improve housing standards, provide home financing through insurance of mortgage loans, and stabilize the mortgage market.

Federal Pell Grant: a type of federal grant for undergraduate students that have financial need.

Federal Perkins Loan: a type of federal student loan for undergraduate and graduate students who demonstrate financial need.

Federal Work Study: a type of federal student aid that provides part-time student employment to help pay for education expenses.

FFEL: see *Federal Family Education Loan Program*.

FHA: Federal Housing Administration.

Fiduciary: as a legal and ethical relationship of trust between two parties.

Financial planner: a professional who prepares financial plans that cover multiple aspects of the personal finance environment.

Financial planning: a process that guides the creation of a financial plan and the development of a detailed strategy.

Financial Risk Manager: an international professional certification offered through the Global Association of Risk Professionals.

Financial services provider: a bank, an insurer, and/or an investment house.

First-time home buyer: an individual who is purchasing a principal residence for the first time.

Fixed annuity: a type of contract that an insured (i.e., policyholder) has with an insurance company. The insurer guarantees that the insured will receive fixed periodic payments.

Fixed-income security: a type of investment vehicle that provides a return that is in the form of fixed periodic payments.

Fixed index annuity: see *Indexed Annuity*.

Fixed rate mortgage: a fully amortizing loan where the interest rate on the loan remains the same.

Fixed-rate bond: a bond whose coupon remains constant throughout the term of the bond.

Floating rate notes: a type of bond that has a variable coupon and is often linked to a reference rate of interest.

Forecasting: market timing or stock picking.

General liability insurance: a type of business insurance that covers the business when a claim or lawsuit arises.

Goodwill: intangible assets that provide a "prudent value."

Government bond: a type of bond that represents the safest form of investment.

Grantor: the person who creates a power of attorney.

Growth fund: a type of fund that invests in the stocks of companies that are experiencing rapid growth.

Health care directive: a type of living will where a person outlines his or her wishes regarding the continuation of medical treatments.

Health care proxy: see *Power of Attorney*.

Health insurance: type of insurance product that hedge against the risk of incurring medical expenses particularly among individuals.

Health insurance policy: contract between an insurance provider and an individual.

Hedge fund: a type of fund that often trades stocks to reduce the risk of investments.

High-limit disability insurance: type of disability insurance that will help to maintain an individual's disability benefits at 65% of income.

High-yield bond: a type of bond that is typically rated below investment grade by a credit rating agency.

Holographic will: wills that are written by the hand of the testator.

Home income plan: a type of lifetime mortgage.

Home reversion: reverse mortgage when the borrower agrees to sell all or part of their home to a third party.

HUD-1 Form: See *Settlement Statement*.

Husband and wife will: wills made by two or more parties (typically between spouses) that mirror provisions that are in favor of the other.

IA: Investment Adviser.

IAR: Investment Adviser Representative.

Income fund: term that refers to a type of fund that invests in the stocks of companies that have a long history of paying dividends.

Indemnify: compensation from the insurance provider to the provider for a qualified event.

Independent fee-only advisor: a type of advisor legally required to act as a fiduciary to the client. Advisors don't receive commissions; instead, they receive a fee that represents a percentage of the amount of money he or she manages for the client.

Indexed annuity: a special type of contracts between an insurance company and the insured.

Index fund: a type of mutual fund.

Individual development account: a type of account offered by community organizations to people with a lower income.

Individual disability insurance: type of insurance is for individuals whose employers do not provide benefits and individuals who are self-employed.

Individual Retirement Account: a type of retirement plan.

Initial public offering: a public offering where a private company sells shares of its stock to the general public to raise expansion capital, monetize the investments of private investors, and become a publicly-traded company.

Installment debt: an account where the consumer pays a set amount each month.

Institutional money fund: a type of fund that requires a high minimum investment, but offers a low expense share class.

Insurance: the transfer of risk of loss between one or more entities in exchange for payment.

Insurance carrier: a company selling insurance.

Insurance policy: an official contract issued by the insurance carrier to the policyholder, or insured.

Insured: the policyholder of an insurance contract.

Internet-Only Bank: a type of institution without any physical bank branches. It wholly operates on a network of computers. See *Direct Bank*.

Interest: the percentage of payment added to the principal on a mortgage loan; term also refers to the money the bank pays a depositor for putting money into a checking.

Interest only: a reverse mortgage a process where the capital is repaid when the borrower dies.

Interest-only mortgage: where the borrower delays paying the principal and only makes the interest payment.

Interest rate risk: the value of an investment and how it contributes to the change in the absolute level of interest rates; these changes usually affect securities.

Inter vivos trust: a settlor who creates a trust at the time he or she is still living.

Investing: an economic principle generally related to saving.

Investment bank: a type of financial institution that provides assistance to individuals, corporations, and governments by helping each raise capital through underwriting or by acting on the client's behalf as an agent in issuing securities.

Investment banking: the process by which financial and banking institutions enter the financial markets.

Investment cash flow: term that refers to how cash is received from the sale of long-life assets; cash may also be spent on capital expenditures, which include investments, acquisitions, and other long-life assets.

Investment vehicle: any product used by investors for the purpose of earning a positive return.

IPO: initial public offering.

IRA: Individual Retirement Account.

Irrevocable trust: a type of document that cannot be amended or revised; the terms of the trust must be fully executed and completed.

Join tenancy: a legal principle regarding property owned by one or more parties at a single time.

Joint tenancy with right of survivorship: a process where upon the death of one of the owners (or tenants), ownership of the property passes to the surviving tenants who are also called successors.

Jumbo reverse mortgage: a type of mortgage structured and supported by private companies.

Junk bonds: high-yield bonds. See *High-Yield Bonds*.

Key-person disability insurance: type of insurance that protects the company from financial hardship due to a loss of a key employee; the loss of this type of employee is often due to a disability.

Level term: a type of term insurance policy that is fixed for at least a year.

LIBOR: London Interbank Offered Rate. See LIBOR rate.

LIBOR rate: the average interest rate calculated by leading banks in London.

Life insurance: type of contract between two parties: the insurer and the insurance policyholder.

Lifetime cap: the establishment of a maximum and a minimum interest rate throughout the term of a loan.

Lifetime mortgage: a reverse loan secured against the borrower's home. See also *Equity Release.*

Limited Liability Company: a type of legal business structure where either the owner or the manager has management authority. An LLC allows an unlimited number of shareholders.

Limited-pay life insurance: term that refers to a type of permanent life insurance that requires premiums to be paid over a specific period.

Living will: a legal document within which an individual outlines his or her wishes regarding the continuation of medical treatments.

Long-term care insurance: a type of insurance product that provides benefits for individuals needing long-term care related to dressing, bathing, eating, continence issues, transferring (getting in and out of bed or a chair), and walking.

Market price: an additional feature of a bond; market price is influenced by currency, timing of interest payments, amount of capital repayment due, credit quality of the bond, and available redemption yield.

Maturity date: a date a bond issuer is required to repay a nominal amount to a bondholder.

MBS: mortgage-backed security.

MIBOR: Mumbai Interbank Offered Rate.

Minimum daily balance requirement: the least amount of money kept in the checking account that is sufficient to meet the requirement.

Mirror will: wills made by two or more parties (typically between spouses) that mirror provisions that are in favor of the other.

Money market fund: an open-end mutual fund that invests in short-term debt securities, which include U.S. Treasury bills and commercial paper.

Monthly fee: a fee charged to a checking account and is defined as payment to the institution for managing it.
Mortality and expense risk charge: a percentage used in calculating a rate per year (1.25%).

Mortgage: a mortgage loan secured by real property.

Mortgage-backed security: a type of asset-based security, claim on the cash flows that result from mortgage loans; the process is called securitization.

Mortgage bond: a type of bond that is issued and/or guaranteed by government agencies, which include the Federal National Mortgage Association (Fannie Mae), the Federal Home Loan Mortgage Corporation (Freddie Mac), and the Government National Mortgage Association (Ginnie Mae).

Mortgage life insurance: the declining face value of this type of product.

Mortgage note: term that refers to the evidence of the existence of a mortgage loan.

Mortgage note buyers: companies and investors who purchase mortgage notes.

Municipal bond: a bond issued by a state, city, local government, agency, and/or a U.S. territory.

Mutual fund: a collection of both stocks and bonds. It is a type of collective investment vehicle that pools together money from multiple investors for the purpose of purchasing securities.

Mutual will: wills made by two or more parties (typically between spouses) that mirror provisions that are in favor of the other.

Mystic will: wills that are sealed until death.

National Credit Union Administration: an independent federal agency that was created by the U.S. Congress for the purposes of regulating, chartering, and supervising federal credit unions.

National debt: See "Public debt."

National social insurance programs: public social disability programs such as Social Security Disability Insurance (SSDI) and Supplemental Security Income (SSI).

NAV: net asset value.

NBCC: National Board for Certified Counselors.

NCC: National Certified Counselor.

NCE: National Counselor Exam.

NCUA: National Credit Union Administration.

Negative amortization: where the loan payment is less than the charged interest; the outstanding balance on the mortgage loan increases.

Net asset value: the value of an entity's assets less the value of its liabilities.

Nonsufficient funds fee: a type of fee assessed when a consumer authorizes a withdrawal when there is no actual money in the checking account.

Non-tax qualified policy: type of long-term care policy where the policy and the receipt of care are taxable.

Notarial will: a will in public form.

NTQ: non-tax qualified.

Nuncupative will: wills that are oral or dictated.

Offshore bank: a type of bank that is located in a non-U.S. jurisdiction.

Open-end funds: a common type of mutual fund.

Operational cash flow: term that refers to how cash is received and/or expended as a result of internal business activity.

Offshore trust: a type of instrument where the trust is resident in a jurisdiction other than the resident of the settlor.

Ordinary income: income that is other than capital gain. See *Capital Gain*.

Partnership: a type of legal business structure where at least two parties come together to form a business, where both parties make the decisions, where the business expenses are deductible, and where each partner is taxed at an individual level and not as partners.

Passive investing: see *Passive Management*.

Passive management: indexes that typically rely on a computer model that requires little or no human input.

Payment shock: when the monthly mortgage payment continues to jump from month to month making the mortgage unaffordable.

Payout phase: the period of time when the insurer makes payments to the annuitant.

Permanent life insurance: a type of insurance product that accumulates a cash value and reduces risk.

Persistent vegetative state: a type of disorder of consciousness.

Personal cash flow: term specific to personal finance budgeting

Physician's directive: a type of living will where a person outlines his or her wishes regarding the continuation of medical treatments.

PLUS Loan: a type of loan that is available to graduate students and also a parent of a dependent undergraduate student.

Pool: the activity of an entity that owns a set of mortgages and submits them to an investment institution that pools them together.

Postal savings bank: a type of bank associated with a national postal system.

Power of attorney: a type of written authorization for an appointed person to represent and/act on someone's behalf.

Pre-approval letter: a document that reflects the lender's process in verifying an applicant's financial information to determine eligibility for a mortgage loan.

Preferred stock: a type of shareholder who is not entitled to voting rights, but has a higher claim on the corporation's assets and/or earnings.

Premium: the amount the policyholder pays to the sponsoring organization to purchase coverage.

Prepaid 529 Plan: an option where an investor is allowed to purchase tuition credits at the current rate and the credits are used in the future.

Prepayment: the prepayment of the principal of a mortgage loan.

Pre-qualification letter: a document sent by a financial institution that has processed the applicant's information without the process of in-depth verification.

PRIBOR: Prague Interbank Offered Rate.

Principal: the face amount of a bond; also an estate planning term that refers to the person authorizing another.

Prior authorization: the obligation of the insured to request permission to receive certain medical services **Short-term care insurance:** type of insurance product that can be used with a long-term care insurance product; the policy provides for help with out-of-pocket expenses.

Private bank: a type of bank that requires a higher minimum deposit; this product is typically tailored to high net worth individuals.

Private banking: a banking product tailored directly to high net worth individuals and families where private banks provide wealth management services.

Private debt: money that individuals and businesses owe within a given country. It is a loan given by a private entity.

Private Loan: a type of non-federal loan that is made by a lender to a borrower. The lender is typically a bank, credit union, state agency, or school.

Product liability insurance: a type of business insurance that covers those claims that arise from the use of a defective product, provided that the product causes injury and/or harm.

Professional liability insurance: a type of business insurance known as "errors and omissions insurance."

Property insurance: a type of business insurance offered as a commercial product.

Proprietary reverse mortgage: see *Jumbo Reverse Mortgage*.

Protection policies: a type of life insurance contract where the beneficiary receives a lump sum payment.

Public debt: government debt.

Rate cap: the limit on how much the interest rate can change.

Real estate owned property: a type of property owned by a bank.

Reciprocal will: wills made by two or more parties (typically between spouses) that mirror provisions that are in favor of the other.

Reconciliation sheet: term that refers to a bank document used to reconcile a checkbook.

Redemption yield: see *Yield to Maturity*.

Reference rate: a type of rate that determines the pay-off outlined within a financial contract; the pay-off is determined outside the control of all parties to the contract.

Registered Investment Adviser: a registered professional with the Securities and Exchange Commission or a state securities agency.

Registered investment companies: three types of entities established by the Investment Company Act of 1940.

REO: acronym stand for real estate owned.

Retail banking: the process by which banks conduct business and execute transactions with consumers instead of corporations.

Retail broker: a type of advisor whose compensation is based upon the number of trades he or she generates and selling of investment products; retail broker is limited to selling only the investment products that are approved by the firm.

Retail money fund: a type of product offered primarily to individuals.

Retirement: the time at which a person stops working completely.

Reverse mortgage: a type of loan that is available to homeowners who are of retirement age.

Revocable trust: a type of document that can be amended, altered, or revoked by the settlor.

Revolving debt: an account in which the lender doesn't require the borrower to repay the outstanding balance in full every month.

RIA: Registered Investment Adviser.

RICs: registered investment companies.

Risk management: a process of identifying, assessing, and prioritizing risks.

Roth IRA: a type of retirement savings plan where an employee makes contributions with after-tax assets.

Sample career questionnaire example: a type of document that provides insight into the types of questions generated to measure a respondent's interests.

Savings 529 Plan: an option where the growth of donated funds is based upon the market performance of one or more of the underlying investments, usually mutual funds.

Savings bank: a type of bank that only accepts savings deposits.

Savings Incentive Match Plan for Employees: a plan that requires an employer to match the contributions of its employees.

SEC: the U.S. Securities and Exchange Commission.

Secondary market: a financial market that allows for the buying and selling of previously issued financial instruments.

Sector fund: a type of fund that invests in a particular area of industry.

Secured debt: debt secured by collateral.

Securities exchange: an environment for stock brokers and traders to trade bonds, stocks, and related securities.

Securitization: the process of pooling together types of contractual debt.

Self-Directed IRA: a type of retirement savings plan that allows the account holder to investment on behalf of the retirement plan.

Self-proved will: wills that include affidavits of subscribing witnesses.

SEP IRA: Simplified Employee Pension Individual Retirement Arrangement.

Serviceman's will: a will of a person in who is an active-duty military servicemen.

Settlement Statement: a type of document prepared by a closing agent; the document details the sale of the transaction, which references the sale price, amount of financing, loan fees and charges, proration of real estate taxes, and amounts due by the seller and the buyer to third-party agents.

Settlor: a person who transfers some or all of his or her property to a trustee.

Shared appreciation mortgage: when the receives a loan from the lender. The loan is a capital sum. In return for the loan, the lender receives a share of the increase in the property's value.

Shareholder: a holder of stock.

Short sale: the process where the bank takes less than what is owed on a property to satisfy the defaulted borrower's debt obligation to the bank.

SIBOR: Singapore Interbank Offered Rate.

Simple Indexed Annuity: see *Indexed Annuity*.

SIMPLE IRA: Savings Incentive Match Plan for Employees.

Simplified Employee Pension Individual Retirement Arrangement: a type of individual retirement account in the United States used by small business owners and self-employed persons.

Social security number: a nine-digit number that is issued to U.S. citizens, permanent residents, and temporary residents.

Sole proprietorship: a type of legal business structure where the owner of the business maintains complete control, makes all of the decisions, and earns all of the profits.

Sound mind: the mental capacity of a person to draft his or her own will without the necessary services of a lawyer.

Sovereign wealth fund: a state-owned investment fund that is composed of multiple financial assets, which include stocks, bonds, precious metals, property, and relate financial instruments.

SSDI: Social Security Disability Insurance.

SSI: Supplemental Security Income.

Stock: a type of security instrument that reflects ownership in a corporation.

Stock fund: a fund that invests in stocks, which are called equity securities.

Stock market launch: the means by which a private company transforms into a public company.

Subsidized loan: a type of federal student loan that is based on financial need.

Surrender charge: a fee charged to the life insurance policyholder for cancelling the insurance policy; the fee covers costs related to keeping the insurance policy on the insurance company's books.

Surrender period: a time when the charge to the annuity account declines gradually over a period of years.

Syndicated loan: debt granted to companies that wish to borrow millions of dollars with greater risk to the lender.

Statement of cash flows: See Cash Flow Statement.

Tax-qualified policy: type of long-term care policy where the policy and the receipt of care are not taxable.

Tenancy by the entirety: a type of concurrent estate where real property is held by a husband and wife. Each party owns the whole of the property, which is undivided.

Tenancy in common: a legal principle where one or more owners own a distinct share of the same property. In essence, with tenancy in common, all co-owners own equal shares.

Term (Loan): the period of time for repayment of a mortgage loan.

Term insurance: a type of policy that does not accumulate a cash value.

Testamentary trust: the product of a will that takes effect upon the death of the testator; and a court order.

Testator: the person who has written and executed a last will and testament that takes effect at the testator's death.

TIBOR: Tokyo Interbank Offered Rate.

TIL: Truth in Lending.

TQ: tax-qualified.

Traditional IRA: a type of IRA account where contributions are tax-deductible; transactions and earnings have no tax impact; and withdrawals are taxed as income.

Tranche: one of many related securities a part of the same transaction.

Transfer: the process of withdrawing money from one account and putting it into another account at the same time.

TransUnion: a credit reporting agency.

Treasury bond: a government bond.

Trust: a relationship whereby real, personal, tangible, or intangible property is held by one party that will serve to benefit another; it is also a common law principle that outlines a relationship between parties and property.

Trustee: a person who holds the property in trust for the benefit of the beneficiaries.

Truth in Lending Statement (TIL): a type of form that reflects corrected changes.

UIT: unit investment trust.

UL: universal life insurance.

Underlying fund expenses: charges imposed by mutual funds within the variable annuity.

Underwriting: a process that large financial services providers use to determine the eligibility of customers that want to receive the institution's products.

Unit investment trust: shares sold to the public one time; and this only when they are created.

Unit trust: the right of the beneficiaries, or unitholders, to possess a certain share (called units) of the trust and request that the trustee pay money out of the trust in direct proportion to the units they hold.

Universal life insurance: type of permanent life insurance that offers flexibility and growth of cash value as a benefit.

Unsecured debt: debt uncollateralized.

Unsolemn will: a will in which the executor is named.

Unsubsidized loan: a type of federal student loan where the borrower is responsible for both the principal and the interest.

Value fund: a type of fund that invests in value stocks.

Variable annuity: when the insured makes a lump sum payment or a series of payments to an insurance company.

Variable-income security: when payments often change due to short-term interest rates.

Vehicle insurance: see **car insurance**.

Whole life coverage: a type of permanent life insurance that provides death benefits for a level premium.

WIBOR: Warsaw Interbank Offered Rate.

Will: a written declaration, or testament, by a person, the testator, who names one or more persons to manage the estate and provide for the transfer of property.

Will in solemn form: a will that is signed by both the testator and the witnesses.

Worker's compensation: type of **employer-supplied disability insurance**.

Workman's compensation insurance: a type of business insurance that covers medical expenses and loss of income for an injured employee.

Yield: the rate of return that a bondholder receives from investing into the bond.

Yield to maturity: the redemption yield, or measurement of return of a bond.

Appendix: Forms

The following pages contain all of the forms used in this book's chapters. You can photocopy or reproduce them for your own use and any non-commercial use.

Financial Coaching Interview Questionnaire & Worksheet

When seeking the advisory services of a financial coach, use the following document to prepare your answers for the meeting.

1. What prompted you to seek out a financial coach?

_____
_____
_____

2. What is going well with your finances?

_____
_____
_____

3. What is *not* going well with your finances?

_____
_____
_____

4. What are your goals for your time with your coach?

_____
_____
_____

5. At the end of your coaching package, what do you hope to have accomplished?

_____
_____
_____

6. Where do you see yourself in the next year? 5 years? 10 years?

_____
_____
_____

7. Do you currently use a working/functioning budget?

    Yes or No

8. What are you willing to sacrifice to see the results you want?

_____
_____
_____

9. Are you committed to not borrowing? Is your spouse committed to not borrowing?

    Yes or No

FINANCIAL PLANNING INTERVIEW QUESTIONNAIRE & WORKSHEET

When seeking the advisory services of a financial planner, use the following document to prepare your answers for the meeting.

Current Status

Age: _____
Net Monthly Salary _____
Monthly Expenses _____
Disposable Income _____

Current Investments and Insurance

Investment Type #1_____Maturity_____
Investment Type #2_____Maturity_____
Insurance Type #1_____Premium _____
Insurance Type #2_____Premium _____
Related Investments_____Maturity _____

Current Financial Goals

Goal #1: _____

Goal #2: _____

Goal #3: _____

Goal #4: _____

Goal #5: _____

Current Emergency Fund

Fund Type #1: _____

Fund Type #2: _____

Fund Type #3: _____

Research & Cost Considerations

Term Insurance
___
___
___

Health Insurance
___
___
___

Child Education Funding
___
___
___

Goal Planning

Annual Vacation Fund
___
___

Retirement Fund
___
___

Home Loan Fund
___
___

Annual Child School Expenses Fund
___
___

Estate Planning Fund
___
___

Notes
___
___
___

BASIC CAREER QUESTIONNAIRE (HIGH SCHOOL)

Name: _____

Current Course: _____

Graduating Year: _____

Address: _____

City, State, Zip: _____

Email Address: _____

1. When participating on a team, how do you identify yourself in relationship to your teammates?

    a. Competitor
    b. Fellow student
    c. Team partner

2. Of the following responses, which of the two represents your preferences?

    a. Team-structured events
    b. Indoor events
    c. Outdoor events
    d. Individual events

3. Rank the following subjects under each column according to preference.

General	*Science*	*Social Science/Business*
a. English_____	Life Science_____	Accounting_____
b. Science_____	Earth Science_____	Psychology_____
c. History_____	Chemistry_____	Economics_____
d. Math _____	Physics_____	Law_____

4. Which of the following represents a primary interest? Rank according to preference.

Sports _____ Photography _____ Boating ___ Computers _____ Technology ___

5. Which of the following appeals to you most? Rank according to preference.

Nike __ Apple ___ Sony __ Wall Street __ Facebook __ Twitter __ UNICEF ___

6. What word best describes you and how you think? _____

CAREER QUESTIONNAIRE (SUBJECT-BASED)

Name: _____

Current Course: _____

Graduating Year: _____

Address: _____

City, State, Zip: _____

Email Address: _____

Please answer the following questions.

1. What is your favorite subject interest?
   _____
   _____

2. What is your preferred method for learning? Reading? Video instruction? Lecture? Explain.
   _____
   _____

3. Do you plan to choose this subject as a major in college?
   _____
   _____

4. What are some requirements for the major?
   _____
   _____

5. What do you hope to do with a degree in the major?
   _____
   _____

6. How long do you want to study for this degree?
   _____
   _____

7. What have you done to prepare for the major?
   _____
   _____

8. Do you plan to enroll in advanced coursework to gain more insight about the major?

9. How would you rate your overall efforts to prepare for the major on a scale of 1 to 10? Provide a reason.

10. Have you established transitional goals?

Kids' Career Questionnaire

Name: _____

Age: _____

Current Course: _____

Graduating Year: _____

Address: _____

City, State, Zip: _____

Email Address: _____

Please answer the following questions.

1. What do you want to become when you grow up?
    a. Doctor
    b. Lawyer
    c. Scientist
    d. Mathematician
    e. Own your own business
    f. Other: _____

2. How much money you want to make?
    a. $5,000 dollars
    b. $10,000 dollars
    c. $1,000,0000 dollars
    d. $50,000 dollars

3. Which of the following would you choose as a career? Rank 1 to 4.

Police _____ Doctor _____ Lawyer _____ Judge _____

4. Which is your favorite subject?

History _____ English _____ Math _____ Science _____ Writing _____

5. If you became a teacher, what subject would you like to teach?

_____

JOB QUESTIONNAIRE (WORKPLACE SKILLS)

Candidate's Name: _____

Address: _____

City, State, Zip: _____

Email Address: _____

Department and Designation (if employed): _____

Please answer the following questions.

1. Are you currently working?
   _____

2. How long have you worked for the organization?
   _____

3. Which of the following do you possess?

a. High School Diploma/GED
b. Associate's degree
c. Bachelor's degree
d. Master's degree
e. Doctorate degree
f. Vocational training certificate

4. What is your computer literacy?

a. Expert
b. Use some computer programs/software
c. Knowledge of computer hardware
d. Create computer software

5. What are your organizational skills?

a. Sales and marketing
b. Public Relations
c. Human Resource Management
d. Leadership Management

JOB APPLICATION QUESTIONNAIRE

Job Title: _____

Job Code:
_____

Name: _____

Address: _____

City, State, Zip: _____

Email Address: _____

Please answer the following questions.

1. How did you come to learn about this position?

Newspaper _____ Television ad _____ Friends/Family _____
Company website _____

2. What other positions have you applied for with the company?

Job Title: _____ Job Code: _____

3. Application Type

Online _____
Telephone _____
In person _____
Mail _____
Email _____

4. Have you read the company profile? Yes _____ No _____

5. What is your preferred start date? _____

Job Search Questionnaire

Job Title: _____

Job Code: _____

Name: _____

Address: _____

City, State, Zip: _____

Email Address: _____

Home Phone: _____ Cell Phone _____

Alternate Phone: _____

Please answer the following questions.

1. Job Experience: Years _____ Months _____

2. Which company did you work for prior to coming here?
_____

3. Description of the company.
_____
_____

4. What was the title of your position?
_____

5. What were your responsibilities?
_____
_____

6. What was your ending salary/wages?
_____

7. How did you find out about this employment opening?
_____

8. Do you have an updated resume?
_____

9. What is your preferred pay rate/salary?
_____

10. Do you have any computer skills?
_____

11. Describe how your skills closely match the requirements of the job.
_____
_____
_____
_____
_____

DETERMINING PAYMENT METHOD WORKSHEET

Category	Amount	Cash	Debit Card	Check
Rent/Mortgage				
Electric				
Water				
Gas				
Food/Grocery				
Homeowner's Ins.				
Life Ins.				
Car Ins.				
Car Monthly				
Credit Card #1				
Credit Card #2				
Cable				
Toiletries				
Other: _____				
Other: _____				
Other: _____				

This worksheet will help you to prepare your budget as well as prepare for how you will expend money. This worksheet also will help you keep track of your spending in general.

RECORD OF AUTOMATIC DEDUCTIONS SCHEDULING REGISTER

Category	Withdrawal Date	Amount	Pay Period	Cancellation

RECORD OF TRANSFERS AND SCHEDULING REGISTER

Account #1	Transfer Date	Amount	Account #2	Pay Period	Cancellation

SURVEY OF SAVINGS ACCOUNTS WORKSHEET

Bank	Minimum Opening Deposit	Interest Rate/APY	Monthly Fee	Minimum Daily Balance

BUSINESS BANKING PRODUCTS RESEARCH

Institution	Bank #1	Bank #2	Bank #3	Notes and Comments
Minimum to open				
Monthly Service Fee				
Check Safekeeping Fee				
Image Statement Fee				
Check Return Fee				
Monthly Transactions Allowed				
Cash Deposit Limit				
Non-Bank ATM Inquiry or Transfer Fee				
Non-Bank ATM Withdrawal				
Overdraft Protection				
Business Online Services				

RECORD OF CHECKS REGISTER

Check Date	Pay to the Order of	For	Check #	Amount

BUSINESS BANKING PRODUCTS RESEARCH SHEET

	Bank #1	Bank #2	Bank #3	Notes and Comments
Minimum to open				
Monthly Service Fee				
Check Safekeeping Fee				
Image Statement Fee				
Check Return Fee				
Monthly Transactions Allowed				
Cash Deposit Limit				
Non-Bank ATM Inquiry or Transfer Fee				
Non-Bank ATM Withdrawal				
Overdraft Protection				
Business Online Services				

RECORD OF TRANSFERS AND SCHEDULING REGISTER

Account #1	Transfer Date	Amount	Account #2	Pay Period	Cancellation

RECORD OF AUTOMATIC DEDUCTIONS SCHEDULING REGISTER

Category	Withdrawal Date	Amount	Pay Period	Cancellation

Determining Payment method Worksheet

Category	Amount	Cash	Debit Card	Check
Rent/Mortgage				
Electric				
Water				
Gas				
Food/Grocery				
Homeowner's Ins.				
Life Ins.				
Car Ins.				
Car Monthly				
Credit Card #1				
Credit Card #2				
Cable				
Toiletries				
Other: _____				
Other: _____				
Other: _____				

HIGH SCHOOL REQUIREMENTS CHECKLIST

Subject	Years Required	Years Completed
History & Social Science		
English		
Math		
Laboratory Science		
Visual and Performing Arts		
College Preparatory Elective		

History & Social Science: includes U.S. history, civics, or American government, social science

English: includes college preparatory English, composition, literature

Math: includes Algebra I, Geometry, Algebra II, higher mathematics

Laboratory Science: includes biological science, physical science

Visual and Performing Arts: includes dance, drama, theater, music, or visual art

College Preparatory Elective:

Test Prep Planning Criteria
(High School Proficiency Requirements)

Reading

Question Type	Number of Questions

Time Allotted:
_____
_____

Special Notes:
_____
_____
_____
_____

Writing

Question Type	Number of Questions

Time Allotted:
_____
_____

Special Notes:
_____
_____
_____
_____

Math

Question Type	Number of Questions

Time Allotted:
_____
_____

Special Notes:
_____
_____
_____
_____

Science

Question Type	Number of Questions

Time Allotted:
_____
_____

Special Notes:
_____
_____
_____
_____

Social Studies

Question Type	Number of Questions

Time Allotted:

Special Notes:

TEST PREP PLANNING CRITERIA (GED)

Language Arts, Writing

Question Type	Number of Questions

Time Allotted:
_____
_____

Special Notes:
_____
_____
_____
_____

Social Studies

Question Type	Number of Questions

Time Allotted:
_____
_____

Special Notes:
_____
_____
_____
_____

Science

Question Type	Number of Questions

Time Allotted:
_____
_____

Special Notes:
_____
_____
_____
_____

Language Arts, Reading

Question Type	Number of Questions

Time Allotted:
_____
_____

Special Notes:
_____
_____
_____
_____

Mathematics

Question Type	Number of Questions

Time Allotted:
_____
_____

Special Notes:
_____
_____
_____
_____

TEST SCORES OVERVIEW WORKSHEET
(HIGH SCHOOL)

State: _____

Overall Score: _____

Writing Score: _____

English Language Arts Score: _____

Mathematics Score: _____

Reading Score: _____

Science Score: _____

Social Studies Score: _____

TEST SCORES OVERVIEW WORKSHEET (GED)

State: _____

Overall Score: _____

Language Arts, Writing Score:
_____

Social Studies Score: _____

Science Test Score: _____

Language Arts, Reading Score: _____

Mathematics Score: _____

State GED Certificate: _____

ACT Overall Score: _____

English Score: _____

Mathematics Score: _____

Reading Score: _____

Science Score: _____

Scores Sent:
Home_____School_____
Scores Sent:
Home_____School_____
Scores Sent:
Home_____School_____

SAT Overall Score:
_____

Critical Reading Score: _____

Math Score: _____

Writing Score: _____

Scores Sent:
Home_____School_____
Scores Sent:
Home_____School_____

HIGH SCHOOL ACADEMIC ADVISING CHECK

Course Number	Courses (For AP courses, place a star near the course.)	Credits Required/ Credits Completed	Grade	Fulfills College Requirement Y/N
		/		
		/		
		/		
		/		
		/		
		/		
		/		
		/		
		/		
		/		
		/		
		/		
		/		
		/		
		/		
		/		
TOTAL		/		

Note: See next page for questions.

Questions:

1. If a course doesn't fulfill a requirement for the college I want to attend, which course can I take to fulfill it?

College #1:
_____
_____

College #2:
_____
_____

College #3:
_____
_____

College #4:
_____
_____

2. Can I take the course as a dual registrant at a local community college?
    Yes_____No_____
    When is the course offered:
    Fall_____Spring_____Summer_____Other_____

College: _____
Course Number: _____ Course Title: _____
Time: _____ Professor: _____
Department Contact: _____
Admissions & Registration Contact: _____

Notes (Advisor Suggestions):
_____
_____

3. Can I take the course at my high school?
    Year:
    Fall____Spring_____Summer_____

Notes (Advisor Suggestions):
_____
_____
_____

ADMISSION REQUIREMENTS WORKSHEET

Category	Completed?	Notes
Application Fee		
Application Filing Period		
Fall Semester		
Spring Semester		
Summer Semester		
Term applied for		
Ordered transcripts		
College #1		
College #2		
College #3		
Financial Aid Application School code: _____	_____	
School code: _____	_____	
School code: _____	_____	
School code: _____	_____	
H.S. Graduation Test PSAT SAT ACT	_____ _____ _____ _____ _____	

Other: _____		
Admission Essay Scholarship Essay	_____ _____	
Letter of Recommendation		

ADMISSION REQUIREMENTS WORKSHEET (INTERNATIONAL STUDENT)

College _____

Application Filing Period
Fall: _____ Spring: _____ Summer: _____

Application Deadline _____

Letter of Recommendation
Recommender:
_____

Contact Information
Phone:
_____

Email:
_____

Postal:
_____

Tests

Test	Test Dates	School Code	Completed?
SAT			
ACT			
TOEFL			

Admission Essay
Finished_____ Need to Write_____ Need to Type_____
Need to Send_____ Sent_____

Exit Examination Scores

Test	Test Dates	Transcript Certified/Evaluated?	Notes

ADMISSION REQUIREMENTS WORKSHEET (INTERNATIONAL STUDENT) CONT'D

Statement of Financial Resources
Academic Program: _____

Tuition and Fees: _____

Expenses (College): _____

Total Cost of Attendance: _____

Category	1st Year	2nd Year	3rd Year	4th Year
Personal				
Savings				
Parents/Sponsor				
Scholarship/Loan				
Other Assets				
Total				

Sponsor Information:
_____
_____

Additional Documentation Checklist
Employment Letter: _____
Bank Statement: _____
Parent/Friend/Relative Letter: _____
Scholarship Award Letter: _____
Approved Personal Recommendation (Graduate): _____

Medical Insurance
Type: _____ Provider: _____

ADMISSION REQUIREMENTS WORKSHEET (INTERNATIONAL STUDENT) CONT'D

Visa Applications (Completed?)
F1 Visa: _____
J1 Student Visa: _____
M1 Student Visa: _____
Green Card: _____

Department Major Admissions
Major:
_____
_____

Affected?
_____
_____

TAX & FINANCIAL INFORMATION CHECKLIST (FAFSA APPLICATIONS)

Category	Status	Need to do
Social Security card/driver's license/identification card		
W-2 forms; record of earned income		
Federal Income Tax Return		
Record of untaxed income Welfare benefits, Social Security benefits, TANF, ADC, military or clergy allowances		
Current bank statements; records of stocks, bonds, investments		
Alien registration number		

HEALTH INSURANCE RESEARCH & PLANNING WORKSHEET

Date:
_____

Health Insurance Company:
_____

Contact Information:
_____
_____

1. What type of coverage do I need? Short-term? Long-term?
_____
_____

2. What is basic coverage? What is comprehensive coverage?
_____
_____

3. Will my doctor and/or hospital be covered with the plan?
_____
_____

4. Does the plan's network require a referral?
_____
_____

5. Will the health plan cover me while traveling?
_____
_____

6. What services are important to me? Will the plan cover those services?
_____
_____

7. Will the plan cover my family? What is the limit?
_____
_____

8. Will the plan cover preexisting medical conditions? What is the limit?
_____
_____

9. Will the plan work with a health savings account? What is the limit?
_____
_____

10. Will prescription drugs be covered?
_____
_____

Notes and Considerations
_____
_____
_____
_____

Use this worksheet to help you focus and meet your insurance planning objectives.

Disability Insurance Calculation Worksheet

Monthly Income: _____

Other Sources of Income: _____

Total Gross Monthly Income (Pre-tax): _____

Estimated Tax (% of Gross Monthly Income): _____

BALANCE (Gross Monthly Income – Tax %): _____

Essential Monthly Expenses:
    Monthly housing (mortgage, rent, insurance, taxes): _____

    Utilities (telephone, electricity, gas, oil, cable TV, internet):_____
    Food: _____
    Transportation (car payments, gasoline, insurance): _____
    Education (tuition, books, supplies): _____
    Healthcare (out of pocket expenses, insurance premiums): _____
    Debt Payments (credit cards, other debt): _____
    Other (dependent care, life insurance premiums): _____

    Total Essential Monthly Expenses: _____

BALANCE (Monthly Income – Essential Expenses): _____

Existing Disability Insurance Benefits
    Group Long-Term Disability (employer): _____
    Social Security Disability: _____
    Other Disability Income Sources: _____
        Total Disability Income: _____

Disability Income Gap:
Essential Monthly Expenses – Total Disability Income: _____

Determining how much disability insurance you will need helps hedge against emergencies related to the disability and will also help to fill the disability income gap.

KEY-PERSON DISABILITY INSURANCE QUESTIONNAIRE

1. What contingencies are in place for when a key employee becomes disabled or leaves the company?

2. What time frame is available to the company to locate and train a replacement?

3. What will be the compensation for the new employee?

4. In terms of percentage, how much revenue will be attributable to new employee?

5. Will the loss of the key person directly correlate to the loss of the company's clients?

6. What are the benefits of a key-man disability insurance policy?

7. What payout options are available?

8. What are additional costs the company must meet to make the change?

Fixed Rate Mortgage Calculations Worksheet

Location	Home Price	Down Payment	Loan Term	Interest Rate	Payment

ADJUSTABLE-RATE MORTGAGE RESEARCH WORKSHEET

Date: _____

Loan Type: _____

Lender: _____

Contact Information: _____
_____
_____

Loan Amount: _____

Initial Interest Rate: _____

Number of Months: _____

What is the **Absolute Minimum Rate** for Term of Loan?
_____

What is the **Absolute Maximum Rate** for Term of Loan?
_____

Number of Months **before** Rate Adjusts: _____
Number of Months **between** Adjusting of Rate: _____
Over the life of the loan, will rate **increase, decrease, or stay the same**?
_____

What is the **assumed rate adjustment** (%)? _____

Notes and Special Considerations
_____
_____
_____

TERMS OF REPAYMENT WORKSHEET

Amount of Principal: _____

Interest Rate: _____

Interest Adjustment Date: _____

Interest Rate Calculated?
Annually: _____ Semi-annually: _____

When will the Principal and Interest Payments be required?
Weekly: _____ Bi-weekly: _____ Monthly: _____

What day of the week will the installment payments come due:
_____

What are the Principal and Interest payments?
_____

Maturity Date:
_____

Are annual prepayments of principal allowed?
_____

When can the prepayment be made?

Anniversary of Interest Adjustment Date: _____
Anytime during the year up to/including Interest Adjustment Date: _____
Percentage of principal can Mortgagor/Borrower prepay: _____

Can Mortgagor/Borrower prepay any amount not prepaid in the previous year?
_____

Is prepayment of entire principal allowed?
_____

Will the Mortgagee/Lender include a power of sale clause*?
_____

*The power of sale clause within a mortgage contract permits the lender to sell the mortgaged property if the mortgagor/borrower defaults.

MORTGAGE NOTE CONTRACT PLANNING WORKSHEET

Borrower's Promise to Pay
_____
_____

Interest
_____
_____

Payments
_____
_____

Time and Place of Payments
_____
_____

Amount of Monthly Payments
_____
_____

Borrower's Right to Prepay
_____
_____

Loan Charges
_____
_____

Borrower's Failure to Pay
_____
_____

Late Charge for Overdue Payments
_____

Default
_____
_____

Notice of Default
_____
_____

No Waiver by Note Holder

Payment of Note Holder's Costs and Expenses

Giving of Notices

Obligations of Persons under Note

Waivers

Uniform Secured Note

FIRST-TIME HOME BUYER MORTGAGE QUESTIONNAIRE

Date: _____

Lender: _____

Mortgage Type: (Based upon pre-approval and/or pre-qualification)

Fixed-Rate: _____

Projected Principal: _____
Projected Interest Rate: _____
Loan Term: _____

Adjustable Rate: _____

Introductory Period:
_____

Introductory Principal: _____
Introductory Interest Rate: _____

Rate Cap:
Adjustment Cap: New Principal: _____ New Interest: _____
Lifetime Cap: New Principal: _____ New Interest: _____

Interest-Only Mortgage (I/O):

Fixed-Rate? _____ *Adjustable-Rate?* _____
Payment Period: _____
Interest Payment: _____
Monthly Principal: Year: _____ *Total:* _____

Notes and Considerations
_____
_____
_____
_____

First-Time Home Buyer Affordability Finance Worksheet

Date: _____

Lender: _____

Gross Income:

Yearly_____ Monthly_____ Weekly_____

Monthly Debt Payments: Monthly _____ Weekly_____

Current Down Payment (Saved): _____

Mortgage Rate (%): _____

Closing Costs (%): _____

Minimum Down Payment (%): _____

Property Tax Rate (%): _____

Hazard Insurance Rate (%): _____

Private Mortgage Insurance Rate (PMI) (%): _____

Housing Expense-to-Income Ratio (%): _____

Long-Term Debt-to-Income Ratio (%): _____

Notes and Considerations

_____
_____
_____
_____

PAYDAY LOAN ACCUMULATION WORKSHEET

Application Date	Institution	Amount	Pay Period	Reason

Resolving Business Debt Planning Worksheet

1. How much money do you have in your personal reserves? Have you allocated it to anything?

2. How much money do you have in your business reserves? Have you allocated it to anything?

_____
_____

3. Determine how much you can take from each to pay down the business debt. What are those amounts?

_____
_____

4. Call the lender. Check to see if the lender will take a minimum payment. If yes, what is that minimum payment?

_____
_____

5. If the lender takes the minimum payment, will the lender consider the account past due?

_____
_____

6. Call the lender. Ask if the lender will allow the business account to be converted from a transactional account to a revolving account. If yes, what are the terms?

_____
_____

7. If the account can be converted, what is the outstanding balance? What is the payment arrangement? Will the lender allow the account to remain in good standing?

_____
_____

8. Do you have a revolving credit card without an outstanding balance?

_____
_____

9. What is the cash advance requirement? What are the standard terms?

_____
_____

10. Can you take out a cash advance against the card?
_____
_____

11. Will the cash advance be enough to satisfy the debt, make the minimum, and/or satisfy a significant chunk of the debt?
_____
_____

12. If this applies, what steps will you take to collect from a delinquent client?
_____
_____

**DEBT RESTRUCTURING
PLANNING QUESTIONNAIRE**

1. What is the quantity of existing assets?

2. What is the value of existing assets?

3. What are possible liquidation scenarios?

4. What is the viability of current business operations?

5. What are the current debtor-creditor issues?

6. What are the current outstanding loans?

7. What are the current commercial transactions?

8. What is the potential for developing new equity?

9. What is the potential for receiving capital injections?

10. What are the current cash flows?

11. What are the company's plans for debt restructuring?

12. How will sustainable debt be restructured?

13. What will be the terms and conditions of the debt restructuring plan?

14. Who or what company will formalize the debt restructuring plan?

Calculating Debt and Repayment Worksheet

1. What is your total income?

Fixed Income Source #1: _____
Fixed Income Source #2: _____
Variable Income Source #1: _____
Variable Income Source #2: _____
Other Source of Income #1: _____
_____

Other Source of Income #2: _____
_____

2. What is your necessity expense?

Housing: _____
Utilities:
        Electricity: _____
        Water: _____
        Gas: _____
        Phone _____
        Trash: _____
        Cable: _____
        Food: _____
Transportation:
        Car Payment: _____
        Bus Fare: _____
        Gas and Oil: _____
        Repairs/Tires: _____
        Car Insurance: _____
Insurance:
        Health: _____
        Life: _____
        Home: _____
Retirement Funding: _____

3. What is your disposable income?

Subtract your necessity expense from your total income. This is your disposable income. You will use this total to determine the percentage of payments you will make to each creditor.

_____

4. List all of your creditors. You will perform calculations for each creditor.

_____
_____

5. What is the total payoff amount for each creditor?

Creditor	Total Payoff Amount

6. Calculate the total payoff amount for all creditors. What is your total debt?

_____

7. For each creditor, calculate the payment amount using the following Dave Ramsey "Pro Rata Debt" payment calculation formula.

Total Payoff Amount **divided by** Total Debt Amount = **Percent**
Percent **multiplied by** Disposable Income = **Payment.**

This formula has been adapted from Dave Ramsey's "Financial Peace University Workbook." All rights reserved.

Dave Ramsey Pro Rata Debt List (Form 11)

Item	Total New Payoff Payment	Total Debt	Percent	Disposable Income
_____	_____ /	_____	= _____ x	_____

= Payment_____

On a separate sheet of paper, create this table to list your debt and calculate what the new payment would be for your debt repayment plan.

SMALL BUSINESS DEBT REPAYMENT & SAVINGS PLANNING WORKSHEET

Establishing Goals

The first part of the process is to establish goals for debt repayment. On a basic level, calculate your disposable income.

Goal #1: Determine your total revenue. List the categories and the amounts.

_____
_____
_____
_____
_____

Goal #2: Determine your necessary business expenses.

Necessary business expenses include salaries, telephone and internet, water and electricity, property rates and taxes, insurance, advertising costs, fuel, stationery and marketing materials, bank charges, and tax expenses.

_____
_____
_____
_____
_____

Goal #3: Calculate disposable income.

After you subtract necessary business expenses from gross revenue, you must consider the disposable income you have to put towards saving for the business. Your goal should be to save the equivalent of what it will cost to fulfill a project, contract, or job. For example, if you charge $1,500 to complete one project, and you have a contract signed, then you will need to have at least three times this amount in a business reserve. From disposable income, what percentage can you put towards creating a financial reserve for the business?

_____
_____
_____
_____

Creating a Business Savings Plan

Now that you have calculated your business's disposable income, you must create a savings plan that will ensure you can meet the requirements of your projects. You need an emergency fund for your business as well as a savings fund to meet business expenses. Establish goals to save for an emergency fund and for the following types of business expenses.

	Month 1	Month 2	Month 3	Total
Emergency Fund				
Salaries Fund				
Overhead Expenses Fund				
Property Rates/Taxes Fund				
Insurance Fund				
Advertising and Marketing Fund				
Banking Fund				
Related Business Expenses Fund				
Project Fund				

To meet a project, you must have at least three times that amount plus the cost of salaries, overhead expenses, property rates, insurance, advertising and marketing, and banking costs. In the same way that a prospective apartment application requires that you have at least three times the rent in the bank, you must consider the same principle for your business.

Going forward, what issues are currently preventing you from creating a strategic savings plan?

_____

_____

Cash Flow Statement Research Worksheet

In this section, you will perform the following exercises to help you plan for this part of your business. You will need your *income statement* and *balance sheet* in order to create the cash flow statement. You can find sample worksheets of these forms in the appendices section of this book.

1. List all cash receipts the company received from customers. What is the total?
_____
_____

2. How much cash was paid to suppliers? How much cash was paid to employees? Total both.
_____
_____

                    Sum of cash generated from operations: _____
                                      Change in total: _____

3. What interest did the company pay?
_____
_____

4. How much did the company pay in income taxes?
_____
_____

                    Net cash flow from operating activities: _____
                                        Change in total: _____

5. What equipment did the company sell? What were the proceeds from the sale?
_____
_____

6. What dividends did the company receive? What were the proceeds from the process?
_____
_____

                    Net cash flow from investing activities: _____
                                        Change in total: _____

7. What dividends did the company pay out? Do the payout of dividends fall under multiple categories.
_____
_____

                    Net cash flow from financing activities: _____
                                        Change in total: _____

Special Notes: What other factors need to be considered before finalizing the statement.
_____
_____

Now that you have researched the figures and have had time to think about what they mean and how they should be represented within a statement of cash flows, it is time to enter the data. Use the following sample form to enter the data. The form will help you to view the figures more comprehensively.

Cash Flow Statement Worksheet

Cash Flows from Operating Activities
Cash receipts from customers _____
Cash paid to suppliers and employees _____
Cash generated from operations (sum) _____
Interest paid _____
Income taxes paid _____
Net cash flows from operating activities _____

Cash Flows from Investing Activities
Proceeds from sale of equipment _____
Dividends received _____
Net cash flows from investing activities _____

Cash Flows from Financing Activities
Dividends paid _____
Net cash flows from financing activities _____
Net increase in cash and cash equivalents _____
Cash and cash equivalents, beginning of year _____
Cash and cash equivalents, end of year _____

Budgetary Expense Policy

Housing (Rent): _____

Utilities

In order to create the Utilities budget policy, you will need to conduct some market research. For now you are just submitting considerations to Jane. You don't know if she can yet afford one or more of the utilities.

Market Research Estimates
Time Warner: _____
AT&T: _____
Gas/Electric: _____
Water: _____

Budgets for Jane
Electric: _____   Gas: _____   Trash: _____
Water: _____   Phone: _____   Cable: _____

Food

Jane will need to budget for groceries and for eating out. If she doesn't budget for this, then she will be blindsided. Develop reasonable budgets based upon her take-home monthly pay.

Groceries: _____   Restaurants: _____

Transportation

Transportation has multiple sub-categories. Jane wants to get a car, but she also lives by a bus stop in Dallas, Texas. The transit system also offers multiple train lines. You will need to research the market to determine the best option(s) for Jane. Should she purchase a car or ride the bus? For how many months or years should she do this? Since you do not know what kind of car Jane wants, suggest to Jane what she should consider based upon her monthly pay.

Bus Fare: _____   Train Fare: _____
Gas Cost: _____   Car Repair: _____
License: _____   Taxes: _____

Mark Research Estimates
Car Payment: _____
Car Insurance: _____

Suggestions:
_____
_____

Clothing

_____
_____

Medical

Future medical costs will include a health insurance premium, a deductible, doctor bills, and medications. Since you do not know if Jane's company offers medical insurance and if Jane will have to make co-pays, develop a budgetary policy based upon your market research. Choose Aetna or BlueCross BlueShield as the basis for your estimates. Make a suggestion to Jane.

_____
_____

Personal

Personal costs include toiletries, hair care, and life insurance. Develop budgetary policy for the bare minimum in this area. However, you will need to research life insurance estimates. Jane lives in Dallas, Texas. Therefore, research two or three life insurance companies and provide suggestions to Jane on which type of life insurance would be of greater benefit.

Toiletries: _____   Hair Care: _____
Market Research Estimates
Life Insurance #1: _____
Life Insurance #2: _____
Life Insurance #3: _____
Suggestions:

_____
_____

Debt

Jane will undoubtedly graduate with some student loan debt. Jane can elect to sign up for the Income Contingent Plan through Direct Loans. Figure for Jane a minimum of $200 per month.

_____
_____

Now that you have developed budgetary policy for Jane, enter the numbers on the following worksheet. Don't worry about the Actual Spent and Total columns yet. This sheet gives you an idea of what to expect and how to plan your budget.

MONTHLY CASH FLOW PLAN BUDGET WORKSHEET

Category	Budget	Actual Spent	Total
Housing (rent)			
Utilities			
Electric			
Water			
Gas			
Phone			
Trash			
Cable			
Food			
Groceries			
Restaurant			
Transportation			
Car Payment			
Car Insurance			
Gas			
Repairs			
License/Taxes			
Clothing			
Medical			
Personal			
Toiletries			
Hair Care			
Life Insurance			
Debt			
Student Loan			

Projected Allocated Spending Plan Sheet

Pay Period (week/month)	___/___	___/___	___/___	___/___
Income	$1,250	$1,250	$1,250	$1,250
Charitable	$20 / $1,230	___/___	___/___	___/___
Saving	___/___	___/___	___/___	___/___
Emergency Fund	___/___	___/___	___/___	___/___
Retirement Fund	___/___	___/___	___/___	___/___
Housing	___/___	___/___	___/___	___/___
Utilities				
Electric	___/___	___/___	___/___	___/___
Water	___/___	___/___	___/___	___/___
Phone	___/___	___/___	___/___	___/___
Trash	___/___	___/___	___/___	___/___
Cable	___/___	___/___	___/___	___/___
Food				
Groceries	___/___	___/___	___/___	___/___
Restaurant	___/___	___/___	___/___	___/___
Transportation				
Car Payment	___/___	___/___	___/___	___/___
Car Insurance	___/___	___/___	___/___	___/___
Gas	___/___	___/___	___/___	___/___
Repairs	___/___	___/___	___/___	___/___
License/Taxes	___/___	___/___	___/___	___/___
Bus Fare	___/___	___/___	___/___	___/___
Clothing	___/___	___/___	___/___	___/___

Medical	___/___	___/___	___/___	___/___
Personal	___/___	___/___	___/___	___/___
Toiletries	___/___	___/___	___/___	___/___
Hair Care	___/___	___/___	___/___	___/___
Life Insurance	___/___	___/___	___/___	___/___
Debt	___/___	___/___	___/___	___/___
Student Loan	___/___	___/___	___/___	___/___

BALANCE SHEET PLANNING WORKSHEET

Company Name: _____

Ending Quarter/year: _____

ASSETS

CURRENT
Cash   _____
Accounts receivable   _____
Deposits and prepaid expenses   _____
Inventory   _____

PROPERTY, PLANT, EQUIPMENT   _____
INVESTMENTS   _____

LIABILITIES

CURRENT
Bank Overdraft   _____
Bank Loan   _____
Accounts payables/accrued liabilities   _____
Long-term debt—current portion   _____
Income tax payable   _____

LONG-TERM DEBT   _____

SHAREHOLDER'S EQUITY

Stated Capital   _____
Retained Earnings   _____

Note: The figures under **ASSETS** should match the totals of **LIABILITIES** and **SHAREHOLDER'S EQUITY**. In other words, they should balance. Consult a standard textbook on the subject for help.

STATEMENT OF INCOME PLANNING WORKSHEET

Company Name: _____

Ending Quarter/year: _____

REVENUE _____

COST OF SALES
Opening Inventory _____
Delivery _____
Purchases _____
Closing Inventory _____

GROSS PROFIT _____

OPERATING EXPENSES _____

INCOME FROM OPERATIONS _____

OTHER INCOME (EXPENSES)
Loss on disposal of property, equipment, plant _____
Gain on sale of investment _____
Miscellaneous _____

NET INCOME BEFORE TAX _____
INCOME TAX EXPENSE _____
NET INCOME _____

Note: Most companies combine the income statement with the statement of retained earnings. If you choose this method, the line items after NET INCOME would be **(DEFICIT) – Beginning of Year**, if your company has a deficit; **DIVIDENDS**; and **RETAINED EARNINGS (DEFICIT) – End of year**. Enter the line items in the above order.

Independent, Fee-Only Questionnaire & Worksheet

Date: _____

Advisor/Contact: _____
Fee: _____

Custodian: _____
Contact: _____

Questions

1. What is the advisor's investment philosophy?
_____
_____
_____

2. What are the advisor's professional qualifications?
_____
_____

   Financial Designations*:
   CFP_____CFA_____CPA_____

3. What is the advisor's educational background?
_____
_____
_____

4. What is the advisor's level(s) of experience with financial services and accounting?
_____
_____
_____

5. What is the current business structure of the advisor's business?

Sole Proprietorship_____Partnership_____Unincorporated Business_____
Other: _____

6. What services does the advisor offer? Is a brochure available for evaluation?

_____
_____
_____

7. What are the advisor's current clients? How long have they been with the advisor?

_____
_____
_____

Special Notes & Considerations

_____
_____
_____
_____
_____

*Certified Financial Planner (CFP); Chartered Financial Analysis (CFA); Certified Public Accountant (CPA)

CREATING AN INVESTMENT PLAN
QUESTIONNAIRE & WORKSHEET

Part One: Creating the Plan

1. What are your goals?
2. What are your current savings?
3. What is the value of your current assets?
4. What are your potential returns? Provide an estimate.

Part Two: Developing Diversification Objectives

1. What are your diversification objectives?
2. What asset classes are you considering?
3. What are your long-term considerations? What are your short-term considerations?
4. Which asset classes will reduce risk?
5. Does your portfolio hold both value and growth stocks? If not, what are your plans for diversifying by equity style?
6. Does your portfolio hold bond securities? What are the maturities?
7. How are assets allocated?

Part Three: Establishing Periodic Checkup Objectives

1. What are your periodic checkup objectives?
2. How often and when will you evaluate your current portfolio to ensure risks are minimized?

Part Four: Reevaluating Benchmarks

1. What are benchmarks objectives?
2. How often will you reevaluate these objectives?

Special Notes and Considerations

_____
_____
_____
_____
_____
_____

VARIABLE ANNUITY PLANNING QUESTIONNAIRE & WORKSHEET

Date: _____

Company/Contact:
_____
_____

Preliminary Questions

1. Is the purpose of the variable annuity to save for retirement?

    Yes_____ No_____

2. Is the purpose of the variable annuity for another long-term goal?

    Yes_____ No_____

What is the long-term goal?
_____
_____

3. Is the investment in the variable annuity through a retirement plan?

    Yes_____ No_____

    Is the investment in the variable annuity through an IRA?
    Yes_____ No_____

    Note that investment through an IRA means that you will not receive additional tax-deferral benefits from the variable annuity.

4. Do you understand the risk that the account value may decrease as a result of underlying mutual fund investment performing poorly?

    Yes_____ No_____

    What are the risks?
_____
_____
_____
_____

Worksheet

Research a prospective variable annuity contract. Answer the following questions.

5. What are the features of the variable annuity?

___

6. What are the fees and expenses that the variable annuity charges?

___

7. What is the policy on the variable annuity for surrender charges related to withdrawing money?

___

8. What is the policy on bonus credits? Do they outweigh any other higher fees?

___

9. What are the features of the variable annuity? Is long-term care insurance a feature?

___

10. What are the tax consequences of purchasing a variable annuity?

___

Special Notes & Considerations

___

Retirement Planning Research Worksheet and Questionnaire

Date:
Plan: 403(b)____ 401(k)____ Roth IRA____ Traditional IRA___ SEP___ SIMPLE IRA___
Custodian: _____

Plan Investments:
Mutual Fund_____ Stock_____ Bond_____ CD_____ Other_____
Tax-deductible contribution:
                                       Yes_____ No_____   _____
Withdrawals taxed as ordinary income:
                                       Yes_____ No_____   _____
Withdrawals tax-free: Yes_____ No_____   _____
Early withdrawal penalty: Yes_____ No_____   _____
Contribution limits: Yes_____ No_____   _____
Employer match: Yes_____ No_____   _____
Rollovers/Conversions/Transfers:
                                       Yes_____ No_____   _____
Prohibited transactions: Yes_____ No_____   _____
Income limits: Yes_____ No_____   _____
Distribution penalty: Yes_____ No_____   _____
Waivers: Yes_____ No_____   _____
Loans: Yes_____ No_____   _____

Notes & Special Considerations
_____
_____

1. What are my retirement planning goals?

Goal #1: _____

Goal #2: _____

Goal #3: _____

2. What is my current budget for retirement planning investment?
_____

3. Based on my current budget, how much money can I allocate per month to creating a retirement plan?
_____

ESTATE PLANNING CHECKLIST

When developing a sound estate plan, consider the following checklist. It provides insight overall into the documents required and steps you will need to take in order to make a sound transition.

	Done	Need to Do	Comments
Will/Living will			
Health care directive			
Financial power of attorney			
Assignment of custodian of children's property (protection)			
Beneficiary forms (bank accounts, insurance)			
Life insurance			
Reviewed estate tax laws			
Prepaid funeral arrangements			
Succession plan			
Named executor/attorney-in-fact			
Trust			
Certificates in stock, bonds, securities			
Bank accounts, mutual funds, safe deposit boxes			
Debts and unpaid taxes			
Letter of instruction			

BUSINESS QUESTIONNAIRE

1. Why are you in business? Are you passionate about your business?

2. What is going well in your business? What is not going well?

3. What do you enjoy about your business? What do you not enjoy?

4. What is your business mission statement? What are your business goals? Do these goals relate well with your personal goals?

5. Where do you see your business in the next year? 5 years? 10 years?

6. Do you currently use a working/Functioning Business Budget?

7. What are your main marketing efforts? (Internet, advertising, referrals, networking)

8. Who are your clients? (Other businesses, individuals, international)

Printed in the USA
CPSIA information can be obtained
at www.ICGtesting.com
LVHW041241091224
798679LV00007B/43